The Flame Tree Cookbook

Sue Carruthers

This book is dedicated to my parents,
Britta and Bernard

Acknowledgements

I would like to thank all the Flame Tree staff for their support and encouragment while this book was being written. Special thanks to Wendy Mani and Ifrieme Bubuluquile for their help with perfecting the recipes, as well as Tauri Ama and Pati Rua.

I would like to thank Lorna Walters, Helen Syme and Bill Carruthers for their assistance with the text, and Bill Carruthers for his cover photography.

Thanks to all my friends and Flame Tree customers who showed their confidence and support, and lastly, very special thanks to Robert Brown for his all his constant encouragment and patience.

First published in 1993 by GP Publications,
10 Mulgrave Street, Wellington, New Zealand

Reprinted 1994, 2000
New Edition Printed in 2003
Copyright © Sue Carruthers 1994

Design by Bill Wieben
Edited by Jane Parkin
Printed by Printlink, Wellington, New Zealand

ISBN 1-86956-080-9

Contents

Preface

This book is the result of many years spent living in the tropics, in Africa, Asia, South America, the Caribbean and, most recently, the Pacific Islands. For the last eight years I have lived on Rarotonga in the Cook Islands, where I own and manage The Flame Tree Restaurant. I named the restaurant after the large African flame tree that grows in the restaurant garden and which reminds me of my own birthplace near the coffee-growing area of Thika in Kenya – it is, of course, the same tree referred to in Elspeth Huxley's wonderful book, *The Flame Trees of Thika*.

Many of the dishes we prepare at The Flame Tree, and which are included in this book, reflect similarly diverse cultural influences. We try as much as possible to use locally grown produce – from fish and other seafoods to a variety of tropical fruits and vegetables – but the ways in which we use them are many and varied. Here the familiar flavours of the Islands are supplemented by those brought by different immigrant groups, mainly from South East Asia and the Indian subcontinent, whose cuisine is ideally suited to a tropical climate and lifestyle. The result in this book is a range of recipes reflecting the cultural melting pot that is the Pacific. Some are hot and spicy, others are cool and subtle – all, I hope, will enable readers who have spent even a short time in the tropics to recreate the flavours and aromas enjoyed there in their own kitchens.

Ingredients used in the book are easily obtained in most supermarkets and speciality food stores, and substitutes for seasonal or particularly unusual items are listed in the brief glossary. I have tried to ensure that all the recipes are nutritionally balanced, and that they make best use of fresh ingredients. For readers who are on a low-fat eating plan, recipes containing little or no fat are marked with a ♥.

I hope that *The Flame Tree Cookbook* is as much a joy to use as it has been a pleasure to put together. I hope too that it will satisfy all those who have requested recipes from me at the restaurant over the years.

A Comprehensive Conversion Chart

For simplicity and easy application, measures have been rounded off as follows. One metric cup, used in New Zealand and Australia, is equivalent to 250g dry ingredients and 250 ml liquids, whereas the Imperial cup used in the UK and USA is 225g and 225 ml respectively. In this book, the cup has been rounded off to be equal to 240g dry ingredients and 240 ml liquids, making the quantities much easier to divide into halves, quarters and thirds.

Dry measures		Liquid measures		
kilograms	pounds/ounces	cups	litres/mls	fl.ounces
1 kg	2 lb	4 cups	1 litre	32 fl.oz.
750g	1 1/2 lb	3 cups	750 ml	24 fl.oz.
600g	1 lb 4 oz	2 1/2 cups	600 ml	20 fl.oz.
500g	1 lb	2 cups	500 ml	16 fl.oz.
300g	10 oz	1 1/4 cups	300 ml	10 fl.oz.
240g	8 oz	1 cup	240 ml	8 fl.oz
180g	6 oz	3/4 cup	180 ml	6 fl.oz.
160g	5 oz	2/3 cup	160 ml	5 fl.oz.
120g	4 oz	1/2 cup	120 ml	4 fl.oz.
80g	2 1/2 oz	1/3 cup	80 ml	2 1/2 fl.oz.
60g	2 oz	1/4 cup	60 ml	2 fl.oz.
30g	1 oz	1/8 cup	30 ml	1 fl.oz.

Measures for Dry Ingredients

I have used either cup or metric measures as the standard for all recipes (and in most baking recipes, where exactness is particularly necessary, have included both metric and cup/tbsp measures for butter, to accommodate personal preferences). Otherwise conversions can be made using the following chart.

If you do not own a set of scales or cups, a standard teacup can be used, as long as the same-sized cup is used throughout.

	Cups and tablespoons	Metric	Imperial
Breadcrumbs (fresh)	1 cup	60g	2 oz
Breadcrumbs (dry)	1 cup	120g	4 oz
Butter	1 cup	240g	8 oz
Butter	1/4 cup (4 tbsp)	60g	2 oz
Cheese (grated)	1 cup	120g	4 oz
Coconut (fresh grated)	1 cup	120g	4 oz
Coconut (desiccated)	1 cup	90g	3 oz
Currants, Raisins, Sultanas	1 cup	180g	6 oz
Flour	1 cup	120g	4 oz
Icing sugar	1 cup	150g	5 oz
Lentils or beans (uncooked)	1 cup	240g	8 oz
Macaroni (uncooked)	1 cup	120g	4 oz
Nuts (chopped)	1/4 cup	30g	1 oz
Rice (uncooked)	1 cup	180g	6 oz
Sugar (white or brown)	1 cup	240g	8 oz
Sugar (white or brown)	1/4 cup	60g	2 oz
Fresh fruit (purée or chopped)	1 cup	240g	8 oz
Fresh vegetables (grated or chopped)	1 cup	240g	8 oz

Lengths

Cm	In
5 mm (1/2 cm)	1/4"
1 cm	1/2"
2 cm	3/4"
2.5 cm	1"
5 cm	2"
20 cm	8"
23 cm	9"
30 cm	12"
46 cm	18"
77 cm	30"

Oven Temperatures

Very slow	120°C	250°F
Slow	150°C	300°F
Mod. slow	160°C	325°F
Moderate	190°C	375°F
Hot	200°C	400°F
Very hot	230°C	450°F

Note

All recipes are recommended for 4-6 servings, unless otherwise stated.

Glossary

Utensils

Baking tin = cake/baking pan
Baking tray = baking sheet
Greaseproof paper = waxproof paper
Large saucepan = kettle
Plastic wrap = Gladwrap
Sieve (flour) = sifter
Tin = can
Tinfoil = aluminium foil

Cooking Terms

Baste: To moisten meat, chicken or fish while it is being roasted or barbecued, with oil, cooking fat or a marinade.

Blanch: To put food such as vegetables quickly into boiling water and then to rinse in cold water. This cooking method helps to retain the colour and texture of the vegetables.

Cream: To beat ingredients until light and fluffy.

Dredge: To coat food such as fish fillets with flour or breadcrumbs or a similar coating ingredient before cooking.

Entrée: This term is used to describe an appetiser or first course in Europe, New Zealand and Australia, and is used to describe the main course in the USA.

Fold in: To mix ingredients without losing air bubbles, by gently bringing liquids from the bottom of the bowl up to the top, using a large metal or wooden spoon, until all ingredients are blended.

Julienne: To cut vegetables into matchstick-like pieces.

Marinade: An oil and acid (such as wine or vinegar) mixture used to flavour and tenderise food such as tough cuts of meats.

Purée: To turn food into a thick liquid, either by passing through a sieve or by using a blender or food processor.

Sauté: To cook lightly in a frying pan with a little oil or butter.

Ingredients

Lists of tropical vegetables and fruits are given on pp. 51–72 and 141–49. In the list that follows, some temperate-climate substitutes are given, where appropriate. Other ingredients that may be unfamiliar are also included.

Banana leaves: Banana leaves are used in tropical countries to wrap around food for baking and barbecuing. This seals in the juices and gives the food a special flavour. To use banana leaves, make pliable by holding over a gentle flame and move back and forth. Aluminium foil can be used where banana leaves are unavailable.

Breadfruit: In most recipes, breadfruit can be substituted by potatoes.

Capsicums: Also known as bell peppers, sweet peppers or pimentos.

Cashewnuts: If unavailable, almonds or macadamias can be substituted.

Caster sugar: A fine sugar used in desserts and baking. If unavailable, put ordinary white sugar in a food processor with blade, and blend until fine.

Cayenne: A type of chilli pepper – any hot chilli pepper can be substituted.

Daikon: A white radish used extensively in Japanese cuisine. An important garnish with Sashimi.

Fish sauce: Made from a combination of dried fish and soya sauce, fish sauce (or Nam Pla) is an important ingredient in Asian and especially Thai cuisine. Oyster sauce can be used instead.

Golden syrup: Substitute honey or maple syrup, or light or dark corn syrup.

Lemon grass: An important ingredient in Thai and other Asian dishes. Not widely available in most stores, substitute chopped young lemon leaves or grated lemon rind.

Mangos: If fresh mangos are unavailable, canned mangos or mango pulp can be used in most recipes. Canned or fresh apricots also make a good substitute.

Mirin: A Japanese rice wine used for cooking. A dry sherry can be substituted.

Passionfruit: There is no substitute for this fruit, but canned passionfruit pulp can be used in most recipes calling for fresh fruit.

Pawpaw (papaya): Ripe or canned peaches or yellow-fleshed melons can be substituted if necessary in most recipes.

Rosewater: Made from essence of rose petals, rosewater is used in many Asian desserts and drinks. It is usually available from Asian food stores and pharmacies.

Shallots: A small cluster of onions similar in shape to cloves of garlic. They are not the same as spring onions, although they are incorrectly referred to as such in Australia.

Shrimp paste: A very strong-flavoured paste made from dried shrimps. Anchovy essence or anchovy sauce can be substituted. Although the flavour of the dish may be somewhat altered, oyster sauce may also be used in the ratio of 1 level tbsp oyster sauce to 1 tsp shrimp paste.

Spring onions: Otherwise known as scallions, these small tender onions with green leaves are much milder in flavour than regular onions. Do not confuse with shallots.

Soya sauce: A variety of soya sauces is available. The best for dipping sauce is generally a Japanese soya sauce called shoyu. For cooking, a heavier Chinese soya sauce can be used, but avoid those that are too heavy.

Tamarind: The tamarind used for cooking is the flesh from the large seedpod of the tamarind tree. Available in compressed packaged form from Asian food stores, tamarind is first soaked in hot water, then strained. Use the strained liquid to flavour curries, stews and drinks.

Taro leaves: Spinach can be substituted for taro leaves.

Taro root: Potato can be used instead.

Soups

2

When avocados come into season on Rarotonga, there is such an abundance that many are fed to the pigs, or are left on the ground for chickens and other birds to feed on. However, avocados can be frozen for use in recipes such as this, as well as for dips and savoury or sweet mousses.

This is a delicious soup and very easy to make, especially if you have home-made chicken or vegetable stock in the freezer.

Iced Avocado Soup

2 large ripe avocados
juice of 1/2 lemon
1 small onion, very finely chopped
4 cups hot chicken stock or
    vegetable stock
1 cup natural yoghurt

salt and freshly ground black
    pepper
a few drops Tabasco
chopped parsley
extra yoghurt for garnish

Peel avocado and scoop out flesh. Mash till very smooth with the lemon juice. (A food processor can be used for this step, and for chopping the onion very finely.) Put the avocado and onion in a large bowl, stir in the hot chicken stock and blend thoroughly. Add the yoghurt, salt and pepper to taste, and the Tabasco. Chill till very cold.

Serve in chilled soup bowls, topped with a swirl of yoghurt and chopped parsley.

This refreshing soup is easy to prepare and is always a success on hot summer nights. Use home-made stock, if possible. It can also be prepared without the seafood, as a light vegetarian soup.

Chilled Cucumber and Crayfish Soup

Serves 6-8

2 large cucumbers, washed
1/4 cup finely chopped parsley
4 spring onions, chopped, or
    1 small chopped onion
2 cups plain yoghurt
1 cup chicken or vegetable stock
2 cups milk or thin coconut cream
salt to taste
2 tbsp fresh lemon juice or lime
    juice

2 tbsp minced fresh dill
freshly grated nutmeg
1/2 cup cream or thick coconut
    cream
250g cooked and chopped crayfish,
    or cooked shrimps or small
    prawns
extra yoghurt or sour cream for
    garnish
extra parsley for garnish

Cut 6 to 8 very thin slices from 1 unpeeled cucumber. Wrap in plastic wrap and refrigerate. Peel remaining cucumber, halve lengthwise and remove seeds. Roughly chop and put in a blender or food processor with steel blade, and purée with all other ingredients except cream and seafood. Transfer to a bowl and whisk in cream, then add chopped crayfish, or whole prawns or shrimps. Refrigerate until very cold. If in a hurry, place in the freezer.

Serve each bowl topped with reserved slices of cucumber, a spoon of sour cream or yoghurt and some extra chopped parsley.

Watercress often can be found growing wild along the streams and in the taro swamps on Rarotonga, and makes a really delicious soup that can be served hot or cold. If watercress is hard to obtain, sorrel or any other green-leafed vegetable would also be excellent.

Cream of Watercress Soup

2 tbsp butter
2 onions, finely chopped
250g potatoes, peeled and chopped
1 big bunch watercress
5 cups vegetable or chicken stock or broth

1 tsp freshly ground pepper
salt to taste
1/2 cup cream, and extra for garnish

Wash and chop the watercress, reserving a few leaves for garnish.

Melt the butter in a large saucepan. Sauté the onion till soft. Add the potatoes and cook for 1 minute. Add all the remaining ingredients except for the cream, and simmer gently for 30 minutes. Pass the soup through a coarse strainer. (This is important, as watercress stalks can sometimes be stringy. This is not always eliminated in a food processor or blender.)

Reheat the soup gently and stir in the cream. Do not allow to boil. Adjust seasoning to taste.

Serve the soup topped with an extra swirl of cream and the reserved watercress leaves, or chill for several hours until very cold and serve in chilled bowls with a swirl of yoghurt.

Gazpacho is a very popular soup in Spain and Mexico, and both this version, which includes seafood, and the traditional version without, are perfect to prepare in the tropics, where the ingredients are easily obtained.

In the hot summer months we find it a great treat to make, as there is no cooking involved.

This soup is even better made the day before serving, so that the flavours have a chance to develop. Keep well chilled.

Seafood Gazpacho♥

500g assorted seafood such as fresh white fish fillets, shrimps, mussels, oysters, crayfish etc.
1/2 cup white wine
2 cups tomato juice
2 tsp tomato paste
1 medium cucumber, peeled, seeded and chopped roughly
1 large onion, peeled and quartered
1/2 cup olive oil or vegetable oil
2 cloves crushed garlic

4 stalks celery, sliced
2 tbsp wine vinegar
1 tbsp Worcestershire sauce
1/2 tsp chilli sauce or Tabasco
1 tsp salt
1 tsp freshly ground pepper
1 1/2 tsp chopped fresh oregano or basil, or 1/2 tsp dried
2 tbsp chopped fresh parsley
plain yoghurt for garnish (optional)

Cut all the seafood into small pieces and poach quickly in the white wine. Drain and cool. Place all the ingredients except for the seafood and parsley into a food processor or blender and process until well blended but not puréed. Combine the seafood and the tomato mixture, adjust seasoning and chill very well for several hours or longer.

Serve in chilled soup bowls topped with a spoonful of yoghurt and chopped parsley.

Chilled fruit soups are often served in the summer months in parts of northern Europe, but are equally delicious using tropical fruit. I first tasted this version using tropical fruit when dining with friends at Montego Bay, Jamaica. Any fruit in season can be used.

Tropical Fruit Soup ♥

3 cups water
grated rind and juice of 2 lemons or limes
grated rind and juice of 2 oranges
1 tsp grated fresh ginger
1 whole clove
2/3 cup sugar
1 stick cinnamon or 1/4 tsp ground cinnamon

1 cup yoghurt and extra for garnish
1 tbsp fresh mint leaves
2 stalks celery with leaves, chopped
1 cup fresh pineapple, chopped
1 cup fresh pawpaw, chopped
1 mango, peeled and chopped
1 carambola (starfruit), chopped
3 passionfruit, juice only, no seeds

In a saucepan combine water, lemon and orange rind and juice, ginger, clove, cinnamon and sugar. Cook, stirring, for 5 minutes or until sugar is completely dissolved. Strain, and cool the strained liquid.

Keeping 1 cup of the chopped fruit and a few mint leaves in the refrigerator for garnish, blend all the remaining fruit, mint leaves and celery together with 1 cup yoghurt until completely smooth. Stir into the sugar syrup until well combined and chill for several hours. The soup must be very cold.

Serve in chilled bowls with a swirl of yoghurt, a little chopped fruit and a mint leaf in each bowl.

Pumpkin grows very well in the tropics, and we often have this soup on the menu at The Flame Tree. The recipe was given to me by friends in Jamaica, but adapts easily to become a classic Pacific or Thai soup, as indicated below.

Thai-style Pumpkin and Coconut Soup

Follow the same recipe but replace half the stock with thin coconut cream. Add extra chilli powder to taste. After processing, add 1 cup thick coconut cream instead of dairy cream. Add 2 tbsp fresh lemon juice and chopped fresh coriander before serving.

Creole French Onion Soup is very simple to make. If desired, 1/4 cup port, sherry or red wine can be added to the soup at the end of cooking time.

Garlic Bread Croutons

Slice French bread, and butter liberally with garlic butter. Bake till toasted in a hot oven or under a hot grill.

Pacific Pumpkin Soup

6 tbsp butter
2 cloves garlic, crushed
1 large onion, chopped
2 medium potatoes, peeled and cubed
2 carrots, sliced
4 cups pumpkin or squash, peeled and cubed
3 tbsp flour
1 1/2 litres (about 6 cups) chicken or vegetable stock or broth

salt to taste
1/2 tsp curry powder, or more to taste
1/4 tsp chilli pepper
2 1/2 tsp paprika
1 cup cream
1/4 tsp nutmeg
1 tsp fresh ground pepper
extra cream for garnish
chopped parsley for garnish

Melt butter in a heavy saucepan, add onion and garlic and cook gently for 5 minutes until soft. Add vegetables and stir well until coated with butter. Add flour all at once, and cook for 4 minutes. Add stock, salt, curry powder, chilli pepper and paprika. Cook gently, uncovered, for 45 minutes.

Place in a food processor or blender and process until very smooth, or pass through a sieve. Put back in saucepan with cream, nutmeg and pepper, and adjust seasonings. Heat through but do not boil.

Serve sprinkled with chopped parsley and a swirl of cream.

Creole French Onion Soup

Serves 6-8

360g butter or margarine
5-6 large or 10 small onions
2 tsp sugar
1/2 cup plain flour
4 cups fresh chicken stock or broth
4 cups fresh beef stock or broth

salt to taste
1/2 tsp freshly ground black pepper
garlic bread croutons
1 cup grated gruyère cheese, or cheddar and mozzarella mixed
chopped parsley

Place butter in a large heavy saucepan. Add onions and sauté, stirring often, over a gentle heat for about 20 minutes until very limp and transparent. Sprinkle sugar over onions and stir to blend. Increase heat to medium and cook till onions are golden with slightly crisp edges. Add flour all at once, stir well, then slowly add combined stocks and bring to the boil. Reduce heat to low, add salt and pepper and simmer for 1 hour, stirring occasionally. Adjust seasoning to taste.

Place garlic bread croutons topped with gruyère cheese in each bowl, then ladle in the soup. Sprinkle with chopped parsley.

This recipe comes from the island of Tuvalu. It is a simple and delicious soup, and many people have asked for the recipe.

This soup can also be served very well chilled. (Remember to chill the soup bowls as well.)

Elaine's Breadfruit Soup

1/2 small, green, fully mature breadfruit, peeled and chopped
2 onions, sliced
2 stalks celery with leaves, washed and chopped
2 tbsp butter
water
4-5 cups chicken or vegetable stock

1 1/2 cups milk or thin coconut cream
salt and pepper to taste
chopped spring onions or parsley for garnish
1/4 cup cream or thick coconut cream for garnish

Fry the onions and celery in the butter in a large saucepan until soft. Add breadfruit and just enough water to cover the fruit. Cover the saucepan and cook the breadfruit until very tender. (Take care not to let the breadfruit stick and burn.) Purée the breadfruit, onion and celery in a blender or food processor, and return to the saucepan. Add chicken or vegetable stock, heat through, then stir in the milk. Add salt and pepper to taste.
Serve topped with a swirl of cream and chopped spring onions or parsley.

This tasty soup is good served with corn chips. The amount of chilli can be decreased if desired. In season, fresh corn kernels, slightly mashed, can be used instead of the canned creamed corn.

Spicy Corn and Cheese Soup

4 onions, finely chopped
2 tbsp butter
1 tsp crushed garlic
2 medium potatoes, cut into cubes
2 tsp crushed chilli
1 tsp ground cumin
4 cups chicken stock
2 cups peeled tomatoes, canned or fresh
2 tbsp grated parmesan cheese

2 x 440g cans cream-style sweet corn, or equivalent fresh corn kernels
salt and freshly ground black pepper to taste
2 tbsp chopped fresh coriander
1 cup cream
1/4 cup tasty cheddar cheese
chopped chives for garnish

Cook onions and garlic in butter until soft. Add potatoes and cook for a few minutes, then add the chilli and cumin. Cook for 1 minute, then add chicken stock and tomatoes. Cook soup until potato is soft. Add half the corn and cook for a few minutes, or longer if using fresh corn kernels. Add salt and pepper to taste. Purée two-thirds of the soup, return it to the saucepan with the rest of the soup, and stir in the remaining corn. (If using fresh corn, cook until the corn is tender.) Heat soup until almost boiling. Stir in coriander and cream, and cheddar and parmesan cheese. Do not allow to boil.
Serve in bowls topped with chopped chives.

This is a delicious soup that makes an excellent start to an Indian meal.

Dhal (Lentil Purée)

Dhal is served as an accompaniment to curry meals. Follow the recipe given for soup, but use only 2 cups vegetable stock or water. Cover the pan and cook according to directions, but check to see if Dhal becomes too dry. If so, add an extra cup or more of hot water or stock until lentils are tender. Dhal should be like a very thick soup.

Indian Lentil Soup

250g brown or red lentils
1 tbsp ghee or butter
1 large onion, chopped
4 cloves crushed garlic
1 tsp grated ginger
1 tsp turmeric
1 tsp curry powder
1 tsp ground cinnamon

2 tsp garam masala
1 tsp grated lemon rind
1 1/2 cups peeled tomatoes, crushed
5 cups vegetable stock or water
1 1/2 cups coconut cream
1/4 cup chopped fresh coriander
salt and pepper to taste

Wash lentils, then soak in plenty of water. Discard any lentils that float, and keep soaking lentils for several hours. (Brown lentils need more soaking then red.) Heat ghee in a large saucepan and fry onion, garlic and ginger until soft. Add curry powder, turmeric, cinnamon and garam masala, and cook for 3 minutes. Add soaked and drained lentils, vegetable stock, lemon rind, tomatoes and 1 cup coconut cream, and cook, covered but stirring occasionally, until lentils are soft. Add salt and pepper to taste, and extra garam masala if required. Stir in the remaining 1/2 cup coconut cream and chopped coriander, and serve.

In the French islands of the Caribbean, local chefs make excellent use of home-grown ingredients and spices, combining them simply but with great flair to come up with one of the finest cuisines to be found anywhere.

I first enjoyed this soup in a simple, thatch-roofed waterfront restaurant in a small village on the Isles des Saintes, and was given the recipe by the proprietress.

Martinique Cream of Eggplant Soup

1 kg eggplant
2 cloves garlic, crushed
1 onion, finely chopped
1 stalk celery with leaves, finely chopped
1 small capsicum, chopped
2 cups tomatoes, peeled and seeded

4 cups chicken or vegetable stock
1 tbsp chopped fresh basil or parsley
1 tsp sugar
salt and freshly ground pepper
1 cup cream
2 tbsp vegetable oil
extra cream for garnish

Chop the unpeeled, washed eggplants into small cubes. Pass the tomatoes through a sieve to remove seeds. Heat the oil in a large saucepan and cook the onion, garlic, capsicum and celery until the onion is soft. Add the eggplant and cook for 5 minutes. Add the tomatoes, sugar and stock together with fresh herbs, salt and pepper. Cover the saucepan and simmer for 20 minutes or until the eggplant is tender. Purée the soup in a food processor or blender until very smooth. Return to the saucepan, heat, stir in cream and adjust seasoning to taste. Do not boil after adding cream.
Serve soup in bowls, topped with swirl of cream.

This tasty chowder has evolved from many different recipes, but is chiefly based on one from Madras, India.

Madras Seafood Chowder

150g fresh white fish, chopped in small cubes
2 cups chopped fresh seafood such as squid, crabmeat, prawns (small shrimps can be left whole)
1 tbsp good-quality curry powder
2 tbsp ghee or 1 tbsp butter and 1 tbsp oil
1 large onion, sliced
1 large potato or kumara, cut into small cubes
2 cloves crushed garlic
1/2 tsp freshly grated ginger
2 tbsp flour

2 cups boiling chicken stock or seafood stock
4 cups hot milk
4 strips bacon, finely chopped and with rind removed
a can smoked oysters (optional)
1 tbsp oyster sauce (optional)
1/4 cup chopped parsley, and extra for garnish
salt and pepper to taste
juice of 1 lemon
1 cup cream or thick coconut cream, and extra for garnish
1 tbsp oil, extra

Toss the fish and seafood in the curry powder. In a large saucepan, fry the onion in ghee until soft. Add the potatoes, garlic and ginger, and cook for a few minutes. Stir in flour, cook for 1 minute, then slowly add stock, a little at a time, stirring until the mixture is smooth. Add hot milk and simmer over a gentle heat until potatoes are soft.

Fry the fish and seafood with the bacon in the 1 tbsp extra oil, just until sealed. Add to the soup with the smoked oysters and oyster sauce (if using), the parsley, salt, pepper and lemon juice. Simmer for 5 minutes or just until seafood is cooked through. Adjust seasoning. Add the cream or coconut cream, and stir well. Do not allow soup to boil after adding cream.

Serve ladled into soup bowls, topped with a swirl of cream and chopped parsley.

Although some of the Chinese ingredients are necessary for the soup to taste authentic, adaptations can be made. Water chestnuts, baby corn and bamboo shoots are available in cans, but you can use extra fresh sliced vegetables of your choice if you prefer. The soup is very easy to make, and always receives compliments.

Home-made stock or broth is preferred for the recipe, but if you are in a hurry the soup can be made using water and instant stock powder or bouillon cubes made up according to manufacturers' instructions.

Szechwan Hot and Sour Soup♥

Serves 6-8

1 cup finely chopped chicken, pork, ham or beef, or combination
1 cup mixed, finely sliced water chestnuts, baby corn and bamboo shoots
2 cups mixed, finely sliced fresh vegetables such as mushrooms, onions, capsicums, carrots, etc.

5 dried mushrooms, soaked and sliced thinly, or use fresh field or button mushrooms
2 tbsp cornflour mixed with 1/4 cup water
60g thin egg noodles or use soaked cellophane noodles
chopped spring onions
1 egg, lightly beaten

SOUP BASE

6 cups chicken, beef or pork stock or broth, or a combination
1 tsp freshly grated ginger
1 tsp freshly grated garlic
2 tbsp vinegar
1 tbsp dry sherry
1 tsp chilli sauce

2 tbsp tomato sauce
1 tbsp soya sauce
1 tbsp oyster sauce
2 tsp white sugar
2 tsp sesame oil (if available)
lots of ground black pepper
salt to taste

Put all the soup base ingredients into a large saucepan and bring to the boil, stirring, for 5 minutes. Add the meat and all vegetables, fresh and canned, and the dried soaked mushrooms together with the cornflour mixture. Cook for 2 minutes. Add the noodles and cook the soup for about 5 minutes, till the noodles are tender.

Serve the soup immediately in bowls with a teaspoonful of beaten egg poured in each bowl and sprinkled with chopped spring onions.

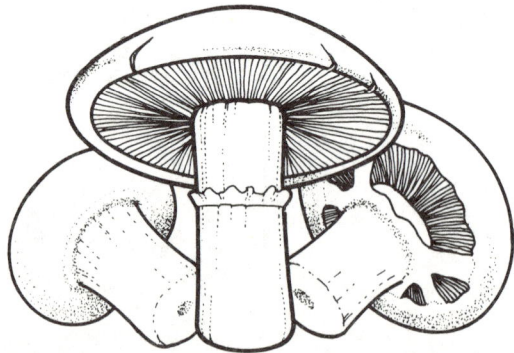

This recipe is similar to a Vichyssoise, and is delicious hot or cold.

Cream of Taro Soup

Taro root, peeled and cut into small cubes and par-boiled, can be used instead of kumara in this recipe.

Cream of Kumara and Pumpkin or Taro and Pumpkin Soup

Add 500g peeled cubed pumpkin to the soup at the same time as the kumara or taro, and reduce the kumara or taro by 150g.

Tahitian Kumara Soup

Serves 6-8

3 kumara weighing 500g total
1 tbsp vegetable oil
1 tbsp butter
3 onions, chopped
3 stalks celery with leaves, chopped
1 tsp curry powder
2 cloves garlic, crushed

4 cups chicken stock or broth
2 cups milk
1/2 cup coconut cream or cream
salt and pepper
yoghurt or coconut cream for
    garnish
1 tbsp chopped parsley

Peel the kumara and cut into small cubes. Heat the oil and butter and sauté the onions and celery until the onion is soft. Add curry powder, garlic and kumara, and cook for 2 minutes. Add chicken stock, bring to the boil, then reduce heat and simmer, covered, for 25-30 minutes or until the kumara is tender. Purée the soup.

Stir in the milk and coconut cream, and add salt and pepper to taste. If serving hot, heat in a clean saucepan till almost boiling; otherwise cool and chill until very cold.

Serve in individual bowls with a swirl of yoghurt or coconut cream and chopped parsley in each. (Remember to chill the bowls if serving cold.)

This tasty soup always receives compliments and is very easy to make. It is similar to the famous Callalloo Soup of the Caribbean.

Variation

Chopped ham or small cooked shrimps can be added to the soup if desired.

Taro Leaf and Coconut Soup

2 tbsp oil
2 onions, chopped
1 tsp (3 cloves) crushed garlic
1 kg taro leaves, or spinach
4 cups chicken or vegetable stock or
    broth
1/4 tsp crushed chilli or chilli sauce

1/4 tsp ground cloves
1 tsp freshly ground black pepper
1 tbsp chopped fresh basil or parsley
    or coriander leaves
salt to taste
2 cups coconut cream

Clean and chop the taro leaves as described on p. 69. In a heavy saucepan cook onions and garlic in oil until soft. Add all remaining ingredients except for 1/2 cup coconut cream, and cook for 30 minutes. Purée in batches in a food processor or blender until smooth. Reheat before serving. Add a swirl of the reserved coconut cream to each bowl of soup.

This soup makes a wonderful start to a Thai meal. It is best made with homemade chicken stock.

Thai Seafood Soup

Use 450g assorted seafood in place of the chicken in the recipe. Seafood may need less cooking time than chicken.

Thai Vegetable Soup

Use 450g assorted sliced vegetables in place of the chicken in the recipe. Use vegetable stock instead of chicken stock.

Thai Chicken and Coconut Soup

Serves 6-8

450g boneless chicken, uncooked
3 cups coconut cream
3 cups chicken stock or broth
2 tbsp grated fresh ginger
1 onion, thinly sliced
freshly ground black pepper
1/4 cup chopped fresh coriander
4 young lemon or lime leaves,
chopped
2 tbsp fish sauce or oyster sauce
1 tsp crushed fresh or bottled chillis
3 tbsp fresh lime or lemon juice
salt to taste
extra coconut cream for garnish
chopped spring onions for garnish

Cut the chicken into strips. Put in a large saucepan with 1 1/2 cups coconut cream, 1 cup stock, the ginger, onion, black pepper, coriander and chopped lemon leaves. Bring to the boil and simmer, uncovered, for about 10-15 minutes until the chicken is tender. Add remaining stock and coconut cream and heat through. Add the fish sauce, chillis and lime juice. Add salt to taste.

Serve topped with a swirl of coconut cream and chopped spring onions.

This recipe suits the tropics well. It is a light and delicious vegetable soup that can be adapted to make use of any vegetables in season.

Tropical Vegetable Soup

2 onions, finely chopped
2 carrots, chopped into small dice
1/4 cauliflower, broken into small florets
250g shelled peas or thinly sliced green beans
1 stalk celery with leaves, chopped finely
100g fresh spinach, chopped
1 cup fresh sliced mushrooms
2 tbsp butter
2 tbsp flour
1 1/2 cups chicken or vegetable stock or broth
2 1/2 cups milk or thin coconut cream
1/4 cup chopped fresh parsley
1/4 cup chopped fresh dill
salt and pepper to taste
1/2 cup thick dairy cream or coconut cream
1/2 tsp mild prepared mustard

In a large saucepan, melt the butter and sauté all the vegetables for about 5 minutes over a medium heat. Stir in the flour, then gradually add the stock, then the milk, parsley (reserving some for garnish) and dill. Add salt and pepper to taste, and simmer the soup gently for 10 minutes or until the vegetables are tender.

Add the cream and mustard. Cook for a further 5 minutes, without boiling.

Serve sprinkled with chopped parsley or dill.

Cold Appetisers and Light Meals

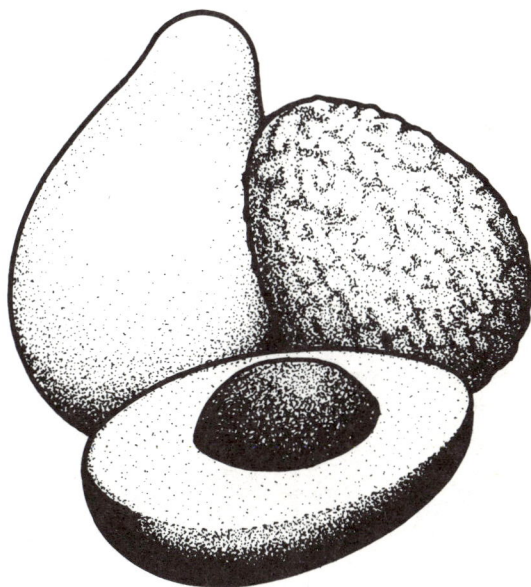

This is a lovely light appetiser which I first tasted at St Lucia in the Caribbean. It translates beautifully to the Pacific.

Avocado Pineapple Cocktail

2 tbsp mayonnaise
1 tsp curry powder
1 tsp fruit chutney
3/4 cup drained pineapple, canned
    or fresh, chopped
2 tbsp finely chopped onion or
    spring onion

1/2 cup cottage cheese
salt and pepper
2 avocados
1 tbsp lemon juice
lettuce for garnish

Mix together the mayonnaise, curry powder and chutney until smooth, then combine with pineapple, onion and cottage cheese. Add salt and pepper to taste.

Cut avocados in half and remove stones. Sprinkle with lemon juice. Fill centres with pineapple mixture and chill for 1 hour. Serve on a bed of lettuce.

This is another simple and light appetiser with a refreshing low-calorie dressing that is perfect with the combination of avocado and oranges.

Avocado and Orange Salad with Yoghurt Mint Dressing

1 large firm, ripe avocado
1 tbsp lemon juice
1 medium orange, peeled, seeded
    and sliced

2 tbsp orange juice
lettuce for garnish

Peel avocado, cut in half and remove stone. Slice the avocado halves and sprinkle with lemon juice, then arrange on lettuce leaves alternately with orange slices. Sprinkle with orange juice.

Spoon dressing all over. Chill for 30 minutes, then serve.

YOGHURT MINT DRESSING ♥
1 cup natural yoghurt
2 tsp honey
1 tsp grated orange rind

1 tbsp chopped fresh mint or mint
    sauce
salt and pepper

Combine all ingredients together until smooth. Season to taste with salt and pepper.

This mousse makes a delicious addition to a cold buffet.

Savoury Avocado Mousse

1 1/2 tbsp plain gelatine
1/4 cup water
1/2 cup hot chicken or vegetable
   stock
3 small or 2 large avocados
1 clove garlic, crushed
1 small onion, finely chopped
2 tsp Worcestershire sauce

1/2 cup mayonnaise
2 tbsp fresh lime or lemon juice
1/2 cup dairy cream
salt and freshly ground black
   pepper
cucumber slices and lime twists for
   garnish

Soften gelatine in 1/4 cup water. Add to hot chicken or vegetable stock, stirring until dissolved, and leave to cool. Halve avocados and remove flesh. Put into a food processor or blender with garlic, onion, Worcestershire sauce, mayonnaise and lime juice, and blend until smooth. Add salt and pepper to taste. Slowly add cooled chicken stock mixture to avocado mixture, stirring constantly. Beat cream until it holds its shape, and fold into avocado mixture.

    Pour into a dampened 1 litre mould or individual moulds, and chill for at least 4 hours until firm. Turn out onto a serving plate or plates, and garnish with thin cucumber slices and lime twists.

Chicken, Pawpaw and Avocado Salad with Honey Lime Dressing

1 firm, ripe avocado, peeled and halved
1/2 medium firm, ripe pawpaw,
   peeled and seeded
3 cups diced, cooked chicken

1 tbsp chopped fresh basil or parsley
lettuce leaves or salad greens
lime slices for garnish

Cut the avocado into small, neat cubes. Cut the pawpaw into thin, neat slices. Combine the avocado and chicken together. Line a serving plate with the lettuce or other salad greens. Arrange the chicken/avocado mixture in a pile in the centre, and surround with a circle of pawpaw slices. Pour over Honey Lime Dressing.

    Garnish the salad with lime slices, and top with chopped fresh basil or parsley.

HONEY LIME DRESSING

1 tsp grated lime or lemon rind
1/2 cup lime juice
1/2 cup honey

1/4 tsp ground coriander
salt and pepper

Place the lime rind, juice, honey and coriander in a small saucepan over a low heat and stir till well combined. Add salt and pepper to taste. Cool completely, then pour over the salad.

16

This salad looks very appealing and tastes superb. The recipe is the result of an attempt to re-create a similar salad I first tasted at a restaurant called The Red Crab in Grenada.

Crayfish and Pineapple Salad with Coconut Dressing

2 crayfish of about 750g each
1 tbsp vegetable oil
1 clove garlic, crushed
3/4 cup thick coconut cream
1/2 capsicum, finely chopped
1/2 cup chopped chives or spring onions
1/4 tsp brown sugar
1/4 cup lime or lemon juice

salt and pepper
a few drops Tabasco sauce
1 tsp soya sauce
1/2 cup fresh or canned drained pineapple, cubed or sliced
2 large ripe tomatoes, sliced
lettuce leaves
cucumber slices
sprigs of parsley, mint or basil

Cook the crayfish in a big pot of boiling water for 7-10 minutes, or until just cooked. Drain and cool under running water. Extract the meat and cut into cubes. Keep the tail tips, legs and claws for garnish.

Heat the oil in a small saucepan and fry the garlic for 1 minute. Add the coconut cream and cook till slightly reduced. Remove from heat and stir in capsicum, chopped chives, spring onion, salt and pepper, brown sugar, lime juice, Tabasco and soya sauce.

Arrange lettuce leaves on a serving plate. Put crayfish meat in the centre, and surround with pineapple, tomato and cucumber slices. Arrange reserved tail tips, legs and claws around the mound of crayfish so that the arrangement resembles a whole crayfish. Pour Coconut Dressing over the salad and chill until ready to serve. Garnish with sprigs of parsley, mint or basil.

This is a fairly economical appetiser that is ideal for serving on a hot summer's evening. It can also be served as part of a summer buffet, and is certain to be appreciated by vegetarians.

For a low-calorie version, substitute cottage cheese for the cream cheese, and yoghurt for the mayonnaise and cream.

Cucumber and Cream Cheese Mousse with Mango Vinaigrette

1 medium cucumber	1/2 small onion, very finely chopped
1 tsp salt	1/2 cup finely chopped canned or
240g cream cheese	fresh pineapple (optional)
1/2 cup mayonnaise	extra salt to taste
1/2 cup cream	freshly ground pepper to taste
1 tbsp lemon juice	1 tsp chopped fresh mint or mint
1 tbsp plain gelatine	sauce
2/3 cup vegetable or chicken stock,	1 recipe Mango Vinaigrette, p. 220
or pineapple juice	pineapple or mango slices, and
2 level tsp caster sugar	parsley sprigs for garnish

Peel the cucumber, slice lengthways and remove seeds using a teaspoon. Grate the cucumber, put into a colander and sprinkle with the 1 tsp salt. Let drain for 30 minutes, and press out excess liquid.

Blend cream cheese with mayonnaise, cream and lemon juice in a food processor or blender until smooth, then turn out into a bowl.

In a separate small heatproof bowl, soften the gelatine in the vegetable stock, chicken stock or pineapple juice, and either set in a pan of simmering water until gelatine is dissolved, or microwave on High for 30 seconds. Stir in caster sugar, then stir the gelatine mixture into the cream cheese mixture, together with the cucumber, onion and pineapple (if using). Add salt and pepper to taste, and chopped mint or mint sauce.

Put into individual wetted moulds, or a larger ring-shaped mould, and refrigerate until set. Allow at least 4 hours. Turn out, and serve with Mango Vinaigrette spooned attractively over. Garnish with sliced fruit and parsley sprigs.

The curried chicken and the fresh mango are delicious together in this recipe.

Fijian Curried Chicken and Mango Salad

4 cups cubed cooked chicken
1 tsp curry powder
1 cup mayonnaise
1/4 cup chopped spring onions
2 cloves garlic, crushed
1/2 tsp honey
1/2 cup chopped celery

1/2 cup chopped tomatoes
1/2 cup freshly grated coconut,
    lightly toasted
2 mangos, peeled and sliced
lettuce or salad greens
fresh sprigs of coriander or basil

Arrange lettuce on serving platter. Mix curry powder with mayonnaise, spring onions, garlic, celery and honey until smooth, then stir in the chicken cubes. Arrange in a pile in the centre of the serving plate, top with chopped tomatoes and sprinkle with coconut. Arrange mango slices to form a circle around the chicken. Garnish with coriander sprigs or basil.

This dish appears in the cuisine of all the Pacific islands, including the Philippines. It is known as Poisson Cru in Tahiti, Kokoda in Fiji and Ika Mata in the Cook Islands. This version is a combination of the best Island recipes.

Ika Mata – Island-style Marinated Fish in Coconut Cream

500g firm fresh fish fillets
lemon juice or lime juice
salt
1 cup thick coconut cream
1 small onion, chopped finely
1/2 small capsicum, chopped finely
1/2 cucumber, peeled and chopped
1 small ripe tomato, chopped

2 cloves garlic, crushed
1 tsp grated fresh ginger
4 tbsp chopped fresh herbs such as
    parsley, dill and basil
1 tsp or less chopped fresh chillis
salt and freshly ground black
    pepper to taste

Cut the fish into small 2 cm cubes. Put in a bowl and sprinkle with about 1 1/2 tsp salt. Cover with juice from 3 large lemons or 6 small limes. Marinate in the refrigerator for 4-6 hours – do not leave too long. The fish should be slightly raw in the centre.

Drain off lemon juice and press fish to remove excess liquid. Combine drained fish with remaining ingredients. Chill until ready to serve.

This dish looks attractive served in a halved coconut shell with flesh intact, or in cocktail glasses lined with lettuce leaves. Garnish with sprigs of herbs and lemon twists.

This unusual fish salad makes a wonderful appetiser on a hot summer evening. The dressing is delicious and the texture of the fish marinated this way is very appealing.

Japanese Fish and Vegetable Salad

500g cubed fish fillets, patted dry
1 cup Tempura Batter, p. 45
oil for deep frying
1 carrot
1 capsicum

1 onion
1 stalk celery
2 tbsp chopped spring onions for garnish

JAPANESE DRESSING ♥

1/2 cup vinegar
1/4 cup dry sherry or mirin
1 1/2 tbsp white sugar
1 tsp grated fresh ginger
1/2 tsp crushed chilli or chilli sauce

juice of 1 lemon
1 1/2 tsp soya sauce
2 tsp cornflour mixed with 1/4 cup water

Mix the cornflour and water together and put into a small saucepan with all the other dressing ingredients. Bring to the boil, stirring, then as soon as the dressing has thickened, remove from heat and cool.

Fry the fish, dipped in Tempura Batter, in hot oil until crisp and cooked (see p. 45). Cut the vegetables into very thin slices. Put the cooked fish and the vegetables into the cooled dressing and refrigerate for at least 4 hours. Serve topped with chopped spring onions.

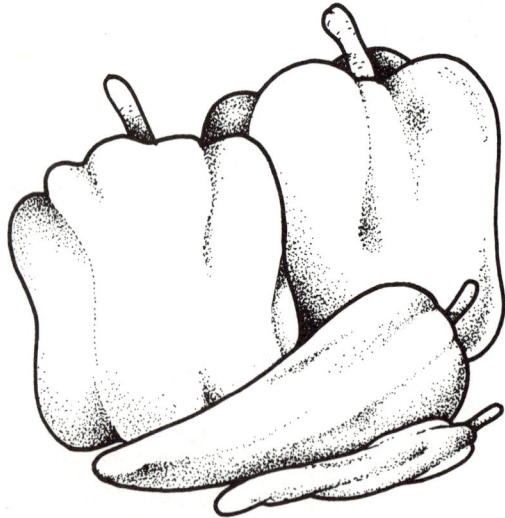

This salad makes a lovely appetiser or an attractive addition to a cold buffet. If fresh mangos are not in season, sliced ripe pawpaw could be used instead. We always leave the heads and tails on the prawns, and remove the body shells.

Prawn and Mango Salad with Avocado Orange Dressing

Serves 8-12 as an appetiser

1 kg cooked prawns
lettuce leaves and a mixture of available salad greens, such as spinach and watercress
2 mangos, peeled, with stones removed

1 onion, very thinly sliced
1 green capsicum, very thinly sliced into circles
1/2 cup grated coconut, lightly toasted
lemon and orange slices for garnish

Arrange lettuce and greens on a serving dish. Cut mango into slices. Arrange prawns in the centre of the bed of greens, and arrange the mango slices around the outside in a circle. Top all with the sliced onion and capsicum. Spoon over the dressing. Sprinkle the toasted coconut over the salad, and serve garnished with lemon and orange slices.

AVOCADO ORANGE DRESSING

1 ripe peeled avocado, stone removed
1/4 cup fresh orange juice
2 tbsp cider vinegar

1 tbsp chopped chives or spring onions
2 tbsp sour cream
salt and pepper to taste

Combine all the ingredients for the dressing in a blender or food processor, and process until smooth. Adjust seasoning, and spoon over the salad.

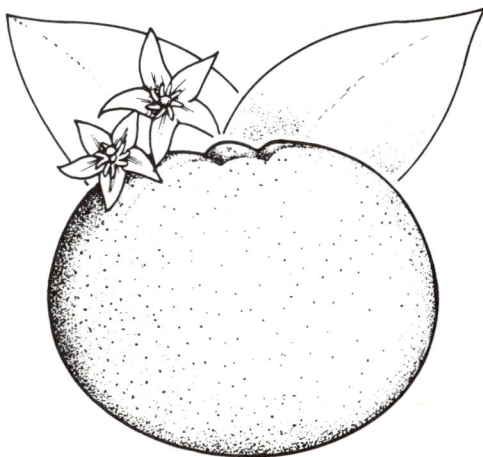

This simple calamari salad has an exotic flavour, and makes an excellent starter to a Thai meal.

Thai Calamari Salad ♥

500g squid, cleaned and prepared (see p. 96)
water

2 tbsp white wine
salad greens such as lettuce, spinach or watercress

CALAMARI DRESSING

1/2 cup fresh lime or lemon juice
1 tbsp fish sauce or oyster sauce
grated rind and juice of 2 small limes or 1 lemon

1-2 small chillis, seeded and chopped
4 spring onions, chopped
1 tsp white sugar

Cut the squid into rings, and marinate if desired, as described on p. 96. (This is often necessary with larger squid.) Bring about 3 cups water to boil in a large pot. Add the white wine. Add the squid, bring the water back to the boil, then immediately remove the squid and run under cold water. Drain.

Combine all the dressing ingredients together in a screwtop jar, shaking well. Combine the squid in a bowl with the dressing and chill until almost ready to serve.

The salad is best served at room temperature, on a bed of salad greens.

Fresh raw squid is often used for Sashimi and served with the tuna or other fresh fish. This looks attractive with the flesh scored with a sharp knife then cut into strips and rolled into pinwheel shapes.

Sashimi ♥

Japanese Sashimi is very popular with westerners today. It is an excellent light appetiser, and here in the tropics there is always a ready supply of fresh fish, including tuna, which makes perhaps the best Sashimi. Experiment with the different fish in your area.

There are various methods of cutting Sashimi. Remember that the fish must be very fresh, and frozen fish should never be used. Chill the fish in the freezer for 10 minutes to make the cutting easier. The fish can then be cut into thin slices or small cubes. Use a very sharp knife and handle the fish as little as possible.

Serve a Soya and Ginger Dipping Sauce (see p. 45) or Sweet and Sour Sauce (p. 225), or both. On the plate with the neatly arranged Sashimi slices can be a small bundle of grated carrot and another small bundle of grated white daikon radish. Fresh edible flowers such as nasturtiums or red hibiscus could also be used for garnish.

This is a quick version of Sushi, using cold cooked rice, which we find we always have left over in the refrigerator from the night before.

Sushi fillings usually consist of a variety of colours, such as pink salmon or tuna, yellow omelette strips, green cucumber or strips of spinach leaf, and orange carrot strips, arranged down the centre of the white rice and then wrapped in the dark-green seaweed wrappers. Sushi rolls make an attractive display when presented with Sashimi but can also be served alone as an appetiser with a variety of different fillings to add interest.

Sushi Rice Rolls♥

2 cups cooked rice   1/2 cup sugar
1 cup vinegar   1 tsp grated fresh ginger

Heat the vinegar, sugar and ginger in a small saucepan and when it is boiling, stir in the rice all at once and keep stirring till the rice is shiny and soft. Remove from heat and allow to cool.

FOR THE FILLINGS

Thin strips of vegetables such as carrots, cucumbers (with skins if possible), green spinach leaves, lengths of spring onion
60g fish such as very fresh raw tuna or smoked salmon or other smoked fish cut into slices, or cooked crayfish meat or other shellfish, as desired.
4 soaked dried mushrooms, cut into strips

1 tsp prepared Wasabi mustard
2 sheets of Nori Seaweed Wrappers
Beat 2 eggs lightly with chopped spring onions or chives, 1 tbsp water and a few drops of soya sauce, and cook in a lightly oiled omelette or crepe pan till just cooked.

A bamboo mat especially for wrapping Sushi can be purchased, otherwise proceed by hand using a clean napkin or square cloth.

Place a sheet of Nori seaweed on a bamboo mat or clean napkin. Divide the rice into 2 portions and spread one portion evenly over two-thirds of the Nori sheet, starting at the end nearest you. In a row down the middle put a thin line of Wasabi mustard and one of the ingredients of your choice, or a combination of ingredients, keeping the end display of colours in mind. Roll up Sushi gently but tightly in the mat or napkin to form a neat cylinder. Repeat with second Nori sheet. Chill the rolls in the refrigerator for at least 30 minutes before cutting each roll into 6 or 8 pieces.

If serving alone, serve with a dish of Soya and Ginger Dipping Sauce (p. 45) and extra prepared Wasabi on the side, and a dish of Sweet and Sour Sauce (p. 225) if desired.

Hot Appetisers and Light Meals

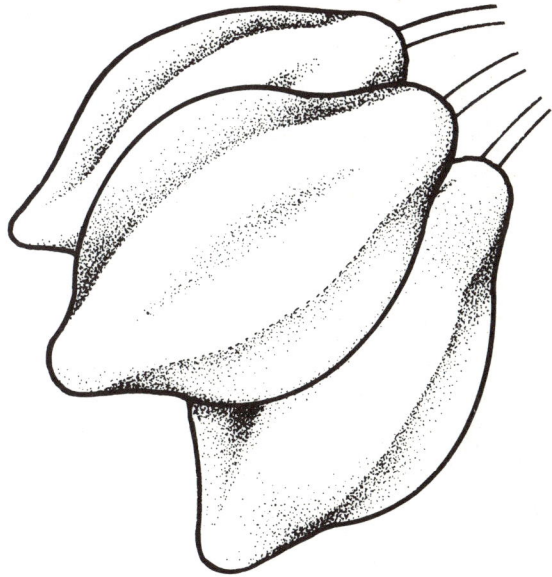

This omelette is perfect for breakfast or brunch, and also makes a delicious light lunch or supper dish served with a green salad and tortilla chips.

Avocado Omelette with Tomato Salsa

Serves 2

1 tbsp butter
4 eggs, lightly beaten
1 tbsp water
1/3 cup sour cream
salt and freshly ground black
    pepper

1/2 cup cheddar cheese
1/2 cup Tomato Salsa
1 tbsp butter
1 avocado, sliced and sprinkled with
    1 tbsp lemon juice

TOMATO SALSA♥

1 tbsp oil
2 cloves garlic, crushed
1 onion, chopped
4 canned or fresh tomatoes, peeled
    and chopped

1 tsp or more chilli sauce
salt and pepper

First make the salsa. Heat oil in a small frying pan and cook onions and garlic until soft. Add tomatoes and cook until sauce is reduced and thickened. Add salt, pepper and chilli sauce to taste.

In a small bowl, combine the eggs, water, salt and pepper, and beat with a fork until just combined. In a small 20 cm omelette pan, heat the butter and pour in half the egg mixture. Cook gently, lifting edges so uncooked mixture flows underneath.

Spoon in 1/4 cup salsa, 1/4 cup cheese, half the avocado slices and half the sour cream. Sprinkle with a little extra pepper and salt, and fold one side over to cover filling. Remove omelette and keep warm. Repeat with remaining egg mixture and filling.

This a really superb dish that is economical to make. Spinach can be used instead of taro leaves but the taro leaves do give a lovely texture to this dish.

The use of coconut cream likewise gives an exotic flavour to the cannelloni, but dairy cream may be used instead.

If you use the 'oven ready' variety of cannelloni, let the cannelloni sit in the baking tray after filling and topping with sauce for about an hour before baking to allow the pasta to soften.

Cannelloni Verde with Taro Leaves and Cottage Cheese

14 cannelloni tubes
2 cups Tomato Basil Sauce, p. 225
1 cup coconut cream or dairy cream
1 cup mozzarella or cheddar cheese, or combination

1/4 cup parmesan cheese
extra chopped basil

CANNELLONI FILLING

1 1/2 cups cooked taro leaves, p. 69
2 tbsp butter
2 cloves garlic, crushed
1 large onion, finely chopped
juice of 1/2 lemon
1 tsp grated lemon rind
1 tbsp fresh basil
1 tsp dried oregano
1/2 cup grated mature (tasty)

cheddar cheese or similar
1 cup cottage cheese or ricotta cheese
1/4 cup parmesan cheese
1/4 cup coconut cream
salt to taste
lots of fresh ground pepper
1/4 tsp grated nutmeg
a few drops Tabasco

Melt the butter, and cook the garlic and onion till the onion is very soft. Add all the remaining ingredients for the filling and stir till well combined. Adjust seasoning to taste.

Preheat oven to 180°C. Butter a large baking dish. Spread 1 cup of the Tomato and Basil Sauce on the bottom.

Fill the cannelloni tubes using a teaspoon and put in a single layer into the baking tray. Top with the remaining 1 cup of Tomato and Basil Sauce, the 1 cup coconut cream, the mozzarella, parmesan and extra chopped basil. Bake for 30 minutes or until hot and bubbly.

It is important that the fresh vegetables are very finely sliced, as in this recipe the vegetables are not cooked before wrapping up in the spring roll wrappers. The vegetables should be crisp.

Use store-bought or home-made spring roll wrappers, see p. 185.

The shrimp can be omitted, as can the chicken, to make Vegetarian Spring Rolls. Or, if you wish, finely shredded cooked pork or other meat or seafood can be used instead. We use whatever suitable fresh vegetables are in season.

Chicken and Shrimp Spring Rolls

oil for deep frying
12 spring roll wrappers

1 egg, beaten

FILLING

100g finely sliced cooked chicken
1/4 cup chopped cooked shrimp
1 small onion, finely sliced
1/3 cup finely sliced carrot
1/2 cup finely chopped celery
1/3 cup finely sliced, fresh mush-
    rooms or 4 dried mushrooms,
    soaked and finely sliced
1 small capsicum, finely sliced
1 cup fresh bean sprouts

2 tsp grated fresh ginger
2 cloves garlic, crushed
1 tsp freshly ground black pepper
1 tbsp oyster sauce or 1/2 tsp
    shrimp paste or anchovy essence
2 tsp soya sauce
1 tsp cornflour
a few drops chilli sauce or more to
    taste

Combine all the ingredients for the filling together. Place a portion (about 2 tbsp) of the filling across the middle of each wrapper, fold the edge nearest you over the filling and roll again. Tuck in the side edges and then roll again, sealing with beaten egg.

Deep fry the spring rolls in hot oil till golden-brown and crisp. Drain on kitchen paper.

Serve immediately with Soya and Ginger Sauce (p. 45) or Sweet and Sour Sauce, p. 225.

Pilaf is the classic rice dish of the Persians, and variations are to be found from as far west as Italy, in the form of risotto, and all along the ancient caravan routes throughout Asia. The north Indian version is called pillau.

Brown Rice Pilaf

Follow the instructions for Plain Rice Pilaf but substitute brown rice. Increase cooking time by 10 minutes and resting time by 10 minutes.

Nut Pilaf

1 cup toasted chopped nuts can be sprinkled on either Plain or Brown Rice Pilaf after cooking.

Plain Rice Pilaf

3 tbsp butter
1 1/2 cups long-grain white rice, washed thoroughly and drained
1 onion, finely chopped

2 cups chicken or vegetable stock
salt
1/8 tsp saffron or 1 tsp tumeric
2 tbsp chopped parsley

Heat the butter in a heavy-bottomed saucepan with a tight-fitting lid and cook the onion until tender. Add rice and stir until well coated with butter. Add stock, bring to the boil and reduce heat to very low. Cover tightly and cook for 20 minutes undisturbed.

Remove from the heat and stand, covered, for another 10 minutes. Fluff with a fork and serve.

The rice can also be baked in the oven in a casserole. After the stock and rice have been brought to the boil in a saucepan, turn into a casserole, cover tightly and bake at 180°C for 20 minutes. Remove from oven and stand for 10 minutes before removing the lid and fluffing with a fork.

This dish, whose origins go back to West Africa, would team up well with any savoury dish cooked in coconut cream, such as the Blanquette of Pork Vanuatu (p. 132). It's also delicious as a light meal on its own, with a salad.

Creole Rice♥

chicken or vegetable stock
1 recipe Creole Tomato Sauce, p. 225

1 tbsp vegetable or olive oil
2 cups uncooked long-grain rice
1 tsp salt

Add enough hot chicken or vegetable stock to the Creole Tomato Sauce to make a total of 4 cups of liquid.

Heat the oil in a heavy-bottomed saucepan with a tight-fitting lid and cook the rice, stirring, until it is shiny. Pour in the tomato/stock liquid and salt, and bring to the boil. Reduce heat to low, cover pan tightly and cook rice, without removing cover or stirring, for 20 minutes. Remove pan from the heat and stand, covered, for 5 minutes. Uncover, toss rice with a fork, and serve immediately.

Dried red beans are mostly used for this dish, but fresh pigeon peas are also used. This recipe makes a delicious accompaniment to casseroles and stews, or to roast chicken or meat. It is also good to serve as part of a vegetarian meal, providing plenty of protein.

Jamaican Rice and Beans

240g dried red kidney or similar
   beans
2 tbsp vegetable oil
1 medium onion, finely chopped
2 cloves garlic, crushed
1/2 tsp chopped fresh chillis or
   chilli sauce, p. 227

2 cups coconut cream
1/2 tsp dried mixed herbs
1 tsp salt
1 tsp freshly ground black pepper
2 cups uncooked long-grain rice

Wash the beans and soak, well covered with water, for at least 12 hours. Put the soaking water and beans into a large saucepan, and add water to cover beans by about 5 cm. Bring to the boil and simmer gently, covered, till the beans are tender. Add extra water if necessary and take care not to let the beans stick and burn. Drain the beans and measure the cooking liquid. Return the beans and cooking liquid to the saucepan.

Wash the rice and drain very well. Heat the oil in a frying pan and sauté the onion and garlic till the onion is soft. Add to the saucepan with the chilli, mixed herbs, salt and pepper and coconut cream, together with the drained rice. Make up the liquid (including the bean liquid and coconut cream) to 3 3/4 cups in total, adding water if necessary.

Cover the saucepan tightly and cook over a very low heat, or bake in a moderate oven in a tightly covered casserole for 20-30 minutes, until the rice is tender and all the liquid is absorbed.

This is one of the most popular appetisers that we serve at The Flame Tree. Some customers even order this dish for dessert!

Grate the coconut on a coconut grater, or use the grating attachment on an electric food processor, rather than an ordinary cheese grater. Dry the grated coconut in a hot oven for a few minutes, or micro-wave on High for a few seconds. This helps the coconut to stick to the camembert.

Coconut-coated Camembert with a Tropical Fruit Sauce

Serves 6

3 camembert cheeses weighing
    about 125g each
1 egg, beaten lightly
1/2 cup milk
plain flour

flesh of 1 coconut, grated
oil for deep frying
orange twists and fresh fruit slices
    for garnish

TROPICAL FRUIT SAUCE♥

1/2 cup chopped ripe pawpaw or
    mango
1/2 cup chopped fresh pineapple
juice of 3 passionfruit, strained to
    remove seeds

1 tbsp brown sugar
1 tbsp lemon or lime juice
1 cup fresh orange juice

Combine all the ingredients for the sauce in a blender or food processor till smooth.

Cut each camembert in half, then each half into 4 wedges. Combine the egg and milk. Coat the wedges with flour, then dip in egg mixture, then roll in the coconut. Deep fry without overcrowding the pan just till the camemberts are golden-brown. Take care not to cook too long – the cheese should not seep out.

Spoon some sauce onto 6 individual plates and arrange 4 wedges of camembert on each plate. Garnish with orange twists and fresh fruit slices. Serve with crackers, if desired.

This is one of the classic rice dishes of India. This vegetable version is good to serve with curries, or as part of a vegetarian meal. Lamb or Chicken Biriyani is often served in northern India, and is really a meal in itself.

It is important to wash the rice well in advance of preparing the recipe, and to allow it to dry. Use a colander and shake the washed rice from time to time to ensure that it dries well.

Vegetable Biriyani

VEGETABLE MIXTURE

2 tbsp ghee or 1 tbsp oil and 1 tbsp butter
2 onions, finely chopped
1 tbsp grated fresh ginger
1 tsp crushed fresh garlic
2 tbsp curry powder or curry paste, p. 228
1 potato, peeled and diced
2 carrots, peeled and diced
1 small capsicum, thinly sliced

1/2 cup fresh or frozen peas
1 cup thinly sliced green beans
1 cup peeled fresh or canned tomatoes, crushed
1 cinnamon stick
2 tsp garam masala
4 whole cloves
1 1/4 cups water

RICE

1 1/2 cups long-grain rice
water
2 tbsp ghee or 1 tbsp oil and 1 tbsp butter

vegetable or chicken stock
1 bay leaf
1/2 cup cashewnuts or almonds, toasted

Heat the ghee and cook the onions till soft. Add the garlic, ginger, curry powder or paste and cook for a few minutes. Add the remaining ingredients and cook until the vegetables are tender and the sauce is thick.

Wash the rice well. Soak the rice in water for 10 minutes, then drain very well for at least 1 hour. Heat the ghee in a saucepan and cook the rice till shiny, then add just enough hot stock to cover the rice. Add the bay leaf and cook for 10 minutes, covered. Do not stir. Then let the saucepan stand off the heat for 10 minutes. The rice should now be tender.

Stir the hot rice and hot vegetable mixture gently together, turn out onto a serving platter and top with chopped nuts.

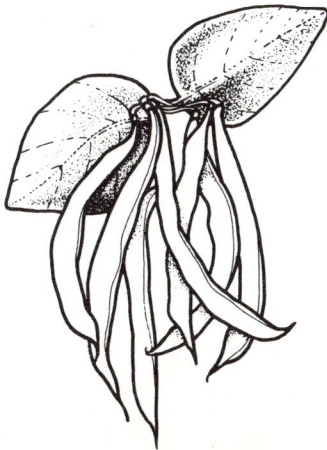

The recipe for the pumpkin curry comes from Trinidad, and the idea of combining this with crepes and serving it with the yoghurt sauce came about when I was creating a special vegetarian lunch for friends.

The crepes make an excellent appetiser or a vegetarian main course served with rice and a selection of salads and sambals (pp. 211–13)

Curried Pumpkin Crepes with Minted Yoghurt Sauce

Serves 8-10 as an appetiser, or 4-6 as a main course

CREPES

2 eggs	1 cup firmly packed wholemeal
1 1/4 cups milk	flour, or a mixture of plain and
3/4 tsp salt	wholemeal flour

Place all ingredients in a blender or food processor, liquid ingredients first. Blend until smooth.

Place a heavy-based frypan, about 16 mm in diameter, over a moderate heat and grease it with a little melted butter or oil. When hot, pour in 2-3 tbsp batter and rotate the pan quickly so that the batter thinly coats the base of the pan. When bubbles have appeared and the batter has set, turn with a spatula or fish slice and cook on the other side. If the first crepe has a solid, rubbery appearance, thin the mixture with a little extra milk.

Pile the cooked crepes on top of one another, ready for filling.

FILLING

500g pumpkin, peeled and cut into small cubes	1 cup peeled chopped tomatoes (canned or fresh)
2 tbsp vegetable oil or ghee	2 small fresh chillis, seeded and chopped
1 large onion, chopped	
3 cloves garlic, crushed	1 tsp ground black pepper
1 green capsicum, chopped	1 tsp salt, or more to taste
2 tsp curry powder	2 tbsp chopped fresh coriander
1/4 tsp ground cloves	1/4 cup chopped spring onions

Heat the oil or ghee in a heavy saucepan, add the onion, capsicum and garlic, and cook, stirring, until the onion is soft. Add the curry powder and cook for 2 minutes. Add the cloves, tomatoes, chillis, pumpkin, and salt and pepper. Stir to combine and cook over a very low heat, stirring occasionally, until the pumpkin is very tender. Add a little water only if necessary. Stir in the coriander and spring onions, and adjust seasoning to taste.

Put about 2 tbsp filling on one side of each crepe, and then roll up, folding in the ends. Put seam side down in an ovenproof dish. Repeat with remaining crepes.

Cover with Minted Yoghurt Sauce, and bake for 20 minutes at 180°C.

Omit cream from yoghurt sauce, and use trim milk in the sauce for a low-fat verison.

MINTED YOGHURT SAUCE♥

2 cups natural yoghurt
1 cup cream or thick coconut
   cream
2 tbsp chopped fresh mint

1 tbsp lemon juice
1 tbsp brown sugar
1/2 tsp salt
1/2 tsp freshly ground black pepper

Combine all ingredients for the sauce together in a bowl, and pour over the filled crepes.

This adaptation of a classic Italian pasta sauce has resulted from a desire to keep a tropical flavour to the fore in the dishes on the menu at The Flame Tree. The most successful chef in recent times to match the flavours of east and west has been Ken Höm, and it is his example that has inspired me.

This colourful dish is tasty and fairly quick to prepare and can be as spicy as you wish to make it.

East/West Spaghetti with Lamb, Peppers and Coconut

Serves 8 as an appetiser, 4 as a main course

500g lamb, cut into thin strips
2 tbsp vegetable or olive oil
2 tbsp butter
1 onion, very thinly sliced
1 tbsp vinegar
2 red capsicums, thinly sliced
1 green capsicum, thinly sliced
3 cloves garlic, crushed
1 tsp paprika
1 tsp crushed chilli, or more to
   taste

2 tsp brown sugar
1 cup coconut cream
450g dried spaghetti
1/2 cup grated coconut, toasted
chopped spring onions for garnish
1/4 cup grated parmesan cheese
   (optional)
salt and freshly ground black
   pepper to taste

In a heavy skillet, wok or saucepan, heat 1 tbsp oil and 1 tbsp butter, and sauté the lamb strips till just browned. Add the onions, cover the pan and cook for 5 minutes. Add the vinegar, stir, remove the pan from the heat and put aside.

In a separate pan heat the remaining 1 tbsp oil and the 1 tbsp butter, and sauté the sliced capsicums for several minutes, stirring. Stir in the garlic and paprika with the chilli, and cook over a gentle heat for about 6 minutes.

Stir the capsicum mixture into the lamb mixture, and return the lamb mixture to the heat. Add the brown sugar and the coconut cream, and simmer over a very gentle heat for 5 minutes. Add salt and pepper to taste.

Meanwhile, cook the spaghetti in boiling salted water till just 'al dente'. Drain and transfer to a warm serving dish or individual dishes. Top with the lamb sauce, followed by the grated coconut and chopped spring onions. Serve the parmesan separately.

This dish makes a simple appetiser when eggplants are abundant. I have used cashewnuts for the pesto base but almonds, pinenuts or macadamias can also be used.

Grilled Eggplant with Coconut Pesto Sauce

2 medium-sized eggplants or 6 long
    thin oriental eggplants

oil, preferably olive, for cooking
salt

Cut the medium eggplant horizontally into thin wedges, or cut the oriental eggplant vertically in half. Sprinkle well with salt and let stand in a colander to drain for 30 minutes. Rinse the eggplant slices and dry with a clean cloth. Brush each side with oil and place on a shallow oiled baking tray. Cook under a preheated grill or in a moderate oven for about 15 minutes, brushing with oil several times, until the eggplant is tender. Do not overcook as the skin should still be soft and pleasant to eat.

Arrange the eggplant on a serving platter and spoon the pesto over the eggplant

COCONUT PESTO SAUCE

1/4 cup cashewnuts, lightly toasted
    but still pale, and roughly
    chopped
3 cloves garlic
1/2 cup vegetable or olive oil
1 cup chopped spinach leaves

1/2 cup basil leaves
2 tbsp lemon juice
2 tbsp grated parmesan cheese
1/4 cup thick coconut cream
pepper and a little salt to taste

Put the nuts, garlic and oil in a blender or food processor and grind till smooth. Add the spinach and basil, and purée till smooth. Add the lemon juice and parmesan, pulse for a few seconds, then add the coconut cream and blend just until well combined. Turn out into a bowl and add salt and pepper to taste.

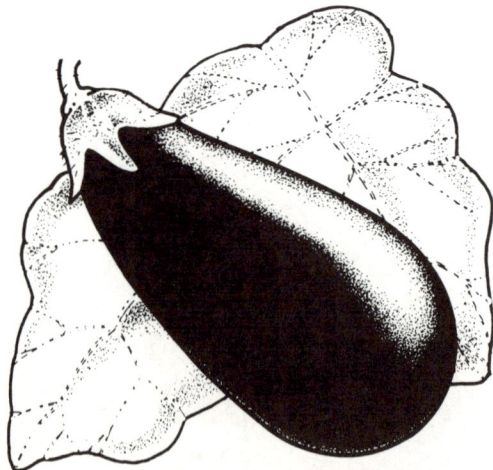

This is a wonderful recipe from Java. The unusual addition of mango chutney is not strictly Indonesian but gives a delicious taste to the curry sauce.

The recipe is very easy to make and is ideal for a light supper or lunch dish with rice or noodles and a salad, or as an appetiser served on a small bed of rice, or as part of an Indonesian buffet.

Indonesian Eggs in a Curried Tomato and Chilli Sauce♥

Serves 6-8

2 tbsp vegetable oil
2 onions, finely chopped
3 cloves garlic, crushed
2 tsp grated fresh ginger
1 tbsp good-quality curry powder
1 tsp crushed fresh chilli or chilli
   powder, or more to taste
1/2 tsp shrimp paste or anchovy
   essence, or 2 tsp oyster sauce

2 cups peeled chopped tomatoes,
   canned or fresh
1 tbsp vinegar
2 tbsp mango chutney or similar
1 tbsp brown sugar
2 tbsp soya sauce
1/2 cup water
6-8 hard-boiled eggs, shelled
salt and pepper to taste

Heat oil in a medium saucepan, add the onion, ginger and garlic, and cook till the onion is soft. Add the curry powder and chilli and cook for a few minutes. Add shrimp paste, tomatoes, vinegar, chutney, brown sugar, soya sauce and water. Cook till smooth and thick, about 20 minutes, over a gentle heat. Season to taste with salt and pepper. Add the eggs carefully and heat through.

This recipe was created at The Flame Tree for some special vegetarian guests, and was voted a great success. Served with a salad and perhaps a Nut Pilaf (p. 30), it makes a very nutritious and interesting main course, but the parcels also make a delicious appetiser.

Keep remaining phyllo sheets covered with a sheet of greaseproof paper covered with a damp cloth.

Kumara and Zucchini Parcels with Pumpkin Coconut Sauce

Serves 8 as an appetiser, or 4 as a main course

FILLING

2 tbsp butter
2 cups grated kumara
3 cloves garlic, crushed
1 onion, chopped very finely
2 tsp curry powder
2 cups grated zucchini
250g cottage cheese
1 egg, lightly beaten

1/2 cup yoghurt
1/2 cup cheddar or gruyère cheese
2 tbsp chopped basil or coriander
few drops chilli sauce
salt and pepper to taste
16 sheets phyllo pastry
1/4 cup melted butter

Grate kumara into a bowl of salted water to prevent discolouring. Drain well, squeezing out all excess liquid. Melt the 2 tbsp butter in a frying pan, and cook the onions, garlic and kumara for about 3 minutes until softened. Stir in the curry powder and zucchini, and cook for 1 minute. Combine the cooked vegetables in a bowl with the cottage cheese, yoghurt, cheese, egg, chopped herbs, chilli sauce, salt and pepper. Mix well.

PUMPKIN COCONUT SAUCE

1 cup cooked pumpkin, drained
1 cup thick coconut cream
salt and pepper

2 tbsp finely chopped spring onions
1/4 tsp each nutmeg, cinnamon and
    curry powder

Put all the ingredients in a blender or food processor and blend until smooth. Heat gently in a small saucepan.

TO ASSEMBLE PARCELS
Preheat oven to 190°C.

Fold one sheet of phyllo pastry in half, brush with butter and top with another sheet of phyllo pastry folded in half, giving a total thickness of 4 sheets. Butter well. Put 2 heaped tbsp of filling at one end, fold in the sides, and roll up neatly to make a parcel. Continue with remaining phyllo sheets and filling.

Put seam side down on a buttered baking tray and brush with melted butter. Bake for 20-25 minutes or until golden-brown and crisp.

Serve with pumpkin sauce.

These mussel fritters, based on a recipe using the flesh from the magnificent conch shell in the Caribbean, make wonderful appetisers to serve with drinks. The recipe is also delicious using other molluscs.

Paua (Abalone) Fritters

Be sure to remove and discard the sandy intestinal sac of the paua before grinding. If desired, some of the colourful lip may be removed. I prefer to remove most of this, but other people consider it to be the best part of all. It is a matter of personal preference.

Mussel Fritters with Curry Mayonnaise

500g mussel meat, finely chopped
1 medium capsicum, finely diced
2 onions, finely chopped
1 tbsp chopped parsley
1 tsp fennel, dill or coriander seeds, crushed
1 1/2 tsp chilli pepper or crushed chillis
1 tsp Worcestershire sauce
1 tsp crushed fresh garlic
1 tsp freshly ground black pepper
1 1/2 tsp curry powder
2 tsp salt
1 tsp chicken stock powder
grated rind and juice of 1 lemon
1/2 cup milk
1 egg, lightly beaten
1 1/2 cups flour
1/4 tsp baking soda
2 tsp baking powder
oil for deep frying

Mix all the ingredients together except for the flour, baking powder and soda. Sift in these last three ingredients, stir gently and let the fritter mix rest in the refrigerator for 1 and up to 24 hours.

Drop teaspoonfuls of the mixture into hot oil and deep fry till golden-brown. Drain on paper towels and serve with the Curry Mayonnaise on p. 218 or Tartare Sauce on p. 79.

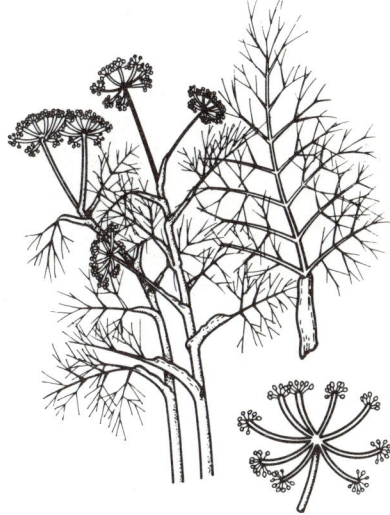

Stir-fried vegetables make an excellent accompaniment to many western as well as far eastern dishes, and make a nutritious light vegetarian meal by the addition of lightly toasted nuts and/or sesame seeds. Serve with brown rice or noodles.

Oriental Stir-fried Vegetables♥

500g vegetables, such as bean sprouts, broccoli, cabbage, Chinese cabbage, capsicums, carrots, cauliflower, celery, eggplant, green beans, mushrooms, onions, snowpeas, spinach, tomatoes, zucchini

2 tbsp oil
1-2 cloves garlic, crushed
1/2-1 tsp grated fresh ginger

ORIENTAL VEGETABLE SAUCE

1/2 cup vegetable or chicken stock
1 tbsp soya sauce
1/2 tsp salt
1/2 tsp sugar or honey

1 1/2 tbsp black bean sauce or oyster sauce (optional)
2 tsp cornflour mixed with a little water (optional)

Wash vegetables and peel where necessary. Cut onions and capsicums into squares or strips. Slice green beans, celery and mushrooms. Cut eggplant into small cubes or thin sticks. Break cauliflower and broccoli into small florets. Cut tomatoes into wedges. Cut carrots and zucchini into slanted, diagonal slices. Cut spinach into strips. Remove ends of snowpeas and leave whole.

Combine all ingredients for the sauce together in a jug or bowl.

Heat oil in a large wok or frying pan. Add the garlic and ginger, and stir once with a large spoon or wok spoon. If using eggplant, add first and stir-fry for 1 minute, then add broccoli, cabbage, carrots, green beans and cauliflower and stir-fry for 2 minutes. Then add zucchini, mushrooms, celery, onions and tomatoes for a further 1 minute, then capsicums, spinach and snowpeas for less than a minute. Add sauce, and beansprouts, and cook just until the sauce is combined with the vegetables and slightly thickened. All the vegetables except for eggplant must still be crisp/tender. Serve immediately.

These crepes have a superb flavour, and even people who claim to dislike eggplant always enjoy them. The crepes can be served as a starter or as a vegetarian main course accompanied by a simple rice dish such as the Brown Rice Pilaf (p. 30), and a green salad. The Ratatouille recipe is also delicious as a side vegetable, or served as a simple meal or appetiser with rice or pasta.

It is important that the eggplant is cooked until tender in this and any other dish – underdone eggplant is very unpalatable.

Ratatouille Martinique
Add 1 cup thick coconut cream to the Ratatouille at the end of the cooking time.

Ratatouille Crepes with a Mild Mustard Sauce

Serves 8-10 as an appetiser, or 4-6 as a main course

RATATOUILLE
2 medium-sized eggplants
salt
3 tbsp oil, preferably olive
3 tsp crushed fresh garlic
1 large onion, peeled, halved and thinly sliced
1 stalk celery with leaves, thinly sliced (optional)
2 small carrots, halved and thinly sliced (optional)
4 zucchini, sliced
1 capsicum, halved and thinly sliced
2 cups peeled tomatoes, fresh or canned
3 tbsp chopped fresh basil
1 tsp dried oregano
1/4 cup vinegar
1 tbsp sugar
salt and freshly ground black pepper to taste
1/4 cup black olives, stoned (optional)

Slice and then dice the eggplants into small, neat cubes. Sprinkle lightly with salt and stand for an hour in a colander. Rinse, then dry in a clean cloth.

Heat the oil in a large, heavy frying pan, or wok, and sauté the onion, garlic and celery and/or carrots until the onion is soft. Add the rinsed and dried eggplant to the pan, stirring until well coated with oil. Add the zucchini and capsicum and stir for a few minutes. Add the tomatoes, basil, oregano, vinegar, sugar, salt and pepper, and cook the mixture over a gentle heat for about 30 minutes. The vegetables should be tender but still hold their shape. Stir in the olives and adjust seasoning to taste.

CREPES
1 quantity Crepe Batter, p. 34, making 10 crepes

MUSTARD SAUCE
1 recipe Bechamel Sauce, p. 221
2 tsp mild mustard
1 1/2 cups cheddar cheese

Stir the mustard into the Bechamel Sauce, together with 1/2 cup cheese, keeping the remaining 1 cup cheese for topping.

TO ASSEMBLE
Preheat the oven to 180°C.

Put about 2 tbsp of Ratatouille filling down one side of each crepe, then roll up, folding in the ends. Place seam-side down on a well-greased ovenproof dish. Top with the mustard sauce, and sprinkle on the extra grated cheese. Bake for 20 minutes, or until cheese is melted and golden.

These delicious cakes can be made instead with chopped prawns or crayfish meat, or a mixture of white fish and any of the above.

Samoan Crab Cakes

1 tbsp butter
1 large onion, finely chopped
2 stalks celery, finely chopped
2 cloves garlic, crushed
1 1/4 cups fresh breadcrumbs
1 cup mayonnaise
1 1/2 cups cracker crumbs
2 tbsp grated lemon rind
1/2 tsp ready-made mild mustard

a few drops Tabasco
500g crabmeat, fresh or canned, drained
1 egg, beaten
1/3 cup ghee, or oil and butter mixed for frying
salt and pepper
lemon wedges for garnish

Heat the 1 tbsp butter, and fry the onion, celery and garlic until the vegetables are tender. Mix all the ingredients together in a large bowl, except for the ghee for frying. Shape into cakes and fry in hot ghee for 3-4 minutes each side, turning carefully. Serve with lemon wedges and Tartare Sauce (p.79), or the Curry Mayonnaise on p. 218.

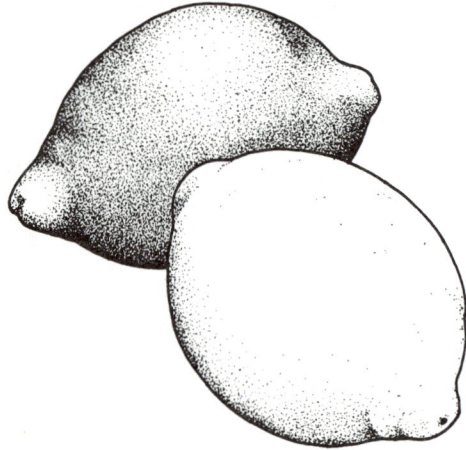

This seafood lasagne is a rich and impressive dish to serve to friends. If you have some Tomato and Basil Sauce and cooked spinach in the freezer it is not very difficult to prepare, and the compliments you receive will make any effort very worthwhile.

If using oven-ready lasagne sheets, let the dish rest for a hour or so after assembling and before baking to allow the pasta to soften.

The blue cheese gives a wonderful flavour to the dish that even people who don't like blue cheese really enjoy.

Seafood Lasagne with Spinach and Blue Cheese

250g fish fillets
1 1/2 cups assorted chopped seafood, such as mussels, prawns, shrimps (small ones left whole), crabmeat and crayfish
1/2 cup white wine
juice and grated rind of 1 lemon
400g par-cooked or about 6 sheets oven-ready lasagne
1 quantity (2 cups) Tomato and Basil Sauce, p. 225
1 quantity (2 cups) Bechamel Sauce, p. 221

2 cups grated cheese such as cheddar, mozzarella or gruyère, or a combination
1 1/2 cups cooked taro leaves (see p. 69) or spinach
60g blue cheese or gorgonzola
1 cup cream or coconut cream
1/4 cup parmesan cheese
2 tbsp chopped fresh basil
1 tsp grated nutmeg
salt and pepper

Poach the fish and seafood in the white wine and grated lemon rind and juice for just 30 seconds.

Combine the fish, seafood and the poaching liquid with 1 cup of the Tomato and Basil Sauce, leaving the other cup of sauce for the top of the lasagne. Combine the spinach, blue cheese and cream or coconut cream, and add salt and pepper to taste. Preheat oven to 180°C.

Butter a baking dish approximately 30 x 23 cm and about 6 cm deep. Spread in 1/4 of the Bechamel Sauce, then a layer of lasagne, followed by half of the seafood mixture, half of the spinach mixture, 1/3 of the cheese, 1/4 of the Bechamel Sauce, and then a layer of lasagne. Repeat once more. Top the last layer of lasagne with the reserved 1 cup of Tomato and Basil Sauce, the 1/4 cup of Bechamel Sauce, and 1/3 of the cheese. Sprinkle on the 1/4 cup parmesan, 2 tbsp chopped basil and grated nutmeg.

Bake at 180°C for 45 minutes. Let stand for 10 minutes before serving.

Samosas are an excellent appetiser to serve at any time. They go especially well with a cold beer and are delicious before a curry lunch or dinner. I spent my childhood in Kenya, where there is a very large Indian community, and I have fond memories of munching on these crisp, spicy little pastry triangles whenever I was hungry. Those made at a wonderful, simple and very basic little Indian restaurant in Mombasa called The Blue Room were the finest samosas I have tasted anywhere. I am always delighted when I go back to Mombasa to find The Blue Room is still, after more than thirty years, in the same place and serving samosas that are as good as they ever were.

Spring roll wrappers can also be used to make triangular samosas and can be a great time-saver if you purchase commercially made ones. To make your own, see p. 185.

Other fillings, such as chopped curried vegetables or chicken, can be used to fill the samosas.

Samosas

SAMOSA PASTRY

1 1/2 cups plain flour	1/4 cup water
1 tbsp oil	

Sift flour, stir in oil and water, and knead until smooth. (A food processor with blade makes the kneading much easier and produces a light pastry.) Rest the pastry, covered, for 1 hour.

Roll the pastry out into a large, thin rectangle. Cut pastry into rounds, using a 10 cm cutter if you are going to make semi-circular or half-moon-shaped samosas, or cut into 20 cm circles if you are going to make triangular-shaped samosas, and then cut this 20 cm circle in half.

MEAT SAMOSA FILLING

250g minced steak or lamb	1 tsp ground cumin
1 tbsp ghee or oil	1 tsp chilli sauce or more to taste
1 large onion, finely chopped	2 tbsp tomato sauce
1 capsicum, finely chopped	1/2 tsp beef stock powder
2 cloves garlic, crushed	salt and pepper to taste
2 tsp curry powder	1 tbsp chopped fresh coriander
1 tsp chopped fresh ginger	

Cook minced meat in a saucepan without any ghee, oil or water until the fat in the meat is released and becomes liquid. Drain the meat in a metal colander, and discard the fat (not down the sink!)

Heat the ghee and fry the onions, capsicum and garlic until they are tender. Add curry powder, ginger and cumin, and cook for 1 minute. Add the mince and cook for 5 minutes.

Add chilli sauce, tomato sauce, beef stock powder, salt and pepper and cook gently for 30 minutes, adding a little water if necessary. Add chopped fresh coriander and adjust seasoning. Cool before filling samosas.

POTATO AND PEA FILLING

Make as for the meat filling, but substitute 300g potatoes (cut into small cubes and cooked) for the minced meat, together with 3/4 cup frozen peas, thawed. Substitute 2 tbsp lemon juice for the tomato sauce, and vegetable stock for beef stock.

TO MAKE UP SAMOSAS

Half Moons: Place a heaped tablespoon of the mixture on half the pastry circle. Fold over the other half, wet the edges and press together with a fork.

Triangular Samosas: Put a teaspoonful of filling on one side of the half circle and brush edges with water. Fold dough over and press edges together firmly.

Phyllo pastry can be used for making samosas and spring rolls and, treated with care, can be deep fried very successfully. To make triangular phyllo parcels, use the same method of folding the pastry as for spring roll wrappers, cutting 3 thicknesses of phyllo with a sharp knife to desired width for the phyllo triangles. Use melted butter to seal.

To wrap samosas using ready-made spring roll wrappers: Cut wrappers lengthways into strips about 8 cm wide. Working with the nearest end of one of the strips to you, put a teaspoon of filling at the left corner of the strip, then fold the right corner over diagonally to form a neat triangle. Repeat the diagonal folding, keeping the triangular shape, until you reach the end of the strip. Moisten the edges with beaten egg, and press to seal.

TO COOK
Deep fry in hot oil until golden and crisp.

Tempura makes a delicious appetiser or light meal with rice and salad. The vegetables and seafood must be very fresh and can be varied according to what is available and in season.

Seafood and Vegetable Tempura

BATTER
1 cup plain flour
1/3 cup cornflour

1 egg or 1 egg white
3/4 cup iced water

VEGETABLES AND SEAFOOD
12 green beans
1 onion, sliced into rings
1 zucchini, sliced into rings
4 mushrooms, halved
1 capsicum, sliced into rings

8 large prawns, de-veined with
   bodies shelled
4 small, thin fish fillets
4 mussels or scallops, cleaned with
   shells removed

Prepare the batter 1 hour before serving time if possible. Beat egg or egg white and iced water together with a balloon whisk. Sift the flours into a bowl, and lightly stir in the egg/water mixture. Do not over-stir. Keep batter, fish and vegetables chilled until serving time.

Heat oil in a large saucepan or deep fryer to a temperature of 170°C. (A bread cube dropped in should turn golden in less than a minute.) Dip fish and vegetables one by one into the batter, then deep fry until golden-brown and crisp. Drain on kitchen paper and serve with dipping sauce.

SOYA AND GINGER DIPPING SAUCE♥
8 tbsp light soya sauce
4 tbsp sherry or mirin
1 tbsp grated ginger

1 tbsp honey
1 tbsp toasted sesame seeds
1 tbsp lemon juice

Mix all the ingredients together until well combined.

I first tasted these peanut fritters in Bali many years ago, when I stayed in a little guest house at Kuta Beach in the days when there was no electricity, no hotels, and the few of us travellers who were there would gather on the beach in the evening to watch the most amazing sunsets. I don't suppose I would recognise Kuta today as it has become so overdeveloped. Recently, however, I was very happy to be able to re-create the delicious peanut fritters that I associate with the place after experimenting with a number of recipes found in various Asian cookbooks, and adding some ingredients such as the coconut cream that I felt important to the flavour of the end product.

The fritters, which are best served at room temperature, make an excellent appetiser to serve with drinks, especially cold beer. They are good to serve before spicy curries, with a coconut sambal (p. 211).

To remove skins from raw peanuts, roast in a hot oven for 10 minutes or until skins slip off easily when rubbed.

Spicy Peanut Fritters

210g raw skinned peanuts
2 cloves garlic, crushed
1 onion, finely chopped
1 tbsp crunchy peanut butter
2 tsp ground coriander
1/2 tsp cumin powder
1/2 tsp turmeric
1 cup self-raising flour
2 tbsp chopped fresh coriander
1/4 cup milk
1/4 cup coconut cream
1 egg, lightly beaten
1/2-1 tsp salt
1 tsp freshly ground black pepper
2 tsp crushed chillis
1 tsp vegetable or herb stock
　powder
oil for deep frying

Roughly chop the skinned peanuts, leaving some whole. Do *not* mince in a food processor. Combine the peanuts with the rest of the ingredients in a large bowl to make a thick, fairly stiff batter. Deep fry by dropping teaspoonfuls into the hot oil and cook until golden-brown and crisp.

We often make these easy corn fritters as an appetiser before our special Thai dinners. They are economical to make. You can serve them with any of the sambals on pp. 211–13, but we usually serve the fritters with the Coconut Mint Sambal on p. 211.

The fritters can be served hot or cold.

If frying in a deep fryer, use 2 spoons to flatten the fritters while they are frying. If frying in a shallow pan, press the fritters flat against the bottom of the pan with a metal spatula or spoon.

Thai Corn Fritters

440g can whole-kernel corn, drained, or equivalent fresh corn kernels	1 tsp baking powder
	1/2 tsp crushed fresh garlic
	1/2 tsp turmeric
1 onion, finely chopped	1 tsp ground coriander
2-4 green chillis, seeded and chopped, or 1-2 tsp crushed chilli or chilli sauce, p. 227	1 tsp good-quality curry powder
	1 tsp chopped basil leaves
	2 tbsp chopped spring onions
1/2 capsicum, finely chopped	1/4 cup grated fresh coconut
1 egg, beaten lightly	2 tsp cracked black pepper
1/2 cup rice flour or plain white flour	2 tsp salt
	vegetable oil for frying

Press corn with the back of a spoon or use a fork so that it will not pop when fried. (Do not use a food processor.) The onion and capsicum can be chopped in the food processor but only roughly. Do not allow them to become mushy. Combine all the ingredients except the vegetable oil.

Either shallow fry in a hot pan or deep fry. Drop tablespoonfuls of the corn mixture into the hot oil, press to flatten and cook 2-3 minutes on each side, or until golden and crisp. Do not try to cook too many at once. Drain on kitchen paper.

These spicy fish cakes, which are delicious served with Coconut Mint Sambal (p. 211), make wonderful little appetisers to serve with drinks or as a first course.

Breadcrumbs are not authentically Thai but they do make the fish cakes easier to handle.

Thai Spicy Fish Cakes

1 kg fish fillets, cubed	1/2 cup breadcrumbs
1 egg, beaten	

MARINADE

2 small onions or 1 large onion, chopped	2 tbsp soya sauce
	2 tsp brown sugar
1 tsp crushed fresh garlic	1 cup chopped green beans or snake beans
2 tsp grated fresh ginger	
3 tsp chopped fresh chilli or bottled crushed chilli, or more to taste	8 young fresh lemon or lime leaves
1 green or red capsicum, chopped	2 tbsp chopped fresh coriander, mint or basil
juice and grated rind of 1 lemon or 2 small limes	1 tsp salt
	1 tsp pepper

Mix the fish cubes and marinade ingredients together. Leave for 1 hour. Put in a food processor with blade or meat mincer, and mince. Add the beaten egg and breadcrumbs and mix together well. Shape the mixture into balls the size of an egg.

Flatten and deep fry 5 or 6 at a time for a few minutes in a wok or deep fryer. Remove with a slotted spoon and drain on kitchen paper.

Any vegetables in season can be used for this curry. We serve it as a vegetarian main course with Dhal (p. 8) and Chappatis. A small bowl of this curry can also accompany chicken and meat curries.

Vegetable Curry with Coconut Cream

2 tbsp ghee
1 tbsp mustard seeds
2 onions, sliced
1 capsicum, sliced
2 tsp chopped fresh chillis
1 cup curry paste, p. 228
2 medium carrots, sliced
1 cup par-boiled and cubed potato,
    sweet potato, breadfruit or taro
    root
1 cup sliced green beans
1 cup cauliflower, broken into
florets, or peeled green pawpaw
    in small cubes
1/2 cup chopped eggplant
1/2 cup sliced mushrooms
1 cup in total other vegetables such
    as peas, pumpkin, or whatever is
    in season
1 cup tasty vegetable stock
2 cups coconut cream
salt to taste
chopped fresh basil or coriander

Heat ghee in a heavy saucepan or wok. Cook mustard seeds till they start to pop. Add onions and cook till soft. Add capsicums, chopped chillis and curry paste, and cook till the curry paste releases a pleasant aroma. Add carrots and potato, and cook till well coated with paste. Add other vegetables, adding mushrooms last. Cook 5 minutes. Add vegetable stock and 1 cup of coconut cream, and simmer the curry gently until all the vegetables are cooked but still pleasantly firm. Add salt to taste. Put curry in a serving dish and top with remaining 1 cup of coconut cream and chopped fresh basil or coriander.

Tropical Vegetables and Vegetable Dishes

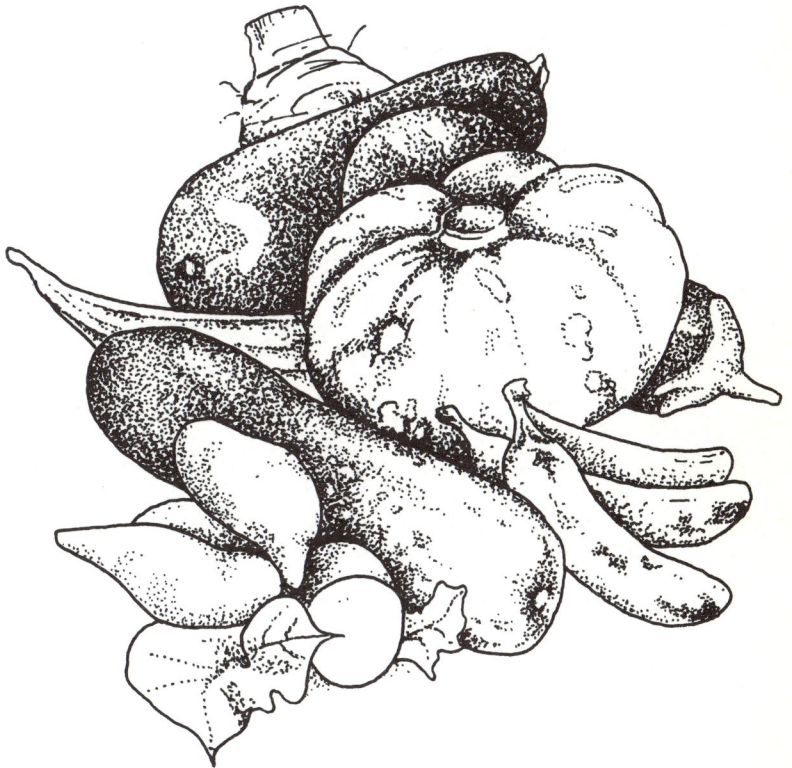

To Prepare

Green beans can be cut into thin slices diagonally or into lengths cross-wise. Young and small green beans can be cooked whole, with both end tips removed.

To Cook

Beans should be steamed or cooked in plenty of boiling salted water for as little as 3 minutes, depending on the cut of the bean. Rinse quickly with cold water to stop further cooking. To reheat, pop quickly into a few tablespoons of boiling water, or toss in a pan with a little melted butter or garlic butter, salt and pepper, and a little lemon juice and/or fresh herbs such as chopped basil or mint, and heat through.

To Freeze

Beans can be blanched in boiling water for 30 seconds, then cooled immediately in iced water. Drain, and pack in plastic bags.

Beans

Green Beans with Cashewnuts

500g green beans
3 tbsp butter

1/4 cup cashewnuts, chopped, or other nuts
salt and pepper

Prepare beans as described, and cook till crisp but tender. In a heavy frying pan heat the butter and sauté the cashewnuts (or other nuts) for 3 minutes. Stir in the beans until heated through, and add salt and pepper to taste.

Green Beans with Coconut

500g green beans, sliced
1 small onion, thinly sliced
1 small capsicum, finely chopped
2 cloves garlic, crushed
1 cup freshly grated coconut

1 tsp ground cumin
1 tsp ground coriander
1/2 tsp ground turmeric
1 tsp salt
4 tbsp butter or ghee

Briefly blend all the ingredients except the butter and beans in a food processor or blender. Melt the butter, stir in the coconut/spice mixture. Cook for a few minutes, add the green beans and cook over a very gentle heat, covered, until the beans are tender – about 10-15 minutes. Uncover from time to time and stir.

Oriental Green Bean Salad♥

500g young green beans

DRESSING

1 tsp juice squeezed from grated ginger
1 1/2 tsp honey

1 1/2 tbsp soya sauce
1 tsp lemon juice
2 tsp sesame seeds, toasted

Leave green beans whole but slice long beans into fairly long lengths. Boil or steam for 4-5 minutes, until tender but crisp. Rinse and drain.

Shake all the salad dressing ingredients except sesame seeds together in a jar until well combined. Toss the beans in the dressing, then sprinkle the sesame seeds over the beans just before serving.

For use as a vegetable, bread-fruit should be mature and fully formed, but green in colour. Once the breadfruit becomes a mottled yellow and brown, it is suitable for use in cakes, scones and desserts.

To Prepare and Cook

Breadfruit can be baked, boiled or steamed. For baking or roasting, the whole, unpeeled breadfruit must first be scrubbed well. Punch a few holes into the flesh, and bake or roast the breadfruit in a moderate oven for about an hour, or until tender. The whole breadfruit can also be boiled, unpeeled, or cut into chunks and baked, boiled or steamed. Once cooled, the breadfruit can be peeled.

The cooked breadfruit can be served hot with melted butter, salt and pepper, or sliced and layered in a roasting or baking dish with salt, pepper and coconut cream and baked for 20 minutes. Breadfruit can be mashed, or curried, and makes excellent chips. It also makes a wonderfully creamy soup (see p. 7) and is good in a salad.

To Freeze

Cooked breadfruit freezes very well.

Breadfruit

Breadfruit Chips

Cut a scrubbed green breadfruit in quarters. Peel and remove core. Put in a bowl of cold water for several hours, then cut into neat chips. Return to cold water until ready to use. Dry with a clean cloth, and deep fry in hot oil until golden. Drain on kitchen paper.

Creamed Breadfruit

Cook a whole mature breadfruit in boiling salted water for 40 minutes. Peel, remove core and mash with 2 tbsp butter and 2/3 cup hot milk, and salt and pepper to taste. Serve as is, or stir in the yolk of 1 egg and fold in the stiffly beaten white. Pile in an ovenproof dish and bake in a moderately hot oven for 10 minutes, or pipe individual mounds on a greased baking dish and bake until golden.

Breadfruit Fritters

Prepare the above recipe with egg yolk and stiffly beaten white folded in. Drop spoonfuls into hot, deep oil, and fry until golden.

Scalloped Breadfruit

1 small cooked breadfruit, peeled
   and sliced
salt and pepper
3 tbsp butter

2 cups Bechamel Sauce, p. 221
1 cup grated mature cheddar cheese
chopped parsley

Put half the breadfruit slices in a layer in a buttered ovenproof dish. Top with salt and pepper, and dot with butter. Pour over 1 cup of the Bechamel Sauce and 1/2 cup cheese. Repeat with remaining breadfruit, sauce and cheese. Bake in a 180°C oven for 30 minutes. Sprinkle on chopped parsley and serve.

Curried Breadfruit Salad

Add 2 tsp curry powder to the mayonnaise, stirring until well combined.

Caribbean Breadfruit Salad

1 small cooked, mature, green breadfruit, peeled and cut into small cubes
1/2 cup vinaigrette dressing
1/2 cup mayonnaise (or more)
1 cup chopped celery
1/2 cup chopped spring onions
2 hard-boiled eggs, chopped
1 tsp honey
1 tsp prepared mustard
salt and pepper to taste

Marinate the breadfruit cubes in the vinaigrette dressing while the breadfruit is still warm. Mix together the remaining ingredients except the egg, and stir into the breadfruit. Top with chopped egg, and serve chilled.

Many types of cabbage grow in the tropics, from the close-leafed, English-type cabbage through to a variety of Chinese-type cabbages.

Uses

As a general rule, the firm close-leafed cabbage is excellent raw in salads, such as coleslaw, or lightly steamed or sautéed in oil or butter, and flavoured with a touch of curry powder or garlic, or cooked in coconut cream. It is always best not to overcook it, but to serve cabbage when it is still a little crisp. Chinese-type cabbages are not generally suitable for use in salads, as they can be bitter when raw, but they are excellent cooked in any of the above ways, and in stir-fried dishes.

To Freeze

The close-leafed cabbage can be frozen to use later in cooked dishes. Remove core, cut into wedges and blanch for 2 minutes, or shred and blanch for 30 seconds. Cool and pack. The Chinese-type cabbage will become soft with freezing. Wash leaves well, trim off ends of stems, blanch for 1 minute only, and plunge into iced water. Drain thoroughly, and pack in bags. Only partially thaw before using.

Cabbage

Caribbean Coleslaw

1 small head cabbage, cleaned, cored and shredded
1 large carrot, peeled and grated
1 stalk celery, very finely chopped
1 medium-sized capsicum, very finely chopped

1 cup Tropical Fruit Mayonnaise, p. 218
1/2 cup sour cream
2 tbsp lemon juice or vinegar
salt and pepper to taste

Combine all the ingredients together until well combined. Chill until almost ready to serve. Allow to come to room temperature before serving.

Carrots can be grown in the tropics during the cooler months.

To Prepare
It is not necessary to peel fresh young carrots. Scrub and cook whole, or slice lengthwise in halves or quarters or cut crosswise into thick or thin slices, or cut into julienne slices.

To Cook
Steam or boil until just tender. Toss with melted butter and/or lemon juice, and chopped fresh herbs or spices such as cinnamon and nutmeg.

To Freeze
Blanch carrots in boiling water for 2 minutes if sliced, or 4 minutes for whole young carrots. Cool in cold water, drain and pack.

Carrots

Orange and Ginger Carrots♥

1 kg carrots
250 ml orange juice
1 tbsp oil
2 tsp grated ginger

1 tsp salt
2 tsp brown sugar
chopped mint leaves

Preheat oven to 180°C. Cut carrots lengthwise into fingers about 5 cm long and 1 cm thick. Put in a baking dish. Mix orange juice, oil, ginger, salt and sugar, and pour over the carrots. Cover and bake for 30 minutes or until just tender. Serve hot or very well chilled, topped with fresh mint.

Carrots in a Parsley and Coconut Sauce

500g carrots
3/4 cup coconut cream
pinch sugar

salt and pepper
1 tbsp chopped parsley

Leave young small carrots whole, and slice large ones. Cook as directed. Drain well, season to taste with salt and pepper, and a pinch of sugar. Return to the pan and add 1/2 cup coconut cream. Bring to the boil and cook until the coconut cream is slightly reduced. Serve topped with remaining coconut cream and chopped parsley.

This is a staple crop of many Pacific islands, and is also important in African diets. As well as being eaten as a root vegetable, the root is also made into flour.

Cassava does not store well, and should be used within 2-3 days. However, the cassava can be peeled and kept in bags in the refrigerator, where it will last up to 2 weeks. Be sure to use fresh, mature roots that are undamaged. The flesh should be white or cream coloured with very little fibre in the centre.

Uses

Grated raw cassava root can be used to thicken soups and stews. The leaves can also be cooked as a green vegetable by boiling in water, uncovered, for 10-15 minutes. (It is important to boil the leaves properly as they may contain toxins.) Cassava is also used as a starch vegetable and in puddings, desserts, cakes and breads. Cassava chips are perfect for serving with drinks.

To Prepare and Cook

Clean roots thoroughly, peel, then trim off ends. Split larger and more mature roots in half and remove fibre from centre. Cut into 6 cm pieces and steam or boil. Discard the cooking water as it may contain a minute quantity of toxins.

To Freeze

Cassava can be peeled and frozen uncooked in plastic bags. To use from the freezer, boil or steam without defrosting first.

Cassava (Manioc, Tapioca, Arrowroot)

Cassava Chips

1 kg peeled cassava
salt

chilli and/or garlic powder
  (optional)
oil for frying

Slice the cassava very thinly, as for potato crisps. (A food processor is ideal for this.) Soak in cold water for about 2 hours. Drain and dry with a clean cloth. Mix salt with chilli and garlic powder.

Deep fry cassava chips in hot oil until golden-brown and crisp. Drain on absorbent paper. Put the chips in a paper bag or bowl, and toss well with salt, chilli and/or garlic. Store in an airtight container.

Savoury Cassava Cakes

1 onion, grated
420g cassava, peeled and cooked
250g of any of the following: cooked
    fish, chicken, prawns, bacon,
    ham, beef, lentils or other pulses
2 tbsp chopped coriander

1/2 tsp curry powder (optional)
1/2 tsp chilli powder (optional)
2 eggs
fine breadcrumbs or seasoned flour
salt and pepper
oil for frying

Grate or mash cooked cassava. Combine with the remaining ingredients except eggs and flour or breadcrumbs. Season the mixture to taste. Separate eggs and add egg yolks to cassava mixture. Beat egg whites with a little water just until frothy. Shape the cassava mixture into flat cakes, dip in egg white, then into breadcrumbs or seasoned flour. Shallow fry in hot oil until golden.

This is a pleasant-tasting, pale green or white pear-shaped vegetable, at its best when young and firm. It keeps well in the refrigerator.

Uses

Chokos have a mild flavour that can be enhanced with the right sauce; they are also good in curries, in chutneys and relishes, and even in desserts. Chokos stewed with sugar, water, lemon and cinnamon or cloves taste similar to pears.

To Cook

Young chokos can be cooked whole, but more mature fruits need to be peeled and sliced. They can be steamed or boiled until tender, and served tossed with butter and fresh herbs, or with an appropriate sauce.

To Freeze

Wash and freeze whole or cut into slices, uncooked and unblanched, packed in plastic bags.

If using macadamias or cashewnuts instead of pecans, these should be lightly toasted.

Choko (Christophene)

Choko au Gratin

Serves 6-8

3 large chokos, peeled and sliced
1 large onion, finely chopped
2 tbsp butter
2 cups Bechamel Sauce, p. 221

1 cup grated mature cheddar cheese
1 cup dry breadcrumbs
2 tbsp chopped parsley
salt and pepper

Cook the chokos in boiling water until tender. Drain well, lay in a buttered ovenproof dish, and sprinkle with salt and pepper. Cook the onion in the butter until soft. Stir into the Bechamel Sauce, along with half the cheese. Season to taste. Pour over the chokos. Top with remaining 1/2 cup cheese, the breadcrumbs and chopped parsley

Bake in a 180°C oven for 20-30 minutes or until top is golden-brown.

Choko Stuffed with Pecans

3 large chokos
1 large onion, finely chopped
1 tbsp vegetable oil
1 clove garlic, crushed
1 tsp mild curry powder
3 medium tomatoes, chopped

1 cup pecans or other nuts, chopped
2 tbsp butter
1/4 cup dry breadcrumbs
1/4 cup grated parmesan cheese
salt and pepper

Boil the whole chokos in salted water for about 30 minutes, or until tender. Remove from saucepan and cool. Cut in halves lengthwise. Scoop out the pulp, including the edible seeds. Reserve the shells.

Heat oil and sauté the onion and garlic until soft. Add curry powder and cook for 1 minute. Add tomatoes and choko pulp. Cook until the mixture is fairly dry. Remove from heat and stir in nuts. Season to taste with salt and pepper, and pack into choko shells. Sprinkle with cheese and breadcrumbs, and dot with butter.

Bake at 180°C for 15 minutes, or until tops are golden-brown.

57

Corn grows well in tropical climates. To choose corn, the ears should have fresh green husks and pale silky ends (not dark brown ones). It is best to eat corn while it is very fresh.

To Prepare and Cook

Corn can be cooked in the husk, with the husk and silk removed after cooking, or you can remove the husk and silk first. Cook in unsalted water for 3-5 minutes only.

When uncooked kernels are needed, cut the raw kernels off the cob with a sharp knife. When cooked corn kernels are needed, cool the cooked corn cob first. Flavour corn after cooking with salt, pepper and melted butter.

Corn is good in soups and fritters, and teamed with fish or chicken. The following recipes are for serving corn as a side vegetable.

To Freeze

Whole ears of corn can be blanched for 2 minutes, then plunged into iced water, drained, and wrapped individually with plastic wrap. Pack in groups in plastic bags. For whole-kernel corn, slice kernels off the cob after blanching and cooling, and pack in plastic freezer bags.

Corn

Corn with Coconut Cream

3 cups cooked corn kernels
2 tbsp butter
1 tbsp flour
1 cup thick coconut cream
1 tsp sugar

1/4 cup milk
1 tsp salt
1/4 tsp freshly ground pepper
pinch nutmeg

In a frying pan melt the butter and stir in flour, and cook for 1 minute. Add the coconut cream and sugar, stirring, then add the milk. Stir until the sauce is smooth. Stir in the corn kernels with the salt, pepper and nutmeg. Heat through and serve.

Creole Corn Pudding

2 cups (about 5-6 ears) cooked fresh corn, or 440g can corn kernels
1 tbsp sugar
1 tsp salt
1/2 tsp freshly ground black pepper
60g butter, melted

5 eggs, well beaten
1 cup milk or thin coconut cream
1 cup cream or thick coconut cream
1 tbsp cornflour mixed with 4 tbsp cold water

Preheat oven to 180°C. Put the corn into a bowl and mash just a little with a fork. Add all the remaining ingredients and stir to combine well. Butter a baking dish and pour in the mixture. Bake for 30 minutes or until a knife inserted comes out clean.

Eggplants grow very well in the tropics, and come in various shapes and sizes, and different shades of purple through to white. Before cooking, eggplants should be shiny and very firm, with no wrinkling of the skin.

To Prepare and Cook

There are many ways of preparing and cooking eggplant. Often it is sliced, cubed and sprinkled with salt, and left to drain in a colander for 30 minutes before cooking. This draws any bitterness from the eggplant and makes it less likely to absorb a lot of oil during cooking. (If sliced or cubed eggplant is microwaved for a short time before frying, it will absorb less oil. It can also be boiled or steamed rather than cooked in oil, but the flavour will be less distinct.) Eggplant can also be roasted whole, the skin pierced in a few places, until blackened and wrinkled, so that the skin can be easily removed and the pulp used in dips and paté.

To Freeze

Eggplant becomes very soft with freezing. It can be frozen, sliced, dipped in lemon juice, blanched in boiling water for 3 minutes, and dipped again in lemon juice. It can also be cut into cubes and cooked in oil with a little onion, then frozen for use in dishes such as Ratatouille.

Eggplant (Aubergine)

Brinjal Bartha (Indian Curried Eggplant)♥

2 large eggplants, unpeeled
2 large ripe tomatoes, peeled or
    unpeeled
2 tbsp cooking oil
2 medium onions, finely chopped
3 cloves garlic, crushed

1 1/2 tsp grated fresh ginger
2 tsp mild curry powder
2 tsp salt
2 tbsp chopped fresh coriander or
    basil

Wash and chop the eggplant and tomatoes into small cubes. Heat the oil in a heavy-bottomed frying pan and gently fry the onion, garlic and ginger until soft and starting to brown. Add the salt and curry powder, and mix in thoroughly. Add eggplant and tomato. Stir well and cover the pan.

Cook over a gentle heat, stirring from time to time, to prevent vegetables sticking to the pan. Cook the mixture until it is thick and like a purée. Stir in the coriander and adjust seasoning to taste.

Serve as part of a curry meal, or as a dip with chips, crackers or sliced pita bread. It can be served hot or cold.

Eggplant Baked in Coconut Cream

2 medium-sized eggplants, sliced
1 onion, thinly sliced
4 tbsp vegetable oil
2 cups coconut cream

salt and pepper
pinch brown sugar
2 tbsp chopped fresh herbs, such as
    parsley, basil or coriander

Trim stalk end from eggplant and cut lengthwise into thin 125 mm slices.

Pour 2 tbsp oil into an ovenproof dish. Arrange eggplant slices in dish and brush with 1 tbsp oil. Fry onion in remaining 1 tbsp oil in a small frying pan until soft. Combine salt, pepper, coconut cream and brown sugar. Pour over eggplant and sprinkle with herbs. Bake at 180°C for 30-40 minutes, or until eggplant is tender.

This dish makes an excellent appetiser, or can be served to accompany a special main course.

Eggplant Stuffed with Cashews and Cheese

2 medium eggplants
salt
1 tbsp oil
1 onion, finely chopped
1 clove garlic, crushed
2 medium tomatoes, peeled and
    chopped

3/4 cup soft breadcrumbs
1/2 cup roasted cashewnuts,
    chopped
1/2 cup grated mature cheddar
    cheese
2 tbsp parmesan cheese
salt and pepper to taste

Slice eggplant in half lengthwise. Scoop out flesh, leaving 50 mm flesh around the inside of the skin. Sprinkle inside of shells with salt and stand them upside-down for 30 minutes. Rinse and pat dry.

Heat oil, and cook garlic and onion until soft. Add tomatoes and eggplant flesh and cook over a low heat for 3 minutes or until soft. Combine this mixture with breadcrumbs, cashewnuts, cheddar cheese and salt and pepper to taste, and spoon into the eggplant. Sprinkle top with parmesan, and bake at 180°C for 30 minutes.

This is a traditional dish from Guam.

Coconut Mashed Eggplant

3 large eggplants
1 medium onion, finely chopped
1 clove garlic, crushed
2 small chillis, seeded and chopped
1 tbsp oil

1 1/2 cups coconut cream
1 tsp salt
1 tsp pepper
juice of 1 lemon

Wash eggplants and prick all over with a fork. Bake in a hot oven (200°C) until skin is blackened and blistered. Cool, remove skin and mash. Fry onion, garlic and chillis in the oil until soft but not brown. Add coconut cream and heat through. Combine onion mixture and mashed eggplant with salt and pepper and lemon juice, and serve.

Green pawpaw are always readily available in most tropical places and make a really delicious vegetable, full of nutrients. The sap of the green pawpaw is good for soothing insect bites and stings, and is also used to tenderise meat and octopus or squid (a little, chopped in a marinade, will quickly tenderise, and the meat needs to be watched carefully so that it does not become mushy).

Green pawpaw can also be used in desserts, chutneys and pickles.

To Prepare and Cook as a Vegetable

Wash, peel and cut pawpaw in half lengthwise, and remove seeds. Cut in even cubes or slices, and cook in a pot of boiling salted water for up to 15 minutes until tender, depending on the recipe.

To Freeze

Freeze whole, washed and unpeeled, or peeled and sliced, uncooked, in plastic bags.

Green Pawpaw (Papaya)

Green Pawpaw Baked with Coconut Cream

Boil cubes of pawpaw as described and drain well. Fry 1 sliced onion in 1 tbsp butter. Put pawpaw and onion in a buttered baking dish, and sprinkle with salt, pepper and a pinch of cinnamon. Cover with 2 cups thick coconut cream, and bake at 200°C for 15 minutes.

Braised Green Pawpaw and Tomatoes♥

1/2 green pawpaw
2 tbsp vegetable oil
1 onion, thinly sliced
3 cloves garlic, crushed
2 stalks celery, sliced
1 capsicum, thinly sliced
1 tbsp chopped fresh basil

4 tomatoes, peeled and chopped
1 tbsp vinegar
1 tbsp sugar
salt and freshly ground black
    pepper
1/2 cup water

Cut the pawpaw into small cubes. Boil in enough salted water to cover, and cook until tender but still firm. Drain well. Heat oil in a large frying pan or wok, and cook onions and garlic until soft. Add celery and capsicum, and cook for 4 minutes. Add pawpaw cubes and cook for 1 minute, then stir in basil, tomatoes, vinegar, sugar, salt and pepper, and the 1/2 cup water. Simmer, uncovered, for 15 minutes, or until all the vegetables are tender, stirring from time to time.

This is good with cold meats, as an accompaniment to curries, or as a side-dish with grilled or barbecued fish. Green mango is also good in this salad.

Green Pawpaw Salad

1 medium green pawpaw
1 tsp salt
juice of 2 limes or 1 large lemon
2 tbsp vinegar

1 tbsp vegetable oil
1/2 cup coconut cream
salt and pepper to taste

Peel and grate the pawpaw, and sprinkle with 1 tsp salt and lime juice. Stand in a colander overnight. Rinse with running water, and drain well. Place in a serving bowl, sprinkle with oil and vinegar mixed together, and pour in the coconut cream. Add salt and pepper to taste. Chill.

This sour curry makes a lovely side dish with a roast dinner or as part of a curry buffet. It is a good contrast to any dish cooked in coconut cream.

Green Pawpaw Curry with Tamarind♥

1 medium green pawpaw, peeled,
    seeded and cubed
1 tsp chilli powder
2 tsp crushed fresh garlic
1 tbsp grated fresh ginger
1 tbsp ghee or oil
1/2 tsp cumin seeds
2 tsp mustard seeds

1 large onion, sliced
1 fresh green chilli, seeded and
    chopped
1/4 cup tamarind liquid
1 1/2 cups water
1/4 cup chopped fresh coriander
salt to taste

Cook the pawpaw cubes in boiling water till half cooked. Grind the chilli powder, garlic, ginger and cumin seeds together in a food processor or by hand to form a paste. Heat the ghee in a medium-sized saucepan and cook the mustard seeds until they start to pop. Add the onion and cook until soft. Add the spice paste and cook 2 minutes, then add the half-cooked pawpaw, green chilli, tamarind liquid and water. Bring the mixture to the boil, then reduce heat and simmer gently until the pawpaw is tender and the curry sauce is thickened. Stir regularly. Stir in the coriander leaves, add salt to taste. Cook for several minutes, then turn into a serving bowl.

Kumara are an excellent source of vitamins. The white and yellow varieties are suitable for use in soufflés, savoury and dessert pies, and any recipe that calls for ordinary potatoes. The purple variety most common in New Zealand is suitable for boiling, baking, steaming and roasting.

Kumara can be stored for up to a month in a cool dark place.

To Prepare and Cook
Kumara can go brown quickly once peeled, so soak in water immediately the root is peeled. Lemon juice added to the cooking water also helps prevent discolouration. The skin can be left on, improving the food value, and can be removed after cooking.

To Freeze
Kumara will darken if frozen raw, but freeze very well when cooked. They can be baked for 10 minutes with the skin on, cooled and frozen, and then they can be rebaked once thawed. They can also be frozen as a purée or cooked in slices – add lemon juice to the purée and dip the slices in lemon juice to prevent darkening. Glazed or candied kumara, and mashed kumara mixed with one part orange juice to every four parts kumara, freeze well.

Kumara (Sweet Potatoes)

French Fried Kumara

Peel the kumara and soak in water. Cut into thin chips and soak again for a short while. Dry in a clean cloth. Fry in hot, deep fat or oil for 3-5 minutes or until golden-brown.

Kumara Soufflé

2 cups hot, mashed, cooked kumara	salt and pepper to taste
2 tbsp butter	1 tsp cinnamon
1 onion, very finely chopped	1 cup milk
2 eggs, separated	1 cup grated cheese (optional)

Preheat oven to 200°C. Combine kumara, butter, onion, beaten egg yolks, salt, pepper, cinnamon and milk. Stir in the cheese. Fold in the stiffly beaten egg whites. Do not over-stir. Put the mixture in a 1 litre soufflé or baking dish, and bake for 20-30 minutes or until risen and golden. Serve immediately.

Candied Kumara

4 medium kumara	3 tbsp butter
salt	cinnamon
paprika	1/2 cup boiling water
1/3 cup brown sugar	

Peel the kumara and immediately soak in water. Cut in half lengthwise and arrange in a buttered baking dish. Preheat the oven to 180°C. Sprinkle the kumara with salt, paprika and brown sugar. Dot with butter and sprinkle with cinnamon. Add 1/2 cup boiling water, cover and bake for 15 minutes. Turn the kumara, add a little more boiling water if necessary, and cover and cook for a further 15 minutes or until tender.

This is delicious with roast pork or chicken.

Indian Kumara with Spinach♥

400g spinach or taro leaves, cooked
400g kumara
2 tbsp ghee or oil
1 large onion, finely chopped
1 clove garlic, crushed
1 tsp freshly grated ginger
1 tsp mustard seeds

1 tsp ground coriander
1/2 tsp ground cumin
1 tsp paprika
1/2 tsp chilli powder
1 tsp freshly ground black pepper
salt to taste
hot water or vegetable stock

Press all excess liquid out of spinach or taro leaves. Chop coarsely. Peel the kumara and cut into 2 cm dice. Put into a pan of boiling salted water and cook until almost tender. Drain

Heat the ghee or oil in a large frying pan or wok, and sauté the onion, ginger and garlic until the onion is soft. Add the mustard seeds and cook for 1-2 minutes, then add the spices and stir for another 1-2 minutes. Add the kumara and sauté for a few minutes. Add the spinach or taro leaves and mix well, adding a little salt. Continue cooking, adding a little hot water or vegetable stock to moisten the mixture when necessary. As soon as the kumara are tender, remove the mixture from the heat, turn into a serving dish and serve immediately.

Kumara, Date and Yoghurt Salad♥

1 kg kumara
1 cup plain yoghurt
1 tsp curry powder
1 clove garlic, crushed

1 stalk celery, cut into thin slices
1 cup chopped dates
1 tbsp chopped spring onions
fresh sprigs of parsley or mint

Peel kumara and cut into cubes. Cook in boiling, lightly salted water till tender. Drain and cool.

Combine yoghurt, curry powder and garlic in a bowl. Season with salt and pepper. Gently fold in celery, kumara and dates. Chill until ready to serve. Sprinkle with spring onions, and serve garnished with sprigs of parsley or mint.

Okra features in Asian, African, Latin American and Cajun Creole cuisines. Okra should be green in colour and snap easily.

To Prepare and Cook

Wash and carefully trim off the stalk ends and tips. Try not to expose the seeds, as this can cause stickiness when cooking. Okra can be sliced for sautéing in hot butter or oil, but for boiling or steaming they are best left whole and prepared as above.

To Freeze

Blanch small whole pods for 2 minutes in boiling water. Larger pods need 3 minutes. Plunge blanched pods in cold water and drain. Pack and freeze.

This is good as a side dish, or as an accompaniment to other curries.

Okra

Buttered Okra

500g okra, washed and prepared
water
salt and pepper
2 tbsp butter

Bring a pot of salted water to the boil, add okra pods and simmer uncovered for 6-8 minutes, depending on the size. (Or steam okra.) Drain and toss with butter and salt and pepper. Serve immediately.

Curried Okra with Coconut Cream

500g okra
2 tbsp ghee
1 onion, thinly sliced
2 cloves garlic, crushed
1 tsp grated ginger
1 small chilli, chopped
1 tsp turmeric

1 tsp ground coriander
1 tsp ground cumin
1 cup coconut cream
1 tsp salt
1 tsp freshly ground black pepper
1 tbsp freshly grated coconut

Slice okra if large, but leave small pods whole with stalks and tips removed. Heat ghee and cook onion until soft. Add garlic, ginger, chillis, okra and spices, and cook for 1 minute. Pour in coconut cream, salt and pepper, and cook, uncovered, over a gentle heat for 10 minutes. Sprinkle with grated coconut.

Although plantains and bananas are a fruit, they are treated as a vegetable when unripe. Green plantains and green (unripe) bananas can be used interchangeably in recipes.

To Prepare

Both green bananas and green plantains are very difficult to peel. To do so, cut off both ends with a sharp knife, peeling away the skin with the knife point, moving around the flesh and trying not to peel lengthwise. Put peeled fruit immediately into a bowl of lightly salted water to prevent darkening. For most uses, fruit can be boiled in the skin until soft and then peeled once it is cooked.

Uses

Peeled uncooked fruit is excellent as thin chips. Slice very thinly (use the slicer on a food processor) and deep or shallow fry in hot oil till golden-brown. Drain and sprinkle with salt and chilli powder, if desired. Fruit that has been cooked in the skin and then peeled can be cut into chunks, then baked with mornay sauce, or coconut cream, or butter and lemon juice, until heated through.

Plantains and Green Bananas

Curried Green Plantains

6 green plantains (or 8 green bananas)
2 tbsp ghee or oil
1 tsp salt
2 tsp curry powder
1 tsp turmeric
1/2 tsp cinnamon

1 large onion, finely chopped
2 cloves garlic, crushed
2 tsp grated fresh ginger
1/2 cup vegetable stock or water
1/2 cup thick coconut cream
1 tbsp lemon juice

Peel and slice plantains diagonally into thick chunks. Combine salt, curry powder, turmeric and cinnamon, and rub onto plantain chunks. Heat ghee and cook onion until softened, add the plantain chunks, garlic and ginger, and cook for 2 minutes, stirring. Add the vegetable stock or water and cook the plantains, covered, until tender. Stir in the coconut cream and lemon juice.

A great variety of pumpkins grow in the Pacific and are usually available throughout the year. Pumpkins store very well, unrefrigerated, for up to a month.

To *Prepare and Cook*

Pumpkin can be baked with the skin, steamed or roasted. Boiling is not always successful owing to the high water content of most tropical pumpkin. For use in pies, quiches, cakes and so on, it is best to bake the pumpkin with the skin (or microwave without water), and then remove the skin and mash the flesh.

To *Freeze*

Cut into cubes or chunks and freeze uncooked, in plastic bags. Defrosted pumpkin can be steamed or baked for use in soups, pies, cakes etc, and also be mashed as a vegetable.

Pumpkin

Mashed Pumpkin

Halve a pumpkin, remove seeds and cut into even chunks. Put into a baking dish peel side down, and bake until tender. Remove peel and mash with butter (1 tbsp butter to every 3 cups pumpkin), and add salt and pepper to taste, together with a pinch of cinnamon or chopped chives. Heat gently and serve.

Honey Baked Pumpkin♥

Cut pumpkin into serving-size chunks after halving and removing seeds. Put peel side down in a buttered baking dish. Sprinkle with cinnamon, salt and pepper. Spoon 1 tsp liquid honey over each chunk, and dot with a little butter. Bake at 180°C for 20-30 minutes, or until tender.

Taro is a staple crop in the Pacific, Caribbean and Africa. Here on Rarotonga every family owns a well-tended taro plantation.

The taro has a turnip-shaped root and heart-shaped leaves. The colour of the root flesh varies from pale cream to a dark purple-grey. Some varieties are dry and crumbly, and some moist and sticky.

To store for longer than a week, wash and dry the roots, cut off the long stem, leaving about 2-4 cm attached and place in large plastic bags in the refrigerator.

To Prepare and Cook

To avoid any reaction to the oxalic acid contained in taro, peel by holding the stem end and peeling downwards with a sharp knife. Remove any soft spots with the tip of a knife.

Cut roots into serving-size pieces, or leave whole for baking. As peeled taro forms a hard skin, whole scrubbed taro can be baked or steamed (trim off the stalk ends) and the skin removed once the taro is cooked.

Cook peeled taro chunks in plenty of boiling salted water until tender. It is important to cook taro well to avoid any irritation of the throat.

Cooked taro can be used in most recipes suitable for potatoes, as well as in cakes, scones and desserts.

To Freeze

Taro can be peeled and frozen uncooked in plastic bags. To use from the freezer, boil or steam without defrosting first.

Taro (Dalo)

Scalloped Taro in Coconut Cream

500g taro, peeled
1 onion, finely chopped

2 cups coconut cream
salt and pepper

Slice taro into thin 1 cm slices. Arrange in layers in a buttered casserole dish. Sprinkle with salt and pepper and chopped onion. Pour the coconut cream over the taro, and cover and bake at 180°C for 1 hour. Remove cover for the last 10 minutes to brown the top.

VARIATION

Cooked taro cut in serving pieces can also be baked in coconut cream. Arrange in a buttered baking dish, top with salt and pepper and a few knobs of butter, pour over the 2 cups of coconut cream and bake uncovered for 10 minutes. Turn and bake for a further 10 minutes.

French Fried Taro

500g cooked, peeled taro

hot oil

Cut taro into thin chips, and deep fry till crisp and golden. It is important to cook the taro completely to avoid unpleasant irritation of the mouth.

The leaves of the taro plant are used extensively in both Pacific and Caribbean cuisine, and are very rich in iron, vitamin C and riboflavin. Good-quality leaves should be tender and young. Some varieties contain oxalate (the substance that causes itchy mouth and throat): if in doubt, ask an experienced local person to pick your taro leaves or check at your greengrocer or market.

To Prepare and Cook

Wash leaves thoroughly before cooking. First pull the stalk out of the leaf and try to remove the central thick veins, then pinch off the tip of the leaf. Place whole or coarsely shredded leaves in a pot with enough water to cover. Young leaves should only take 3-5 minutes; older leaves 10-15 minutes. Drain off the water, mash the leaves with a heavy spoon and reheat with coconut cream or other flavourings. To keep the beautiful green colour of the taro leaves, be sure to have the water boiling, and plenty of it. Cook on a high heat in a pot with a tight-fitting lid.

Cooked taro leaves can be used in any recipe calling for spinach.

To Freeze

Cooked, drained taro leaves freeze well, packed in plastic bags. Partially thaw before steaming or sautéing just to heat through, or thaw and drain well for use in quiches, mousses and so on.

Taro Leaf (Rukau, Rourou)

Taro Leaf au Gratin

1 kg taro leaves, cooked
2 tbsp butter
1 tbsp chopped parsley
1/4 cup chopped spring onion
2 eggs, lightly beaten

1 cup milk
1/2 cup grated cheddar or gruyère cheese
1/2 tsp prepared mustard
salt to taste

Press all the liquid from the cooked taro leaves. Melt the butter and cook the parsley and spring onion till softened. Mix in with the taro leaves. Season to taste with salt and mustard. Spoon into a buttered baking dish. Combine the eggs, milk and cheese, and pour over the taro leaves. Bake at 160°C for 20-30 minutes until puffed and golden on top.

Coconut Creamed Taro Leaf

1 kg taro leaves, cooked
3 tbsp butter
1 small onion, finely chopped

1 tbsp flour
2 cups coconut cream
salt and pepper to taste

Squeeze all excess liquid from cooked taro leaves. Heat butter in a large frying pan and cook onion till soft. Stir in flour and cook for 1 minute, then stir in coconut cream and heat through, stirring to make a smooth sauce. Add taro leaves and heat through. Season to taste with salt and pepper, and serve.

Tomatoes grow in most tropical places all year round. They are an essential ingredient in many hot-climate dishes.

To *Prepare*

For many cooked sauces, tomatoes need to be peeled. This is easily done if tomatoes are blanched in boiling water until the skin is wrinkled. Cool the tomatoes under cold running water, drain and when cool enough to handle, peel off the skins – they should slip off easily.

Some recipes require the seeds to be removed. Halve the tomatoes and squeeze out the seeds.

To *Freeze*

Tomatoes that have been frozen will be good only for cooked dishes, not for salads. Tomatoes can be frozen whole, unblanched and unpeeled. The peel can be removed easily once the tomatoes defrost. However, they can be blanched and peeled before freezing, if preferred. Sprinkle with a little sugar to counteract acidity, and pack in plastic bags.

Tomatoes

Sun-dried Tomatoes

Sun-dried tomatoes have a wonderful flavour, and are very popular for use in sauces, pizza toppings, and so on. If you live where it is hot and dry, tomatoes can be lightly salted and dried on racks in the sun. However, if there is a high humidity, which is the case in most tropical places, excellent 'sun'-dried can be prepared in the oven.

Slice tomatoes in half lengthwise, squeeze out the seeds, then place on oven racks (the air must be allowed to circulate). Sprinkle lightly with salt, and dry in a 70°C oven for about 8 hours. When shrunken and rather leathery, the tomatoes are ready. Pack in sterilised jars in olive oil (or, if necessary, vegetable oil) and keep in the refrigerator. The tomatoes should keep for months. (Sprigs of herbs can be added to the oil in the jars.)

Baked Tomatoes

6 firm, ripe tomatoes
2 tbsp butter
1 clove garlic, crushed
salt and pepper

3/4 cup soft breadcrumbs
1/4 cup grated parmesan cheese
1 tbsp chopped fresh herbs such as
    dill or parsley

Halve the tomatoes by cutting through the widest part of the circumference. Arrange in a buttered baking dish. Sprinkle with salt and pepper. Melt butter and add crushed garlic, breadcrumbs, parmesan and chopped herbs. Stir well to combine. Sprinkle over tomato halves and bake at 200°C until tomatoes are tender and tops are golden-brown.

Spinach Stuffed Tomatoes

6 firm tomatoes
1 cup cooked spinach or taro leaves
1/2 small onion, very finely chopped
1 tbsp butter
1 cup cooked rice or soft
    breadcrumbs

salt and pepper
1/4 tsp nutmeg
2 tbsp roasted peanuts, or toasted,
    chopped cashewnuts (optional)

Cut a 1 cm slice off the top end of the tomatoes and carefully scoop out seeds and pulp with a teaspoon. Strain pulp and discard seeds. Keep pulp for another use, such as a sauce.

Cook the onion in butter over a gentle heat until very soft. Remove from heat and stir in the spinach with rice or breadcrumbs, nutmeg, salt and pepper, and nuts if using. Pack into tomato shells and bake at 190° for 15 minutes.

Zucchinis grow well in the tropics for most of the year.

To Prepare and Cook

Zucchini is good sliced raw in salads, or very lightly steamed or sautéed in a little oil or butter. It is one of the ingredients of Ratatouille, and pairs up well with tomatoes.

Whole zucchini that has been steamed or boiled until almost tender can be halved lengthwise, and stuffed with such ingredients as cheese and nuts or ham mixed with the scooped-out flesh, topped with breadcrumbs or parmesan, and baked or browned under a grill.

To Freeze

Zucchini is best frozen after sautéing in a little oil or butter for 1 minute, then cooled and packed in plastic freezer bags. Reheat gently. It is good to use in Ratatouille, curries, or puréed in a soufflé. Water blanching is not recommended for zucchini, as it becomes very mushy once defrosted.

Zucchini (Courgettes)

Fresh Zucchini Cakes

4 cups grated zucchini, very lightly salted
3/4 cup flour, sifted
1 1/2 tsp baking powder
salt and pepper to taste
1 egg, well beaten
vegetable oil for frying

Combine the zucchini with the flour, baking powder, salt and pepper. Add the egg, and blend all the ingredients together well. Refrigerate for 15 minutes. Heat about 2 tbsp oil in a heavy frying pan and drop the mixture in by the teaspoonful. Press to flatten with the back of a spatula. Cook till brown on both sides. Repeat with the remaining mixture, adding extra oil if necessary.

Zucchini Curry♥

240g zucchini, sliced
1 small green capsicum, seeded and sliced
1 medium onion, sliced
1 clove garlic, crushed
1 tbsp vegetable oil
1 tsp ground cumin
1/2 tsp turmeric
1/2 tsp cinnamon
120g canned or fresh tomatoes, peeled and chopped
2 tbsp water
salt to taste

Heat the oil in a large frying pan and cook the onion and garlic till the onion is soft. Add the cumin, turmeric, cinnamon and tomatoes, and cook for 5 minutes. Add remaining ingredients and cook, covered, for 15 minutes. Add salt to taste.

Fish and Seafood

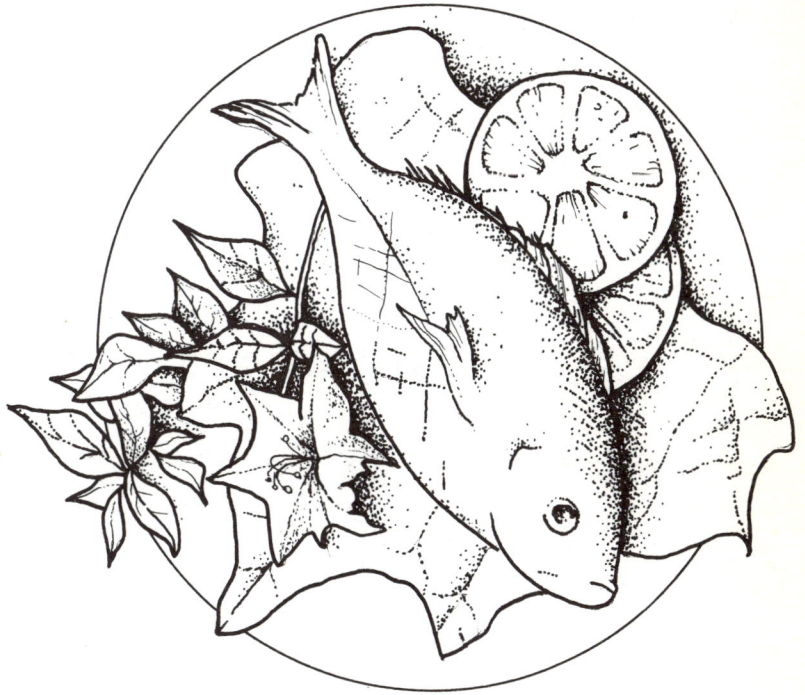

This easy baked fish has a wonderful, exotic flavour – the green peppercorns combine with the mango and coconut very well.

Serve with rice and Creole Corn Pudding (p. 58).

Baked Fish with an Orange and Mango Green Peppercorn Sauce

6 fish fillets or steaks
2 tbsp butter
salt and freshly ground pepper
1 cup orange juice
flesh of 2 mangos, chopped
1 tsp mango chutney
1 tbsp crushed green peppercorns

juice of 1 lemon
2 tbsp brown sugar
1 tsp cinnamon
1/4 cup coconut cream
1/4 cup grated coconut
1 mango, peeled and sliced, for
garnish

Preheat oven to 180°C. Place the fish in a single layer in a buttered baking dish. Dot each fillet with butter, and sprinkle with salt and pepper. Combine the orange juice with the mango flesh, mango chutney, crushed peppercorns, lemon juice, brown sugar and cinnamon. Pour over the fish. Spoon the coconut cream over the top and sprinkle with grated coconut. Bake for 15-20 minutes or until fish is cooked.

Serve garnished with fresh mango slices.

Burmese Tamarind Fish♥

This recipe from Burma is very similar to others found throughout Thailand, Malaysia and Indonesia. The sweet-sour flavour of the tamarind is really delicious with fish, especially when combined with the chillis and soya sauce.

Although the recipe calls for whole fish, fish fillets or steaks, fried or grilled, could be used instead. Grill fish for a low-fat version.

The fish is good with plain steamed rice or noodles.

1 1/2 kg whole fish, preferably 6 fish
of 1/2 kg each
salt and pepper

1/2 cup flour
oil for deep frying

Wash and clean fish, and pat dry. Slash the fish diagonally on both sides almost through to the spine. Sprinkle with salt and pepper inside and out, and dust with flour. Heat oil for deep-frying, and deep fry the fish until cooked through and golden – about 10 minutes. Keep warm.

TAMARIND SAUCE
2 tbsp vegetable oil
4 cloves garlic, crushed
1 large onion, finely sliced
1 tbsp grated fresh ginger
2 tbsp fish or oyster saucer
2 tbsp soya sauce
3 tbsp sugar

1/2 cup tamarind liquid
2 tsp or more chopped seeded
chillis
1 tbsp cornflour mixed with 1/2 cup
water
chopped spring onions for garnish

Heat the 2 tbsp oil (you can use some of the oil from frying fish) in a wok and fry the garlic, onion and ginger until softened. Add remaining ingredients and bring to the boil, stirring well until the sauce thickens.

Pour over the cooked fish. Garnish with spring onions.

This recipe originates in the Bahamas, and is always very popular.

If fresh coconut is unavailable, desiccated coconut can be used instead.

Serve with taro chips (p. 68) and a green salad.

Variation

The Coconut Fish is also delicious with the Avocado Sauce on p. 221.

Grate coconut finely with a food processor with a blade, or blender.

Coconut-coated Fish Fillets with Orange Mustard Sauce

1 kg fish fillets in 6 portions
seasoned flour
2 eggs
1/2 cup milk
2 cups freshly grated coconut

3/4 cup dry breadcrumbs
1/4 cup oil, for frying fish
orange and lemon slices for garnish
parsley or basil sprigs for garnish

ORANGE MUSTARD SAUCE

3/4 cup orange marmalade
1 cup fresh orange juice

1/4 cup fresh lemon or lime juice
1 tsp mild prepared mustard

Put all the ingredients for the sauce in a small saucepan and bring to boil, stirring. Remove from heat, and keep warm.

Combine the coconut and breadcrumbs together in a food processor or blender and blend briefly. Lightly beat the eggs and milk together. Lightly dust the fish fillets with seasoned flour. Dip in egg/milk mixture, then coat in coconut crumbs, pressing well to cover each fillet completely.

Heat the oil for the fish in one large or two small frying pans to fit the fish, and fry the fish for 3-4 minutes on each side, turning carefully. The fish should be golden-brown on both sides.

Serve with the sauce spooned over half of each fillet. Garnish with orange and lemon slices, and parsley or basil sprigs.

This recipe was created at The Flame Tree while experimenting with tropical fruit-based sauces that would best complement fish. This is a tasty, low-calorie dish that is excellent to prepare on an outdoor barbecue.

Other tropical fruit, such as ripe mango or pawpaw, or a combination of fruit, could be used to make the salsa.

Serve with Brown Rice Pilaf (p. 30) and Coconut Creamed Taro Leaf (p. 69).

Fish Kebabs with a Pineapple and Mint Salsa♥

12 wooden skewers
750g fish fillets
2 small onions, cut into quarters

6 mushrooms, halved
3 tomatoes, quartered
2 capsicums, cut into squares

MARINADE
1/4 cup vegetable oil, or less
1 tsp chilli sauce
1 tbsp fresh chopped mint or mint sauce
grated rind and juice of 1 lemon

1 tbsp honey
1 tbsp chopped spring onion
1 tsp grated fresh ginger
2 bay leaves, crumbled

PINEAPPLE MINT SALSA
1 tbsp vegetable oil
425g tin crushed pineapple, drained
2 tbsp mint sauce or chopped mint

2 tbsp honey
1/4 cup chopped spring onions

Mix all marinade ingredients together. Cut fish into even, 4 cm cubes. Marinate the fish cubes in the marinade, in the refrigerator, for 1 hour.

Thread the fish on skewers alternately with the onion, mushroom, tomato and capsicum. (Soak the skewers in water first to prevent burning on the grill.) Grill or barbecue the fish kebabs, brushing with marinade mixture, for about 5 minutes each side, until tender.

Combine all the salsa ingredients together. Serve fish on a bed of rice with the salsa spooned over.

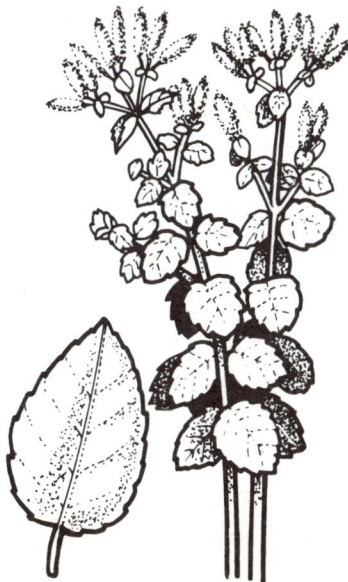

This easy method of preparing fish is perfect for outdoor barbecues. The fish is easiest to handle cut into steaks, but fillets also work well.

Other butters, prepared in the same way, are also wonderful with grilled fish. Here are just two examples – have fun experimenting with some of your own.

Orange and Coriander Butter

Replace the lime rind and juice with orange rind and juice, and the basil with chopped fresh coriander.

Lemon and Dill Butter

Replace the lime rind and juice with lemon rind and juice and the basil with chopped fresh dill.

Grilled Fish Steaks with Basil and Lime Butter

1 kg fish such as tuna or wahoo cut into steaks

FOR BRUSHING THE FISH

1/4 cup oil
1 clove garlic, crushed (optional)
1/2 tsp salt

1 tsp freshly ground pepper
1/2 tsp dried oregano, basil or
    thyme

BASIL AND LIME BUTTER

180g butter, softened
2 tsp finely grated lime rind
2 tbsp fresh lime juice
1/2 tsp prepared mild mustard

1/3 cup chopped fresh basil
1/4 cup chopped spring onions
1 clove garlic, crushed (optional)
2 tsp freshly ground black pepper

Mash all the ingredients for the Basil and Lime Butter together or, for best results, use a food processor. Set the butter aside, or chill until ready to use. (If preferred, the Basil and Lime Butter can be rolled into a neat cylinder in a foil wrapping, chilled until firm, then unwrapped and cut into slices to top each fish steak.)

Combine the ingredients for brushing fish. Brush the fish well with the mixture and cook fish on a hot barbecue grill (or in a ridged frying pan), turning once or twice and brushing generously with the oil mixture until the fish is cooked.

Serve on a plate with some of the Basil and Lime Butter spooned onto each steak.

The fresh herbs are important to this dish, and whatever suitable herbs are available can be used.

Serve simply with breadfruit chips (p. 52) and a salad.

This fish is also good with Curry Mayonnaise (p. 218).

Tartare Sauce

1/2 cup mayonnaise
2 tbsp chopped gherkins
2 tbsp capers
2 tbsp chopped spring onions or chives
1 tsp lemon or lime juice

Combine all ingredients in a bowl, and chill until ready to serve.

Herb-crumbed Fish with Tartare Sauce

1 kg fish fillets in 6 portions
plain flour
2 eggs, lightly beaten
1/4 cup milk
2 cups stale dry breadcrumbs
1 tsp garlic powder
1/2 tsp salt
1/2 tsp pepper

2 tbsp chopped parsley
1 tbsp chopped fresh basil
1 tbsp chopped fresh coriander
1 tsp dried oregano
1/2 cup oil for frying fish
lemon wedges and parsley sprigs for garnish

Combine the breadcrumbs with herbs, garlic powder, salt and pepper. Dust the fish lightly in flour, and shake off the excess. Beat eggs and milk together, and dip the fish in the egg mixture, then the herbed breadcrumbs, taking care to ensure that the fish fillets are evenly coated with the crumb mixture.

Heat oil in a large frying pan and cook the fish for 3-5 minutes on each side, turning carefully. Do not overcrowd the pan, and cook the fish in batches, keeping cooked fillets warm. Drain on kitchen paper. (The fish fillets can be deep fried if preferred.)

Serve the fish fillets with the Tartare Sauce in a separate bowl. Garnish with lemon wedges and parsley sprigs.

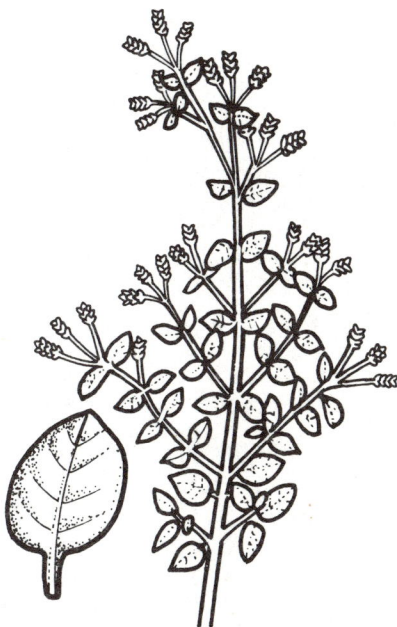

I first tasted this wonderful dish at the Tandoori Restaurant in Hong Kong. More recently on a trip to India I enjoyed the fish many times again.

Although the Tikka is traditionally cooked in a Tandoor or clay oven, I have cooked the fish very successfully on a hot barbecue grill.

It goes well with a vegetable curry, rice, chapatis and raitas.

Chicken Tikka

Use boneless breasts. Cut into cubes smaller than the fish, as the chicken takes longer to cook. Proceed in exactly the same way as for the Fish Tikka.

Indian Barbecued Fish Tikka

1 kg fresh firm fish fillets, such as
    tuna or wahoo
1 onion, chopped
1 tsp crushed fresh garlic
1 tbsp grated fresh ginger
2 tsp ground coriander
1 tsp ground cumin
grated rind and juice of 1 lemon or
    2 limes
1 tbsp vegetable oil
1 tsp chilli powder
1/2 bottle of sweet chilli sauce or
    similar, p. 227
1/2 tsp ground black pepper
1/2 cup yoghurt
2 tsp soya sauce
1 tsp brown sugar
1 tsp salt
2 onions, sliced (extra)
2 tbsp chopped fresh coriander or
    mint leaves

Cut fish into cubes about 4 cm square. Combine all the ingredients (except for the sliced onions and fresh coriander or mint) to make the marinade. Put the fish cubes into the marinade for several hours, turning occasionally.

Thread fish cubes gently onto wooden skewers and cook on a lightly oiled, hot barbecue grill, or under a hot grill, or cook in a hot dry frying pan, turning from time to time, until just cooked. Take care not to overcook the fish or it will fall apart.

Serve topped with thinly sliced onion and chopped coriander, accompanied by lemon quarters.

This is a really superb grilled fish recipe with a tasty golden glaze. It is important to marinate the fish for an hour.

Either whole small fish, cleaned and scaled, or fish steaks or fillets can be used. The fish can be cooked on an outdoor barbecue over warm coals or on an indoor grill.

Omit the butter for a low-fat version.

Serve simply with rice and a green salad or selection of sambals (pp. 211-13).

Javanese Grilled Fish with Chillis and Soya♥

4 whole fish or 4 fillets or steaks
1 tsp salt
2 tbsp brown sugar
4 tbsp soya sauce
2 cloves garlic, crushed
1 onion, finely chopped
1/4 cup water
grated rind and juice of 1 lemon or 2 small limes
1 tsp crushed fresh chillis or sambal oelek
2 tbsp butter

Sprinkle the fish with the salt. Mix together the sugar and soya sauce. Mix half this soya/sugar mixture with the onions, garlic and water. Pour this over the fish in a non-metallic bowl and, turning the fish from time to time, marinate for 1 hour. Add remaining sugar/soya mixture to the marinade.

Remove the fish from the marinade and cook, turning carefully, for 5-7 minutes on each side. Brush the fish with the marinade from time to time.

Add the lemon rind and juice, chilli sauce and the butter to the marinade. Heat in a small saucepan till the butter melts, but do not boil.

Serve the fish on a serving plate with the marinade poured over.

In this wonderful dish for special occasions, mahi mahi fillets are complemented beautifully by the Shrimp Cream Sauce.

Serve with plain steamed rice and Spinach Stuffed Tomatoes (p. 71)

Prawn Stock

shells and heads from prawns
1 chopped carrot and peelings
1 stalk celery and leaves
1 chopped onion, peeled
2 cloves
1 cup white wine
6 cups water
chopped parsley and other fresh
    herbs such as thyme and
    basil
2 tsp seafood or chicken stock
    powder or bouillon cubes
    (optional)
freshly ground pepper

Boil all the ingredients, covered, for 30 minutes. Reduce heat and simmer, uncovered, till reduced by a third. Strain through a fine strainer, and discard prawn peelings and vegetables.

Mahi Mahi Fillets with Shrimp Cream Sauce

1 kg mahi mahi fillets (or any white
    fish) in 6 portions
2 tbsp ghee or oil and butter, mixed
seasoned flour

juice of 1 lemon
1/2 cup white wine
parsley or dill sprigs for garnish
lemon wedges for garnish

SHRIMP CREAM SAUCE

300g small fresh prawns or
    shrimps, shelled and de-veined
1 tbsp butter
2 tbsp flour
150 ml milk

150 ml prawn or fish stock
150 ml cream or coconut cream
1 tbsp chopped fresh dill or parsley
1 tbsp cold butter (extra)
salt and pepper

FOR THE SAUCE

Melt the first 1 tbsp butter in a small saucepan. Stir in the flour to make a smooth roux. Add the milk gradually, stirring, then add the stock and the cream. Add salt and pepper to taste. Keep stirring until the sauce is smooth. Simmer over a gentle heat for 10 minutes. Add shrimp and dill or parsley, and cook just until the shrimp turns pink. Check seasoning. Stir in the extra chopped cold butter, and remove from heat as soon as the butter is melted. Keep the sauce warm. (Cover pan with foil, or place over a pan of simmering water.)

FOR THE FISH

Heat the ghee in one large or 2 small frying pans to fit the fish fillets. Dust the fish very lightly with seasoned flour and fry for a minute or two on each side. Add lemon juice and white wine, and cook until the fish is done, turning carefully once more.

Serve the fish with the Shrimp Cream Sauce spooned over, and garnish with dill or parsley sprigs and lemon wedges.

Serve with breadfruit chips (p. 52), Braised Green Pawpaw and Tomatoes (p. 61) and a green salad.

Panfried Fish with Lemon Butter

Serves 2

360g fish fillets in 2 portions (or fish steaks)
seasoned flour
2 tbsp ghee or butter
1/4 cup white wine
1/4 cup lemon juice or lime juice
grated rind of 1 lemon or 2 small limes

1 tbsp chopped parsley
1/4 tsp brown sugar
30g butter, chopped
freshly ground black pepper
parsley sprigs and lemon slices for garnish

Dust the fish lightly with seasoned flour, and shake off any excess. Heat the ghee or butter in a large frying pan and cook the fish on both sides until well sealed. Add the white wine and cook the fish until almost done. Remove fish from pan and keep warm.

Add the lemon juice, lemon rind and chopped parsley to the pan with the brown sugar, and cook until reduced to about 2 tablespoons. Add the butter, stirring vigorously with a wooden spoon to incorporate into the lemon and wine mixture. Add some freshly ground black pepper, and remove pan from heat before butter separates.

Arrange fish on plates with sauce poured over, and garnish with parsley sprigs and lemon slices.

This delicious recipe is a re-creation of a dish I first tasted in Mauritius, where toasted cashewnuts were used instead of the pecans. Whichever nuts you use, the dish will be sure to win compliments.

Serve with French Fried Kumara (p. 63), Ratatouille (p. 41) and a green salad.

Pecan Baked Fish Mornay

1 kg fish fillets or steaks in 6 portions
juice of 2 lemons
salt and pepper
2 tbsp butter
1/2 cup dry white wine
2 cups Bechamel Sauce, p. 221
1 cup grated mature cheddar cheese

2 tsp prepared mild mustard
1/4 cup chopped spring onions
1/4 cup chopped parsley
2 ripe tomatoes, sliced
1/2 cup breadcrumbs
1 cup chopped pecans (or toasted cashewnuts)
2 tbsp grated parmesan cheese

Preheat oven to 180°C. Arrange fish fillets in a buttered baking dish in a single layer. Sprinkle with salt and pepper and lemon juice. Dot each fillet with butter and pour the wine over the fillets. Mix the mustard into the Bechamel Sauce with the cheese, spring onions and parsley. Pour evenly over the fish fillets. Arrange the tomato slices over the top, then sprinkle on the breadcrumbs mixed with parmesan cheese and nuts. Bake for 15-20 minutes, or until fish is cooked and the top is golden-brown.

Any white fish or tuna fillets or fish steaks can be used for this delicious recipe. The fish could also be grilled or pan fried.

Serve with rice, Baked Tomatoes (p. 70), and a green vegetable or salad.

The poaching liquid can be prepared in advance and kept in the refrigerator for 2 days or the freezer for 2 months.

Poached Wahoo Fillets in White Wine with a Curry Hollandaise

6 portions fish fillets
1 recipe Curry Hollandaise, p. 223
chopped parsley for garnish

paprika for garnish
lemon wedges for garnish

POACHING LIQUID

2 cups white wine
1 cup water
1 tsp chicken stock powder
8 peppercorns
1 bay leaf

quarter onion, sliced
a little chopped carrot
chopped parsley and dill
pinch dried thyme

Heat the ingredients for the poaching liquid in a large covered frying pan or skillet and cook for 15 minutes. Turn off heat and let stand to infuse the flavours. Strain.

Meanwhile make up the Hollandaise Sauce and keep ready in a warm bowl, covered with foil.

Heat the poaching liquid and poach the fish in a large skillet or frying pan, till just done. Do not overcook. Remove the fish with a spatula to individual plates or a larger serving plate. Spoon the Hollandaise over each fillet, sprinkle with paprika, and brown quickly under a hot grill or broiler. Sprinkle with chopped parsley and serve with lemon wedges.

This Flame Tree dish looks very impressive and tastes wonderful. We always serve it with white or brown rice, and a selection of salads.

To enable each pawpaw shell to sit evenly on the serving plate, level off a small slice from the bottom, but be careful not to make a hole through the shell. Or, place a small saucer on the serving plate, and sit the pawpaw shell in the saucer.

Pineapple Fish and Coconut Cream

This recipe can be adapted to use 3 small ripe pineapples instead of pawpaw. Cut the 2 cups of pineapple needed for the recipe into small cubes. Remove most of the remaining flesh from the pineapple. Proceed as in the Fish with Pawpaw recipe.

Rarotongan Fish with Pawpaw and Coconut Cream

Serves 6

3 small ripe, firm pawpaw, halved and seeded
750g fish fillets, cut into 10 cm pieces
seasoned flour
2 tbsp vegetable oil
1 small onion, thinly sliced
1 tsp grated fresh ginger
1 clove garlic, crushed
1 tsp mild curry powder
2 green capsicums, thinly sliced
2 tomatoes, chopped
juice of 1 lemon
2 cups thick coconut cream
salt and pepper to taste
3 tbsp chopped fresh parsley or basil

Using a melon baller, scoop out 2 cups of pawpaw balls from the pawpaw halves (or carefully spoon out pawpaw and cut into small cubes). With a spoon remove the remaining pawpaw flesh, taking care not to damage the shell. (Keep this remaining flesh for another use such as in a fruit salad.)

Heat the vegetable oil in a large frying pan. Add onion slices and cook until tender. Remove from pan. Dust fish pieces lightly with seasoned flour, and fry for 30 seconds only on each side. Add a little extra oil if necessary. Remove fish from pan.

Add 4 tbsp coconut cream to the pan, together with the garlic, ginger and curry powder, and cook for 1 minute. Add 1 cup coconut cream and cooked onions, and simmer gently for 10 minutes. Add a further 1/2 cup coconut cream, together with the thinly sliced capsicum, and cook 5 minutes.

Meanwhile, bring a large pot of water to the boil, and carefully lower in pawpaw shells for 2-3 minutes. Remove and drain well (or place the pawpaw shells in a baking tray in a hot oven for a few minutes). Add the fish to the coconut sauce in the pan, and cook until done (about 3 minutes). Gently stir in the chopped tomatoes and pawpaw balls, the lemon juice, and salt and pepper to taste.

Spoon the fish evenly into the 6 warm pawpaw shells together with the sauce. Top each with a spoonful of coconut cream, sprinkle with chopped parsley or basil, and serve immediately.

Dill grows wild on Rarotonga, as does basil. Interestingly, both are used to decorate the flower garlands worn by the local people, and are used in folk medicine, but are not used at all in the local cuisine. It was with a great deal of amazement that the restaurant staff watched me use these herbs to flavour dishes when I first arrived on Rarotonga, but now they enjoy using these herbs in their own cooking.

This is a delicious recipe that always receives compliments. It is best made with fresh tomatoes in season, but canned tomatoes can be used.

Serve with Rice Pilaf (p. 30) and fresh Zucchini Cakes (p. 72).

Sautéed Tuna Fillets with Dill and Tomato Sauce

1 kg tuna fillets (or similar fish) in 6 portions
2 tbsp ghee, or oil and butter mixed
seasoned flour

1/2 cup dry white wine
juice of 1 lemon
sprigs of dill and lemon wedges for garnish

DILL AND TOMATO SAUCE

2 cups chopped tomatoes
2 cups dry white wine
2 cloves garlic, crushed
1 cup cream

1 tbsp chopped fresh dill
120g butter
salt and freshly ground pepper

FOR THE SAUCE

In a medium saucepan put the tomatoes, white wine and garlic. Simmer, uncovered, until reduced to one-third of the original quantity. Pass through a sieve to remove seeds, and return the strained tomatoes to the saucepan. Add the cream, bring to the boil, then reduce heat and simmer until the mixture is reduced by one half. Remove from heat, add the dill, and pepper to taste, and stir in butter. Add salt to taste, and keep the sauce warm. (Cover pan with foil or place over a pan of simmering water.)

FOR THE FISH

Heat the ghee in one large or 2 smaller frying pans to fit the fish fillets. Dust the fish very lightly with seasoned flour and fry for a minute or two on each side. Add lemon juice and white wine, and cook until the fish is done, turning carefully once more.

Serve the fish with the Tomato and Dill Sauce spooned over, and garnished with dill sprigs and lemon wedges.

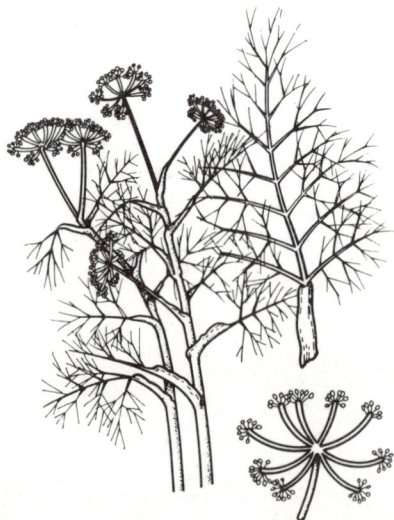

This is a superb dish that I first tasted in the Seychelles. I have tried to re-create the sauce exactly as I remember it, and for the last few years this has been one of the most popular fish dishes at The Flame Tree.

Taro leaves really are the best for this dish as they make a smooth and delicious sauce, but spinach leaves can be substituted quite successfully.

If preferred, the fish fillets can be put into a baking dish with the taro sauce without frying first, and baked in the oven, covered, for 15 minutes or until done.

Seychelles-style Fish Fillets

3 tbsp oil for frying
seasoned flour

juice of 2 limes or 1 lemon
1 kg fish fillets, in 6 portions

SEYCHELLES SAUCE

1 cup cooked taro leaves or spinach,
    well drained
2 tbsp butter or vegetable oil
1 onion, finely chopped
3 cloves garlic, crushed
1/2 tsp curry powder
1/2 tsp ground coriander

1/2 tsp turmeric
1 1/2 cups thick coconut cream
1/4 cup chicken stock
1 tsp black pepper
1 tbsp oyster sauce (optional)
salt to taste

Make the sauce first. In a heavy frying pan heat the 2 tbsp butter or oil and fry the onion and garlic until the onion is soft. Add the curry powder, coriander and turmeric, and cook for a few minutes. Stir in the cooked taro leaves or spinach, 1 cup coconut cream, chicken stock, black pepper and oyster sauce. Add salt to taste.

Meanwhile squeeze the lime juice onto the fish fillets. Heat the oil in another frying pan. Coat the fish very lightly in the seasoned flour and fry just 30 seconds on each side in the hot oil to seal each fillet. Add the fish fillets to the pan containing the sauce and simmer the fish till just cooked – about 5-10 minutes, depending on the thickness of the fillets.

Serve the fish covered with the sauce and topped with the remaining 1/2 cup coconut cream.

These smoked fish strudels make a delicious appetiser or main course, and are a real gourmet treat. Phyllo pastry is very easy to work with, and these strudels can be prepared in the morning, kept chilled, then baked just before serving.

Crème Fraiche

Stir 1 tbsp plain, full-fat yoghurt or 1 cup sour cream into 1/2 cup dairy cream. Leave in a warm place for at least 6 hours until the cream thickens.

Smoked Fish and Avocado Strudels with Lemon and Caper Sauce

Serves 12 as an appetiser, or 6 as a main course

24 sheets phyllo pastry   1/2 cup melted butter

FILLING

1 avocado, stoned, peeled and cut into small cubes
2 tbsp lemon juice
1 tbsp each vegetable oil and butter
1 onion, very finely chopped
1 capsicum, very finely chopped
1 stalk celery, very finely chopped
1 tbsp flour

250g smoked fish
1 tbsp chopped fresh dill
1 tbsp chopped fresh parsley
2 tbsp mayonnaise
2 tbsp yoghurt
1 egg yolk
salt and ground pepper to taste

LEMON AND CAPER SAUCE

1 cup chicken stock or broth
1/2 cup lemon juice
1 tsp brown sugar
1 small onion, finely chopped
1 tsp cornflour mixed with 1 tbsp water

1 tbsp chopped capers
1 tsp chopped parsley
1/2 cup sour cream or Crème Fraiche

FOR FILLING

Toss avocado cubes with lemon juice. Heat oil in a frying pan and cook onion, capsicum and celery until soft. Stir in the flour. Remove from heat and add boneless, flaked smoked fish, dill and parsley. Beat together the mayonnaise, yoghurt and egg yolk, and add to the smoked fish mixture. Stir in the chopped avocado and lemon juice. Add salt and pepper to taste.

LEMON AND CAPER SAUCE

Mix together all the ingredients, except the sour cream or Crème Fraiche. Bring to the boil, reduce heat to low, and stir until thickened. Stir in the sour cream or Crème Fraiche.

TO ASSEMBLE

Using 2 sheets of phyllo pastry at a time, cover the rest with a sheet of greaseproof paper topped with a clean damp towel. Brush the 2 sheets of phyllo pastry with melted butter and fold in half, one short end to meet the other. Place 2 heaped tbsp of filling towards one short end, fold the 2 long edges in towards the centre and bush with butter, then roll up the phyllo to make a neat cylinder. Continue until all the pastry and filling is used up. Place phyllo parcels seam side down on a baking sheet. Brush with melted butter. Bake for 25-30 minutes at 190°C until lightly golden and crisp.

Serve on a bed of Lemon and Caper Sauce, with a little extra sauce spooned over one end of each strudel. Garnish with parsley and lemon wedges.

Do not cover the top of the strudel with the sauce as this makes the pastry soggy.

This recipe is an excellent way to make a little fish go a long way. If using canned fish, your guests will never know! The fish cakes are delicious and can be served on their own without the sauce if desired, with lemon wedges and a salad.

The coconut sauce is a simple one that is equally good with fish fillet portions or other seafood.

South Indian Fish Cakes in Coconut Curry Sauce

FISH CAKES

500g white cooked fish, or smoked fish, or drained canned fish such as mackerel or tuna
200g potatoes
1 tbsp butter
1/4 cup milk
1 onion, finely chopped
1 tbsp mild curry powder

1 tsp chilli powder or seeded and crushed fresh chilli
1-2 tsp salt
1/2 tsp black pepper
2 tbsp chopped fresh parsley or coriander
1 egg
3 tbsp ghee or oil for frying

Boil and mash the potatoes with the 1 tbsp butter and 1/4 cup milk. Add to the flaked fish and remaining ingredients, and mix together until well combined. With well-floured hands, shape into 6 or 8 cakes. Heat the ghee or oil in a large frying pan and fry the fish cakes on both sides until they are golden-brown. Set aside.

COCONUT CURRY SAUCE

1 large onion, roughly chopped
3 cloves garlic
2 tsp finely grated ginger
1/2 cup peeled chopped tomato, fresh or canned
2 tsp curry powder
1 tsp chilli powder or chopped and seeded fresh chilli

1 tsp salt
1/2 tsp freshly ground black pepper
2 bay leaves
1 tsp chutney
2 cups coconut cream
2 tbsp oil or ghee
1 tsp garam masala

Put the onion, garlic, ginger and tomato in a food processor or blender and blend till smooth. Heat the oil in a large frying pan and fry the blended ingredients, stirring for a few minutes. Add the curry powder and chilli, salt and pepper, and cook 2 minutes. Add the bay leaves, chutney and coconut cream, and cook, stirring, for 10 minutes. Add the fish cakes and garam masala and cook gently till the fish cakes are heated through. Remove bay leaves and serve with rice and accompaniments.

For ginger lovers this is a very successful fish recipe that is fairly simple to prepare.

The amount of chilli can be increased for a really authentic Thai flavour, but we find that the amount in this recipe suits most palates.

If crystallised ginger is unavailable, use an extra 1 tbsp fresh ginger and an extra 2 tsp brown sugar.

Thai Ginger Fish with Julienne of Vegetables♥

750g fish fillets
2 cups assorted vegetables, such as carrots, capsicum, celery, onions, dried mushrooms (soaked), baby corn, cut into julienne slices

3 tbsp oil, or less
cornflour seasoned with salt and pepper for dusting fish

THAI GINGER SAUCE

1/2 cup well-flavoured chicken stock
1/4 cup water
2 tbsp soya sauce
2 tbsp sherry
3 tbsp brown sugar
juice of 1 lemon

1 tbsp oyster sauce
2 tbsp grated fresh ginger
1 tbsp chopped crystallised ginger
1/2 tsp crushed chillis, seeded (or more to taste)
2 tsp cornflour mixed in a little water

Mix all the sauce ingredients together in a jug. Cut fish into slices about 7 cm x 10 cm. Dust with seasoned cornflour. Heat the oil in a large wok and cook fish quickly on both sides just to seal. Remove with a slotted spoon. Add vegetables and stir-fry till coated with oil but still crisp. Add sauce until heated through and thickened. Return fish to wok and cook until the fish is done. Do not overcook.

Serve with spring onions sprinkled over, accompanied by plain steamed rice or noodles.

This is a wonderful fish curry that is easy to make because the base of the curry is a paste that is quickly prepared in a food processor.

Serve with steamed rice or noodles and a selection of sambals (pp.211–13).

Thai Green Curry of Chicken

1 kg boneless chicken, cut into cubes of about 2 cm, can be used instead of the fish using exactly the same method. If you wish to use a whole cut-up chicken or chicken portions on the bone, cook the chicken first in a frying pan of hot oil till well sealed. Add the chicken to the curry sauce and cook till the chicken is done. Add chicken stock if required during the cooking process.

Thai Green Curry of Fish

GREEN CURRY PASTE

1 onion, roughly chopped
1 capsicum, roughly chopped
1 tsp crushed fresh garlic
6 young lemon or lime leaves
1 tsp grated fresh ginger
1 tbsp ground coriander
1 tsp ground cumin
1/2 tsp ground nutmeg
1 tsp turmeric
juice and grated rind of 1 large
    lemon

1 tsp freshly ground black pepper
1 tbsp oyster sauce or fish sauce, or
    1 tsp shrimp paste, or 1/2 tsp
    anchovy essence
2 tsp brown sugar
1 tsp salt
1/2 cup coconut cream
1 tbsp finely chopped green chilli,
    seeded, or crushed bottled chillis

Put all ingredients in a food processor or blender, and blend till smooth.

CURRY

2 tbsp oil
2 onions, thinly sliced
Green Curry Paste, above
2 cups coconut cream

1 kg fish fillets, cut into pieces
    approx. 6 cm square
2 tbsp chopped coriander leaves or
    basil

Heat the oil in a large frying pan or wok and fry the onions until soft. Add the curry paste and cook for 5 minutes, stirring constantly.

Add 1 1/2 cups coconut cream and cook for about 20 minutes, covered. Add the fish and the remaining 1/2 cup coconut cream, and simmer gently until the fish is cooked through. Check the seasoning and add extra chillis if desired, then turn out onto a serving plate and top with chopped coriander or basil.

Grilled Crayfish, Pacific Style

Serves 4 as a main course, or 8 as an appetiser

4 medium crayfish, cooked
2 tbsp ghee, or oil and butter mixed
1 large onion, finely chopped
2 cloves garlic, crushed
2 tsp mild curry powder
1/2 tsp crushed chilli (or more to taste)
1/2 cup thick coconut cream

1/2 cup milk
1 cup cream
1 tbsp chopped fresh basil
salt and pepper
1/2 cup grated parmesan or mature cheddar cheese
1/4 cup chopped spring onions

Split crayfish cleanly in half, and remove crayfish flesh from shells. Cut the flesh into small chunks. Heat ghee in a medium-sized saucepan and add onion and garlic, and cook until soft. Add the curry powder and chilli, and cook for a few minutes. Add the crayfish chunks, coconut cream and milk, and cook for 2 minutes. Remove from heat. Stir in the cream and basil, and add salt and pepper to taste.

Pile the crayfish back into the shells, top with parmesan cheese and spring onions, and brown under a hot grill or broiler until golden.

Fresh Steamed Mussels in a Dill and Parsley Cream Sauce

1 kg fresh mussels
2 tbsp butter
1 onion, finely chopped
2 cloves garlic, crushed
1 small carrot, finely chopped
1 stalk celery, finely chopped
1 cup water or chicken stock

1 tbsp chopped fresh dill
1 cup dry white wine
1 tbsp chopped fresh parsley
1 cup cream
salt and freshly ground black pepper

Scrub and de-beard the mussels. Melt the butter in a large saucepan and cook the onion and garlic till softened. Add the remaining vegetables and cook till softened. Add the water and cook for 5 minutes. Stir in the dill. Add the mussels and white wine. Cover the pan and cook until the mussels are opened. Stir in the parsley and cream, and add salt and pepper to taste.

This is a very popular dish, and the hot chilli sauce seems to really complement the crispy prawns.

Singapore Chilli Crab

The Singapore Chilli Sauce is wonderful on crab. Use 3 whole crabs, weighing about 750g each, cleaned and with stomach sac, lungs and any green matter removed. Remove large claws and cut each crab body into 4 pieces.

Heat 1/4 cup oil, and fry crab pieces and claws until they change colour, turning to cook evenly. Add the Singapore Chilli Sauce, and cook the crabs another 3 minutes or so, adding a little water if necessary. Serve as for prawns.

A Tahitian friend, Henri, prepared this prawn dish when I was a guest at his home in Papeete. It is a very easy recipe, and the sauce would be equally delicious on fish fillets or other seafood.

Serve with rice and a green salad.

Singapore Chilli Prawns

500g raw prawns	plain flour
2 cups Tempura Batter, p. 45	oil for deep frying

SINGAPORE CHILLI SAUCE

2 tbsp vegetable oil	1/3 cup tomato sauce
1 tbsp grated fresh ginger	2 tbsp brown sugar
2 tsp crushed fresh garlic	1 tbsp soya sauce
1/3 cup Flame Tree Chilli Sauce (p. 227), or any bottled hot chilli sauce	1 tbsp lemon juice

Combine all ingredients for sauce, and set aside.

Shell only the body of the prawns and de-vein. (We always leave the head and tails on, as the prawns look more impressive and some people love the juices in the heads.) Dry the prawns on paper towels, dust with flour, then dip in Tempura Batter, shaking off the excess.

Deep fry till golden and crispy in hot oil – take care not to overcook. Arrange on a serving platter with heads in one direction and pour the hot chilli sauce in a line over the body sections. Garnish with lemon wedges and parsley, and serve immediately.

Tahitian Prawns with Tomato and Coconut

1 kg large prawns, shelled and de-veined	2 cups coconut cream
1 tbsp oil	2 tbsp tomato purée
2 tbsp butter	1/2 cup cream
1 large onion, chopped	2 tsp cornflour mixed with 1/4 cup water
1 tsp crushed garlic	salt and freshly ground black pepper to taste
1 tsp grated ginger	2 tbsp chopped basil or coriander
1 tsp mild curry powder	
2 tsp crushed chillis	

Heat butter and oil in a medium-sized saucepan, and cook onions until soft. Add garlic, ginger, curry powder and chillis and cook for 1 minute. Add coconut cream and tomato purée, and cook for 15 minutes. Add prawns and cook just till they turn pink. Add salt to taste. Mix cream and cornflour mixture together, add to the pan and cook until sauce is thickened. Season to taste with salt and pepper. Sprinkle with chopped basil or coriander.

To Prepare

If using freshly caught octopus, beat the octopus well with a wooden paddle, large wooden spoon or a piece of smooth timber all over for about 10 minutes. The best place to do this is on a rock at the beach.

Octopus becomes more tender the longer it is in the freezer, so if possible, freeze octopus (after washing and putting in a freezer bag) for at least 2 months.

To Cook

Cook the octopus whole in a large pot of boiling water, covered, for 30-60 minutes. To tenderise the octopus more quickly, add some slices of green (unripe) pawpaw to the pot. Check the octopus from time to time, as it can suddenly become tender and then become mushy and unappealing.

Remove from the pot. Remove suckers if desired – I prefer to do so, but many people really like this part. Cut tentacles into pieces and cut hood into rings, removing eyes and beak.

To Serve

The cooked octopus can be served cold as a salad with the dressing of your choice, or hot, simmered for 10 minutes in the sauce of your choice.

Octopus

Curried Reef Octopus

1 kg octopus, cooked and sliced
2 tbsp vegetable oil or ghee
1 onion, finely chopped
1 clove garlic, crushed
1 recipe curry paste, p. 228
1 tsp chopped chillis

2 cups tomato juice, or chicken or vegetable stock
juice and grated rind of 1 lemon
1 cup coconut cream
3 tbsp chopped coriander or basil
salt and pepper to taste

Heat the oil or ghee and fry the onion and garlic until tender. Add the chillis and curry paste, and cook for 5 minutes over a gentle heat. Add the tomato juice, lemon rind and juice, and the octopus, and simmer for 15 minutes, stirring. Stir in the coconut cream and coriander or basil, and add salt and pepper to taste.

Serve with plain steamed rice and chutney.

To Prepare

Pull the head and body of the squid apart, and cut off the tentacles just below the eyes. Reserve the tentacles and the body. Discard the transparent quill from inside the body, and rinse the body well. Scrape off the purple membrane covering the body.

On larger squid, there is a very thin transparent membrane under the purple membrane, and if this is removed the squid will be very tender when cooked. It is easier to remove this clear membrane if the cleaned squid body has been frozen. Insert a sharp knife under the clear membrane and lift, then peel off.

The squid body can be cut into rings or into small squares of about 5 cm, with the squares scored diagonally with knife. If using baby squid, just slit down one side of the body and open up. Score the body as with larger squid squares. This should make the squid curl attractively as it cooks.

For extra tenderness, squid can be marinated in white wine to cover, with some grated green pawpaw added to the wine. Take care that the squid does not become over-marinated and mushy: one hour is usually long enough.

To Cook:

The secret is to never overcook squid. It should be cooked just until the flesh turns white – about 30 seconds to 1 minute.

Squid Tempura

Squid can also be dipped in flour and then the batter on p. 45. Deep fry till golden and crisp.

Squid

Fresh Herb-crumbed Calamari

500g squid, cut into rings
seasoned flour
2 eggs
1/2 cup milk
1 cup dry breadcrumbs
1/2 tsp salt
1/2 tsp pepper
1/2 tsp garlic powder
2 tbsp chopped fresh parsley
1 tsp dried oregano
lemon wedges
oil for deep frying

Combine eggs and milk, and beat together lightly. Combine breadcrumbs with salt, pepper, garlic powder and herbs. Pat the squid rings dry with paper towels. Dip in flour and egg mixture, and then breadcrumbs, taking time to ensure the rings are well coated. Chill until ready to fry. Deep fry the squid rings in hot oil until golden and crisp. Drain on paper towels.

Serve garnished with lemon wedges, and with Tartare Sauce (p. 79), Curry Mayonnaise (p. 218), or the sauce of your choice.

This recipe also works well with Octopus. Cook octopus first until tender; see p. 95.

Serve with plain steamed rice as part of a Chinese-style meal.

Szechwan Stir-fried Chilli Squid

450g squid, cleaned and prepared
2 tbsp vegetable oil
3 stalks celery, finely sliced
1 carrot, finely sliced
1 small onion, finely sliced
2 tsp crushed fresh garlic

3 tbsp sugar
1/4 cup chicken stock or broth
1/2 cup chopped spring onions
1/2 tsp sesame oil
2 tsp cornflour

MARINADE

1 tbsp grated fresh ginger
2 tbsp soya sauce
2 tbsp dry sherry
1/4 cup white wine
1 tsp black bean sauce

1 tsp oyster sauce
2 tsp chopped seeded fresh chillis or
    Flame Tree Chilli Sauce, p. 227
juice and grated rind of 1 lemon

Combine all the marinade ingredients and marinate the squid for no longer than 2 hours.

Heat the vegetable oil in a large frying pan or wok, and stir-fry the celery, carrots, onion and garlic until fairly tender but still crisp. Add the squid and marinade to the wok. Mix the sugar, chicken stock, spring onions, sesame oil and cornflour together. Add to the wok and cook, stirring, for 1 minute. Serve immediately.

This is a very impressive and flavourful dish to serve to guests.

To balance the coconut shells full of seafood on the serving dish, set each coconut shell in small saucer. However, the recipe can also be cooked and served without placing in the coconut shells. Pile the seafood mixture into a buttered baking dish, cover with foil, and bake in a preheated oven for 10 minutes. Remove foil, and serve from the baking dish.

Serve with plain steamed rice and a selection of salads.

Fijian-style Seafood in the Coconut Shell

2-3 coconuts
300g fish fillets, cubed
8-12 mussels or clams, cleaned and scrubbed
8 small prawns, shelled and de-veined
250g crab claws or crayfish pieces
2 small chillis, seeded and chopped
1 medium onion
1 tsp crushed garlic
1 tsp grated fresh ginger
grated rind and juice of 1 lemon
2 cups thick coconut cream
1/2 tsp ground cardamom
1 tsp salt
1 tsp sugar
2 tsp soya sauce
2 tomatoes, chopped
1 tbsp chopped fresh basil
1 tbsp chopped fresh mint
1 tbsp chopped fresh coriander
6 young spinach or Chinese cabbage leaves, very finely shredded
pepper and extra salt to taste

Saw the coconut shells in half, and grate out most of the flesh, leaving a lining of flesh in the shell. Keep 3 tbsp grated flesh and set aside. (The remainder of the flesh can be used to make the coconut cream for this recipe, although extra grated coconut will be needed to make the required amount.)

Put the chillis, onion, garlic, ginger, and lemon rind and juice with 1/2 cup of coconut cream in a blender or food processor, and blend to a very smooth paste. Heat another 1/2 cup coconut cream in a large saucepan, add the paste from the blender, and cook, stirring, for 2 minutes. Add the cardamom, salt and sugar, stir and add the remaining coconut cream. Bring to the boil, reduce heat and simmer gently for 30 minutes.

Preheat oven to 200°C. Add seafood to the coconut cream mixture, putting in crab claws or crayfish pieces first. Cook for a few minutes, then add the mussels or clams, cook until beginning to open, then add fish cubes and prawns. Stir in the 3 tbsp reserved grated coconut, soya sauce, chopped tomato, basil, mint, coriander and spinach. Add extra salt and pepper to taste.

Pile the seafood mixture evenly into the coconut shells. Cover each shell with foil and bake in the preheated oven for 10 minutes. Remove the foil and serve the seafood in the coconut shells.

Use whatever seafood is available for this recipe.

Seafood Crepes with a Dill Cream Sauce

1 quantity crepe batter (p. 34), making 10 crepes

FILLING

350g fish fillets, cut into small cubes
150g small prawns or shrimps, shelled and de-veined
8 cooked mussels, chopped
180g can salmon, tuna or crab (or use equivalent cooked fresh seafood of your choice)
1 tbsp butter
1/4 cup chopped spring onions or 1/2 small onion, finely diced

1 1/2 tbsp flour
1 cup milk
1 cup sour cream
2 tbsp parmesan cheese
1 tbsp chopped fresh parsley
1/2 tsp prepared mild mustard
1 tbsp tomato purée
a few drops Tabasco
salt and freshly ground black pepper to taste

DILL CREAM SAUCE

1 cup cream
1 cup natural yoghurt
1 tbsp fresh lime or lemon juice

3 tbsp chopped fresh dill or parsley
salt and pepper to taste

FOR THE SAUCE

Combine all the ingredients for the sauce, stirring until well mixed.

FOR THE FILLING

Melt butter in a medium-sized saucepan and cook the spring onions until soft. Stir in the flour and cook for 1 minute. Add the milk gradually, and once the sauce is smooth add the fresh fish and shrimps, and cook till just done. Then stir in the mussels, canned salmon, sour cream, parmesan cheese, parsley, mustard, tomato purée and Tabasco. Season to taste with salt and pepper. Remove from heat and cool.

Divide the filling among the crepes. Roll up the crepes and place seam side down on a buttered baking dish. Top with the sauce and bake in a hot oven for 8-10 minutes.

I have tried many fish and seafood curry recipes over the years, and this has evolved as being the best of all. It is a combination of the best Indian and Thai seafood curry recipes, and although the list of ingredients may seem overwhelming, do not let this put you off.

Serve with rice and a selection of chutneys and sambals (pp. 211–13).

The curry paste can be made up and kept in batches in the freezer, as can the curry sauce, without the seafood added. Keeping the sauce in the freezer makes the preparation much easier on the day.

The Flame Tree Seafood Curry

Serves 6-8

CURRY PASTE

2 onions, chopped
1 capsicum, seeded and chopped
2 tbsp good-quality curry powder
2 tsp ground coriander
1 tsp ground cumin
1 tsp turmeric
1 tsp fennel or dill seeds
2 tsp cardamom seeds
2 tsp garam masala
1/2 tsp ground cinnamon

1/4 tsp ground cloves
2 tsp crushed fresh garlic (about 6 cloves)
1 tsp grated fresh ginger
1 tsp salt
1 tsp freshly ground black pepper
juice and grated rind of 1 large lemon or 2 limes
1 tsp brown sugar
8-10 young lemon or lime leaves

Put all the curry paste ingredients in a food processor or blender, and blend till smooth.

CURRY

500g fish fillets, cut into cubes
12 prawns or shrimps, shelled and de-veined, but with head and tails left on
12 mussels or clams, cleaned
12 crab claws or crayfish chunks, or whatever seafood is available
2 tbsp ghee or oil
1 tbsp mustard seeds
1 cup water

1 cup peeled tomatoes
2 cups coconut cream
1 tbsp chutney such as mango
1 tbsp oyster sauce (optional)
1 tsp garam masala
1/2 cup thick coconut cream, extra
extra salt to taste
lemon wedges for garnish
fresh chopped coriander or basil

Heat the ghee in a large heavy saucepan or wok, add the mustard seeds and cook till they start to pop. Add the curry paste and cook about 5 minutes.

Add the water, tomatoes and 1 cup coconut cream, and cook gently for about 45 minutes, uncovered or until the sauce is thick. (The sauce can be frozen at this stage for up to a month.) Stir in the remaining coconut cream, chutney, oyster sauce, fish and shellfish, putting crab or crayfish in first, followed by mussels or clams and cooking until they start to open, then fish cubes, and lastly prawns. Simmer just until the seafood is cooked.

Stir in the 1 tsp garam masala and 1/2 cup thick coconut cream. Add salt to taste and turn out on to a serving platter with the seafood arranged appealingly and garnished with lemon wedges. Sprinkle with fresh coriander or basil.

Chicken and Duck

This is an easy and delicious chicken dish to serve when mangos are in season.

Serve with mashed kumara and Zucchini Cakes (p. 72).

Low-fat Cooking

In most recipes, chicken can be first baked in a hot oven or grilled, without fat or oil, to seal in the juices. (Always remove skin and fat from chicken.) This makes the initial cooking of the chicken in hot fat or oil unnecessary. Onions, garlic and vegetables can be sautéed in a little stock, water or wine instead of oil. Many recipes in this book, with the exception of those containing coconut cream, can become low-fat recipes by using the above methods.

Baked Mango and Ginger Chicken

1 large chicken, cut up, or 6-8
    chicken portions
flour seasoned with salt, pepper and
    ground ginger
1/2 cup vegetable oil
2 cloves garlic, crushed
1/4 cup brown sugar
1/4 tsp ground cloves
1/2 tsp ground cinnamon

1 tbsp grated fresh ginger
1/4 cup lime juice
2 cups peeled and diced mango
1 cup chicken stock
1 tsp dried thyme or 1 tbsp fresh
    thyme
extra salt and pepper to taste
sprigs of parsley for garnish
1 mango, sliced, for garnish

Remove skin and excess fat from chicken portions, and toss in seasoned flour. Heat oil in a large frying pan or wok and brown chicken portions on all sides. Put chicken in a large baking dish with a tight-fitting lid.

Combine garlic, brown sugar, cloves, cinnamon, ginger, lime juice, chicken stock, thyme, and extra salt and pepper to taste, together with the diced mango. Pour over the chicken. Cover the baking dish tightly and bake in a preheated 180°C oven for 30-40 minutes or until the chicken is cooked through.

Arrange chicken portions on a serving platter with the sauce from the baking dish poured over. Garnish with fresh mango slices and parsley sprigs.

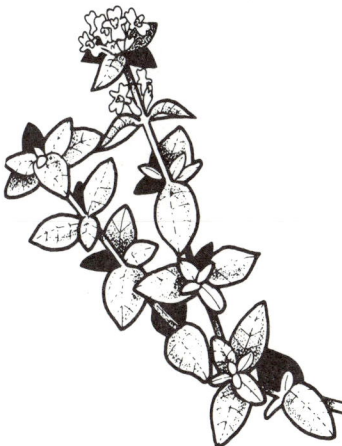

103

The idea for this came from a dish I ate at a buffet lunch some years ago at the Regent Hotel in Fiji. The combination of chicken and prawns may seem unusual, but it works beautifully, and the dish is always in great demand at The Flame Tree.

Serve with rice and sambals or a green salad.

Chicken and Prawns in a Coconut Curry Sauce

12 small prawns, cleaned, shelled
    and de-veined
3 whole boneless chicken breasts
3 tbsp butter
1 medium onion, finely chopped
1 tsp crushed fresh garlic
2 tsp grated fresh ginger
2 tsp curry powder
1 tsp ground cumin

1 tsp turmeric
1 tbsp flour
2 cups thick coconut cream
1 tbsp oyster sauce
2 tsp chicken stock powder
1 cup thick dairy dream or an extra
    cup thick coconut cream
1/2 cup chopped fresh basil
salt and pepper to taste

Cut the chicken into small cubes. Melt the butter, and fry onions and garlic with the ginger until the onions are tender. Add the chicken and cook, stirring, for a few minutes. Remove the chicken. Add the curry, cumin and turmeric to the saucepan and cook, stirring, for 30 seconds. Add the flour and then slowly add the coconut cream, stirring continuously to make a smooth sauce. Add the oyster sauce and chicken stock powder. Add the chicken meat and the prawns. Cook just till the prawns are pink. Stir in the cream and basil. Add salt and pepper to taste.

This is a very impressive dish to serve to guests and takes very little preparation

Serve with Scalloped Breadfruit (p. 52) and a green salad.

Chicken, Pawpaw and Camembert Parcels with Cashewnut Butter Sauce

18 sheets phyllo pastry
6 chicken breasts
1/2 small ripe, firm pawpaw, seeded and sliced into 6
1x125g camembert cheese, cut into 6 wedges
1/2 cup plain yoghurt

1 tsp curry powder
1 tsp brown sugar
1 tsp cinnamon
salt and freshly ground black pepper
120g butter

CASHEWNUT BUTTER

4 tbsp softened butter
2 tbsp very finely chopped onion
1 tsp lemon juice
1/2 cup chicken stock or broth

1/2 cup cashewnuts, toasted and chopped
2 tbsp cream or coconut cream

FOR THE CHICKEN

Heat 60g butter in a frying pan or skillet and cook the chicken breasts, 2 at a time and turning once, till they are well sealed on the outside. Cool the chicken breasts.

Combine the yoghurt, curry powder, cinnamon and brown sugar together.

TO WRAP CHICKEN BREAST

Melt the remaining 60g butter. Fold 3 sheets phyllo pastry in half, brush with melted butter. Set once slice of pawpaw and one slice of camembert in the centre. Top with 1/6 of the yoghurt mixture, then one chicken breast. Sprinkle on 1/8 tsp salt, and lots of freshly ground pepper.

Turn the 2 long sides in to meet in the middle. Brush with melted butter. Turn in the 2 short sides to the middle, one overlapping the other. Brush one and then the overlapping one with melted butter. Turn the parcel seam side down on to a buttered baking tray. Brush top with melted butter. Continue with the remaining 5 chicken breasts. Bake in a moderately hot oven (190°C) for about 25-30 minutes.

CASHEWNUT BUTTER SAUCE

Heat 1 tbsp butter and cook onion till very soft. Add stock and lemon juice and cook for a few minutes. Add the cashewnuts. Chop the remaining butter and beat in a little at a time till sauce is smooth. Add the cream or coconut cream. Do not boil.

Serve immediately in a sauce boat with the chicken parcels, or serve some of the sauce on each plate under the parcel. (Do not pour over the top as this will make the phyllo soggy.)

Everyone who tries this chicken dish asks for the recipe. The fruit can be varied according to what is in season.

For special occasions, serve this dish with the Kumara Soufflé (p. 63) and Spinach Stuffed Tomatoes, (p. 71), and for a simple family meal serve with plain steamed rice and a green salad.

Coconut Roast Chicken with Tropical Fruit

Serves 6-8

2 medium-sized chickens (or 12-16 chicken pieces)

2 cups thick coconut cream

MARINADE

1 onion, finely chopped
2 cloves garlic, crushed
1 tbsp soya sauce
1 tbsp honey
1 cup coconut cream

freshly ground black pepper
2 tsp salt
1 cup white wine
grated rind and juice of 1 lemon or 2 limes

FRUIT MIXTURE

6-8 pineapple rings
3 firm ripe bananas, split length-wise
6-8 slices pawpaw
6-8 slices mango

2 tbsp butter
2 tbsp lemon juice
2 tsp ground cinnamon
1 tbsp brown sugar

Combine the marinade ingredients until smooth. Rub the chicken with the marinade, and refrigerate in the marinade for several hours, turning occasionally.

Preheat the oven to 180°C. Remove the chicken from the marinade, reserving the marinade. Roast the chicken in a roasting pan for 30 minutes (or 20 minutes if using chicken portions). Drain off all the fat from the roasting pan. Arrange the fruit in the roasting pan around the chicken. Dot the fruit with butter, and sprinkle with the lemon juice, brown sugar and cinnamon. Pour the marinade over the chicken and fruit, and bake for a further 15-20 minutes, or until the chicken is completely cooked and the fruit is soft.

Arrange chicken on a serving dish, surrounded by the fruit (carefully lift it out with a spatula). Keep the chicken and fruit warm. Pour the pan juices into a saucepan, bring to the boil, add the 2 cups coconut cream, season to taste with salt and pepper, and heat through. Serve with the chicken and fruit.

Although this recipe is Hungarian in origin, it suits the tropics well as nearly all the ingredients are locally produced. The taste is superb.

Serve with rice or noodles or mashed kumara, and a green salad.

Chicken in a Tomato and Paprika Cream Sauce

Approx. 2 1/4 kg chicken or 12 chicken portions
1 cup flour, 2 tsp salt and 1 tsp pepper
4 tbsp paprika
4 tbsp butter
2 tbsp oil
4 large onions, thinly sliced
2 tsp crushed fresh garlic
3 capsicums, thinly sliced

6 cups peeled tomatoes, fresh or canned
1 tbsp chicken stock powder mixed with 2 cups hot water, or 2 cups well-flavoured home-made chicken stock or broth
1 1/2 cups cream
juice of 1 lemon
lots of chopped fresh parsley
extra salt and pepper to taste

Cut the whole chicken into portions. Mix flour, salt and pepper together with 1 tbsp paprika and toss the chicken pieces in this mixture till well coated.

Heat the butter and oil in a large saucepan and fry the chicken pieces till golden. Remove chicken from pan. Add onions, garlic and capsicums and cook till soft, stirring constantly. Stir in the remaining 3 tbsp paprika, the chopped tomatoes with their juice, and the 2 cups chicken stock liquid. Bring to the boil and stir well, then reduce heat to low. Return the chicken to the pan and cook 30-40 minutes, until chicken is done. Stir in 1 cup cream and add extra salt and pepper to taste.

Stir in the lemon juice and turn the chicken out into a serving dish. Top with remaining 1/2 cup cream and chopped parsley.

This is my own recipe for Hawaiian chicken, which has evolved from experimenting with a number of different versions. Hawaii is a fascinating melting pot of cultures, and the Chinese influence is evident here.

Serve with steamed white or brown rice and a green salad.

Hawaiian Pineapple Chicken♥

8-10 chicken portions   2 tbsp vegetable oil

MARINADE
2 tbsp soya sauce   2 cloves garlic, crushed
1 tsp curry powder   2 tbsp sherry
1/2 cup dry white wine   2 tsp finely chopped fresh ginger

SAUCE
2 onions, sliced   1 red and 1 green capsicum, finely
1 cup chicken stock   sliced
1 cup peeled tomatoes, fresh or   1 stalk celery, sliced
   canned, with seeds removed   juice of 1 lemon
2 tbsp brown sugar   1 tbsp cornflour
salt and pepper to taste   1/4 cup water
450g can pineapple chunks with   1/3 cup toasted cashewnuts
   juice, or equivalent fresh   (optional)

Remove skin and fat from chicken. Combine all the ingredients for the marinade, and marinate the chicken, covered, in the refrigerator for at least 2 hours or overnight. Remove chicken from the marinade, and reserve marinade.

In a large frying pan or wok, heat the oil and cook the chicken until golden. Remove chicken, then add onion to the oil and cook for 1 minute. Then put the chicken back in the pan or wok with the marinade, chicken stock, tomatoes, brown sugar, salt and pepper. Cover tightly and cook gently until the chicken is completely cooked – 20-30 minutes. Remove chicken to a serving dish and keep warm.

Add pineapple chunks, with juice, capsicum and celery to the pan, and cook for 3 minutes only. Add lemon juice, and extra salt and pepper to taste. Blend cornflour with water and add to the pan. Stir until sauce thickens. Stir in the cashewnuts, pour the sauce over the chicken, and serve.

This classic dish from Martinique is very popular at The Flame Tree, and deserves an honourable place in a book with a tropical flavour.

The chicken in this version is marinated in the red wine overnight for extra flavour. If you are in a hurry this step is not necessary, but do try to let the chicken marinate for a few hours at least.

The mushrooms can be omitted if desired.

Martinique Chicken in Red Wine

1.5 kg chicken or equivalent
   chicken portions
60g butter
4 thick rashers bacon, rind removed
250g fresh sliced mushrooms
1 cup dry red wine
1/2 cup brandy

2 cups well-flavoured chicken stock
   or broth
salt and lots of freshly ground black
   pepper
1/2 cup flour
chopped parsley

MARINADE

2 onions, sliced
2 carrots, sliced
3 stalks celery, sliced
3 cloves garlic, crushed
1 cup dry red wine
1/2 cup vinegar

2 tsp brown sugar
1 tbsp chopped parsley
2 tsp chopped fresh thyme or 1 tsp
   dried thyme
1/8 tsp ground cloves
2 tsp French mustard such as Dijon

Cut the whole chicken into pieces. Place the chicken in a non-metallic container with all the marinade ingredients. Cover and marinate overnight, turning occasionally.

Heat the butter in a large saucepan or flameproof casserole. Take the chicken pieces from the marinade (reserve the marinade). Brown the chicken in the butter. Add the bacon and cook 1 minute, then the mushrooms and brandy, and cook 2 minutes. Add the marinade, the 1 cup red wine, the chicken stock, and salt and pepper. Cook in the large saucepan, covered, on top of the stove over a gentle heat, or in a casserole (covered) in a moderately slow (160°C) oven, for 1-1 1/4 hours, or until cooked.

Transfer the chicken to a serving plate. Mix the flour with enough water to make a smooth paste and add to the pan liquid. Heat till thickened. Adjust seasoning. Pour over the chicken and serve sprinkled with extra chopped parsley.

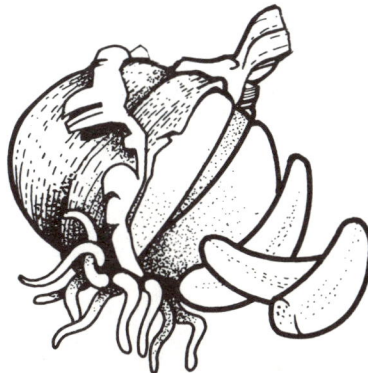

This is a mildly spiced North Indian chicken curry that is delicious. Extra chilli can be added if you prefer a hot curry. Traditionally the cuisine of Northern India uses very little chilli, but a wide variety of spices is very important to the essence of the cuisine.

For a special occasion, serve this curry with the Vegetable Biriyani (p. 33) and Naan Bread or Chapatis (pp. 197–98).

Murghi Dahi (Chicken Curry with Yoghurt and Tomatoes)♥

1.5 kg chicken, cut up (or 8 chicken parts), skin removed
4 tbsp oil or ghee, or less
2 onions, finely chopped
1 tsp chopped fresh garlic
1 tbsp grated fresh ginger
1 tsp cardamom seeds
1 tsp fennel seeds
1/8 tsp ground cloves
1/2 tsp ground cinnamon
2 tsp ground coriander
1 tbsp paprika
1 tsp ground cumin
1 1/2 tsp chilli powder
1 tsp ground turmeric
4 cups well-flavoured chicken stock
2 cups chopped peeled tomatoes, seeds removed
2 potatoes, peeled and cut into small cubes
salt and freshly ground black pepper
2/3 cup yoghurt, plus extra for garnish
1 tbsp honey
2 tsp garam masala
fresh chopped coriander or basil

Heat the oil, add the onion and cook until clear. Add the garlic, ginger, cardamom seeds, fennel seeds, cloves and cinnamon, and cook a few minutes. Add the coriander, paprika, cumin, chilli and turmeric, and cook until the oil separates from the spice mixture.

Add the chicken, and fry for 5 minutes. Add the chicken stock, tomatoes and potatoes, salt and pepper. Cover the saucepan and cook the curry over a low heat for 30 minutes. Stir in the yoghurt, and continue cooking, with the pan uncovered, until the chicken and potatoes are cooked, and the sauce is thick – about another 30 minutes. Add the honey and garam masala.

Adjust the seasoning to taste, and turn the chicken curry out on to a serving dish, topped with a spoonful of extra yoghurt and sprinkled with the chopped fresh coriander or basil.

The sauce for this recipe was created by Phillip Postlethwaite, a talented New Zealand chef who worked with me at The Flame Tree for several years.

Serve with mashed kumara and carrots, or plain steamed rice and a green salad.

Panfried Chicken Breasts with Banana Coconut Sauce

6 chicken breasts
1/2 tsp chilli powder
1/2 cup flour
1 tsp salt
1 tsp black pepper

grated rind of 1 lemon or 2 small
   limes
1/4 cup vegetable oil
1 cup dry white wine
chopped parsley for garnish

BANANA COCONUT SAUCE

1 tbsp butter
1 small onion, peeled and very
   finely chopped
2 cloves garlic, crushed
1 tsp freshly grated ginger
1 tsp curry powder

2 ripe bananas, peeled and cut into
   2.5 cm chunks
1 cup thick coconut cream
1 tbsp lemon juice
1/2 tsp salt
freshly ground black pepper

FOR THE BANANA SAUCE

Melt the butter and sauté the onion, garlic and ginger over a gentle heat until the onion is soft. Add curry powder and cook for 3 minutes, stirring. Add the chopped banana and cook for 2 minutes. Pour in the coconut cream and lemon juice, and simmer for 10 minutes, stirring constantly. Add salt and pepper to taste.

FOR THE CHICKEN

Mix together the flour with the chilli powder, salt, pepper and grated lemon rind. Flatten chicken breasts slightly with a meat mallet or small rolling pin. Heat the oil in a large frying pan. Dust the chicken breasts with the seasoned flour and cook for 5 minutes on each side. Add the wine and cook until the wine is evaporated. Add the banana sauce and cook for 5 minutes.

Serve the chicken breasts topped with the sauce and sprinkled with chopped parsley.

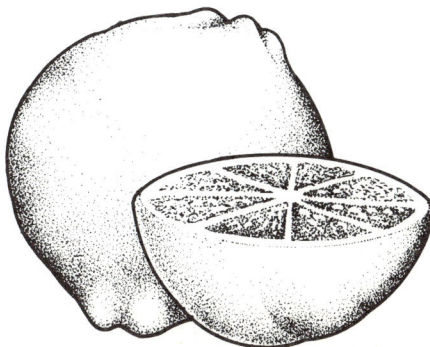

This is a chicken curry that we always have on the menu at The Flame Tree. It is easy to make, especially as we always have a large jar of the Easy Garam Masala made up for the curry paste.

Serve with steamed rice and a raita.

South Indian Chicken Curry

Serves 6-8

1/2 cup ghee or oil
2 whole chickens, cut up (or 8-12 chicken parts), skins removed
4 medium onions, sliced thinly
2 capsicums, sliced thinly
1 tsp crushed fresh garlic
2 cups curry paste, p. 228
1 cup chopped, peeled tomatoes
3 cups well-flavoured chicken stock

2 cups thick coconut cream
2 tsp brown sugar
salt and freshly ground black pepper to taste
juice of 1/2 lemon
1/4 cup chopped fresh coriander or basil
2 tsp garam masala, p. 228

Heat the ghee in a large saucepan or wok, and brown the chicken on all sides. Remove chicken and set aside. Pour off all but about 2 tbsp ghee from the pan. (Keep this surplus ghee, once strained and cooled, in the refrigerator for the next time you are frying chicken.)

Add onions and capsicum to ghee in the saucepan or wok, and sauté until onion is clear. Add garlic and curry paste, and cook quickly until the oil separates and a pleasant aroma is released from the pan. Add tomatoes and chicken stock, and cook for a few minutes. Return the chicken to the pan, and cook very gently, with the pan uncovered, for about 45 minutes, or until the chicken is cooked.

Stir in 1 1/2 cups coconut cream and the brown sugar. Add salt and pepper to taste, and lemon juice. Stir in the chopped coriander or basil and garam masala, and turn out the chicken on to a serving dish, topped with the remaining coconut cream.

This is a very spicy chicken dish that should only be served to people who like incendiary food. It is a delicious recipe, easy to prepare, especially if you can buy boneless chicken or chicken breasts.

Serve with plain rice or noodles and stir-fried vegetables or a plain salad.

The recipe can be prepared an hour or more in advance to this stage. To finish off the dish at serving time, reheat the sauce, stirring until beginning to boil, toss through the chicken for about 10 minutes, and serve immediately.

Szechwan Honey Chilli Chicken ♥

500g boneless chicken
4 tbsp cornflour
1 tsp ground ginger
1 tsp salt

1/4 cup oil, or less
1/4 cup chopped spring onions
2 tsp freshly grated ginger
1 tsp crushed fresh garlic

HONEY AND CHILLI SAUCE

1/2 cup chicken stock
1 tbsp crushed chilli
1/3 cup fresh lemon or lime juice
1 tbsp dry sherry
2 tbsp honey

1 tsp freshly ground black pepper
1/2 tsp sesame oil
1 tbsp soya sauce
2 tsp cornflour mixed in 1/4 cup
    water

Mix all the sauce ingredients together in a jug or bowl.

Mix together the 4 tbsp cornflour with the ground ginger and salt. Cut the chicken into bite-sized pieces and toss in the cornflour mixture, dusting off any excess. Heat the 1/4 cup oil in a wok or large frying pan and cook the chicken pieces (without crowding the pan) until golden. Remove cooked chicken to drain on absorbent paper and cook remaining chicken.*

Pour off most of the oil from the wok and add spring onions, fresh ginger and garlic to the pan, and cook for 1 minute. Add the sauce and cook, stirring, till thickened. Return the chicken to the wok and toss through the sauce.

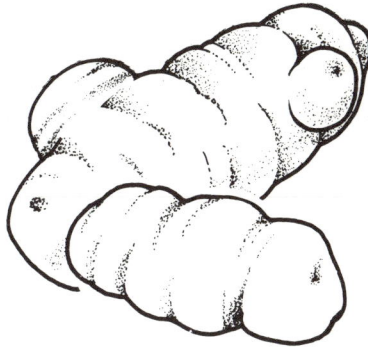

Tandoori Chicken is traditionally a whole chicken marinated overnight in a sauce and then baked. I have found that chicken parts such as thighs or legs work equally well and are easier to serve.

This version is a little spicier than the traditional Tandoori Chicken. You may cut down on the amount of chilli if you wish.

For a low-fat version, omit the butter or ghee, and use low-fat yoghurt.

Serve with Indian bread such as Naan or Chapatis (pp. 197–98), along with a vegetable curry and steamed rice, or Vegetable Biryani (p. 33) and a selection of raitas.

It is important to marinate the chicken overnight to get the real flavour of the Tandoori marinade through the chicken.

Tandoori Chicken♥

Serves 6-8

1 whole large chicken or 2 small chickens or 8 chicken portions

2 tbsp ghee or butter

MARINADE

1/4 cup lime or lemon juice
1 small onion, chopped finely
2 tsp crushed fresh garlic
1 tbsp grated fresh ginger
500g carton (2 cups) plain yoghurt
1 tbsp good-quality curry powder
1 tsp ground cumin
2 tsp ground coriander

2 tbsp paprika
2 tsp chilli powder or crushed fresh chillis
1 tsp garam masala
1 tsp freshly ground black pepper
1 tbsp brown sugar
1 tsp salt or more to taste

Remove skin and fat from chicken or chicken pieces and slash chicken with a sharp pointed knife to allow spices to penetrate. Blend all the marinade ingredients together.

Dry the chicken inside and out (or the outside of the chicken portions) with paper towels. Set the whole chicken or pieces into a large dish and rub well with the marinade. Cover the dish with plastic wrap and leave in the refrigerator to marinate overnight.

Put the chicken or chicken portions with the marinade in a baking or roasting pan. Put the whole chicken breast down in the pan. Dot with the ghee or butter. Roast about 40 minutes for the large whole chicken and less for the smaller chickens. Turn the chicken(s) every 10-15 minutes or so while they are cooking, and baste with juices. Chicken pieces will take about 20 minutes to cook. Turn once during cooking and baste.

This is a simple and delicious recipe for roast duck, that is just as good with roast chicken.

Honey Roast Duck with Pawpaw and Ginger

1 young duck, weighing 2.5 kg,
   cleaned and prepared
1/4 cup honey

salt and pepper
pawpaw slices and parsley for
   garnish

PAWPAW AND GINGER SAUCE

1 tbsp vegetable oil
1 medium onion, finely chopped
1 clove garlic, crushed
1 tbsp grated fresh ginger
1/4 cup chicken stock or broth
1/2 cup thick coconut cream

1 tsp brown sugar
juice of 1 lemon or 2 small limes
1 small ripe pawpaw, peeled, seeded
   and chopped
1/2 cup plain yoghurt

Preheat the oven to 190°C. Truss the duck and place, breast side uppermost, on a rack in a roasting dish. Season with salt and pepper, and spread the honey all over. Roast for 1 hour or until cooked. (Juices will run clear when a skewer is inserted into the duck.)

Serve on a platter garnished with pawpaw slices and parsley sprigs, and accompanied by the sauce.

SAUCE

Heat the oil in a saucepan and sauté the onion and garlic until tender. Add the ginger and cook for 1 minute. Add the chicken stock and coconut cream, and cook for 5 minutes. Stir in the brown sugar, lemon juice, pawpaw and yoghurt, and cook for 1 minute. Serve with the duck.

Beef, Lamb and Pork

This version of the classic Belgian dish comes from the Netherlands Antilles.

Serve with a purée of kumara and carrots, Eggplant Baked in Coconut Cream (p. 59) and Baked Tomatoes (p. 70).

Although the recipe calls for brown ale, lager beer can successfully be substituted.

Antilles Carbonnade de Flamande

1.5 kg braising beef
4 tbsp butter
5 large onions, thinly sliced
750 ml bottle brown ale
1 bay leaf
1 1/2 tsp fresh or 1/2 tsp dried thyme
1 tsp salt

1 tsp freshly ground black pepper
2 whole cloves
1 cup beef stock
grated rind and juice of 1 orange
2 tbsp brown sugar
1 1/2 tbsp flour
2 tbsp wine vinegar

Cut the beef into strips 5 cm wide. Heat butter in a large saucepan and brown meat on all sides. Remove meat from pan. Sauté onions until tender. Remove onions from the pan. Add beer to the pan, let it foam and subside, then add bay leaf, thyme, salt, pepper, cloves, beef stock, orange rind and juice, meat and onions. Cover and simmer gently on top of the stove for 1 1/4-2 hours, or until beef is tender. (The Carbonnade can also be baked in a covered casserole in a moderate oven for 1 1/4-2 hours, or until tender.) Blend the sugar, flour and vinegar together until smooth. Add a little water if necessary. Add to the pan or casserole and stir until gravy is thickened. Adjust seasoning to taste, and serve.

This recipe is perfect for barbecues. It is important to marinate the steaks for at least 6 hours. This recipe should only be served to people who like spicy food.

Serve with French Fried Kumara (p. 63) or rice, and a selection of vegetable salads.

Flame Tree Steak Peri Peri♥

6 steaks such as rump or T-bone, fat or sinew removed

PERI PERI MARINADE

1 tbsp seeded and crushed chillis
1 cup chilli sauce, either bought or home-made, p. 227
1/4 cup sherry
1/2 cup yoghurt
2 tbsp soya sauce
2 tsp crushed garlic
1 tbsp vegetable oil

2 tsp freshly ground black pepper
1/2 cup brown sugar
1 tbsp ground paprika
grated rind and juice of 1 lemon
1 tsp salt
a few drops red food colouring (optional)

Mix all the marinade ingredients together and marinate the steaks for at least 6 hours in the refrigerator. Grill steaks on barbecue grill, brushing with marinade while cooking, and turning occasionally, until cooked as desired.

This version of a classic Cantonese dish is always very popular on our menu. Wok cooking is a great way of preparing food quickly and with very little effort. This recipe is perfect for a warm summer's night when the cook wishes to remain cool and serene. The secret of success in wok cooking is to have all the ingredients for the recipe prepared, sliced and marinated in advance, and then to throw them all together in the wok and serve the dish immediately it is cooked. If serving, have rice or noodles prepared and cooked in advance.

Cantonese Ginger Beef with Cashew Nuts♥

500g beef fillet
2 tbsp vegetable oil

1 tbsp grated fresh ginger
2 cloves garlic, crushed

MARINADE
2 tbsp soya sauce
1 tbsp grated fresh ginger

1 tbsp dry sherry

GINGER SAUCE
1 tbsp dry sherry
1 tbsp oyster sauce
2 tbsp vinegar
1/4 cup sugar or 2 tbsp honey
1 tbsp soya sauce

1/2 tsp crushed chilli, chilli sauce or powder (optional)
1 cup beef stock or broth
2 tsp cornflour mixed in 1/4 cup water

VEGETABLES
1 onion, sliced
1 capsicum, sliced
2 sticks celery, sliced
6 dried mushrooms, soaked (optional)
150g fresh mushrooms, cleaned and sliced

1 carrot, sliced lengthwise
other vegetables of your choice, sliced
60g unsalted cashewnuts, roasted (optional)

Combine marinade ingredients. Cut beef into thin strips and marinate for several hours.

Combine all the Ginger Sauce ingredients in a jug or bowl, and set aside.

Remove beef from marinade. Heat 2 tbsp oil in a wok or large frying pan. Add ginger and garlic and beef and cook for a few minutes. Remove beef, then add all vegetables except fresh mushrooms. Cook, stirring, for 2 minutes. Add mushrooms and cook for a few seconds. Stir the Ginger Sauce and add to the wok with the beef and cashewnuts. Cook till sauce is thickened.

Serve with steamed rice.

This is a very tasty way to prepare meatballs. The dish is economical and simple to prepare. Use all minced beef, if desired.

Serve with plain steamed rice or noodles and some fresh sambals or a green salad.

Indonesian Meatballs in Chilli Fruit Sauce

MEATBALLS
400g lean minced beef
400g lean minced pork
1 tbsp oyster sauce or 1/2 tsp shrimp paste
1 tsp salt
3 tbsp fresh coriander, chopped

3 cloves garlic, crushed
2 tsp freshly ground black pepper
1 egg, lightly beaten
6 lemon leaves, finely chopped
3 tbsp oil, for frying

CHILLI FRUIT SAUCE
1 tbsp oil
1 onion, finely chopped
3 cloves garlic, crushed
2 tsp chopped fresh chilli or bottled crushed chilli, or more to taste
1/4 cup fruit chutney
grated rind and juice of 1 orange
1 tbsp chopped basil

1 1/2 cups beef stock or broth
1/4 cup coconut cream
1 tsp soya sauce
1 tbsp cornflour, mixed till smooth with 1 tbsp water
salt and freshly ground black pepper

Combine all the ingredients for the meatballs except the oil, and mix together thoroughly. With wet hands, shape into balls the size of an egg. Toss in flour.

Heat the 3 tbsp vegetable oil in a large frying pan or wok and brown meatballs on all sides, shaking the pan to prevent sticking. Drain meatballs on kitchen paper, while making the sauce.

Add the 1 tbsp oil to the pan in which meatballs were cooked, and fry onion and garlic until soft. Add chillis, chutney, orange rind and juice, basil and beef stock, and cook gently for 5 minutes.

Add the meatballs and simmer over a low heat until the meatballs are cooked – about 20 minutes. Carefully stir in the coconut cream, soya sauce and the cornflour mixture. Add salt and pepper to taste, and serve once sauce is thickened.

Serve with plain steamed rice, Orange and Ginger Carrots (p. 55) and Oriental Green Bean Salad (p. 51).

Japanese Barbecued Steaks Teriyaki♥

6 portions fillet steak or ribeye fillet, fat and sinews removed
1 cup thinly sliced vegetables such as mushrooms, carrots, capsicum, celery

1 tsp cornflour mixed in a little water
2 tbsp oil

TERIYAKI MARINADE

1/4 cup soya sauce
1/2 cup water
1/4 cup dry sherry or mirin
1/3 cup white sugar

1 tsp freshly grated ginger
1 clove garlic, crushed
1 chopped shallots or spring onions

Mix marinade ingredients together and put the steak in the marinade for about an hour. Remove meat and reserve marinade, putting the marinade into a small saucepan with the vegetables.

Brush the steaks with the oil and cook the steaks on a hot barbecue or griddle until cooked as desired, brushing occasionally with some of the marinade.

When the steaks are done, heat the marinade, add the cornflour mixed in water and heat through till just thickened. Do not let the marinade really boil – this causes it to taste bitter. Serve steaks with the marinade and vegetables spooned over.

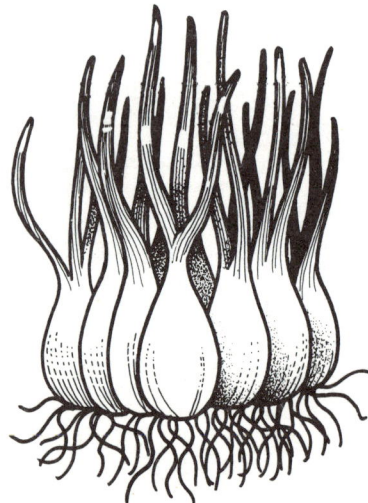

This recipe for minced beef was given to me by a friend from Sri Lanka. It is delicious and very economical to make. The dish also freezes well.

Serve with plain rice and sambals. Or for a simple family dinner, serve on toast, perhaps with a green salad.

Sri-Lankan Spiced Beef with Vegetables

1 kg lean minced beef (or pork or lamb)
1 tbsp chilli powder
1 tbsp good-quality curry powder
1 tsp turmeric
3 tbsp ghee or cooking oil
1 large onion, finely chopped
3 cloves garlic, crushed
1 tbsp grated fresh ginger
4 medium carrots, thinly sliced lengthways
3 small potatoes, peeled and cut into small cubes
1 cup well-flavoured beef stock
2 large green capsicums, sliced thinly
1/2 cup tamarind liquid or lemon juice
1 cup thick coconut cream
3 tbsp chopped fresh coriander or basil
salt and pepper to taste

Mix the minced meat thoroughly in a bowl with the chilli powder, curry powder and turmeric. Heat the oil in a large saucepan or wok, and sauté the onion until soft. Add the garlic, ginger, carrots and potatoes, and cook, stirring, for 5 minutes over a gentle heat. Add the meat and cook, stirring, for 15 minutes. Add the beef stock and capsicum, and the tamarind liquid or lemon juice, and cook until almost all the liquid is absorbed. Stir in the coconut cream and chopped fresh coriander or basil. Season to taste and serve.

Green pawpaw (papaya) makes a delicious vegetable. This is an easy and economical family dish that can be made as spicy as you wish.

For a low-fat version, omit butter and use low-fat cheese.

Serve with Scalloped Taro in Coconut Cream (p. 68) and carrots or a simple green vegetable.

Vegetarian Stuffed Pawpaw

Substitute 2 cups cooked and drained lentils (or chopped cooked soya or kidney beans) mixed with 1 cup wholemeal breadcrumbs for the minced meat, and vegetable or herb stock powder for the beef stock.

A pumpkin or squash can be substituted for the green pawpaw in this recipe.

Stuffed Green Pawpaw♥

1 large green pawpaw
500g lean minced beef (or lamb)
2 tbsp vegetable oil
1 large onion, finely chopped
1 capsicum, finely chopped
1 stalk celery, finely chopped
3 cloves garlic, crushed
3 tsp curry powder, or more to taste
3 medium tomatoes, peeled and chopped
2 tsp beef stock powder or bouillon cube
1 tsp crushed chilli, or more to taste
salt and lots of freshly ground black pepper
2 tbsp tomato sauce
grated rind and juice of 1 lemon
1 cup grated cheddar cheese
1 tbsp butter

Wash pawpaw, peel it and cut in half lengthwise. Remove seeds. Drop into a big pot of boiling salted water and boil for 15 minutes. Drain on a clean cloth or paper towels.

Fry the minced meat in a dry pan to release the fat. Drain off the fat and discard (not down the sink!). Heat oil in a clean, large frying pan or wok, and sauté the onion, celery, capsicum and garlic until soft. Add the curry powder and minced meat and cook for 1 minute, then add the tomatoes, beef stock powder, chilli, salt and pepper, together with the tomato sauce, lemon rind and juice. Cook for 15-20 minutes until the sauce is thick and fairly dry.

Arrange pawpaw halves in a greased baking pan, and fill with the meat mixture. Top with grated cheese and dot with butter. Bake in a 180°C oven for 45 minutes, covering with foil if top becomes too brown.

This is a really delicious beef curry that everyone loves. It is quite spicy, in the traditional Thai manner, but the amount of chilli may be reduced if desired.

Serve with plain rice and sambals.

Thai Red Curry of Beef

BEEF CURRY

3 tbsp oil
2 onions, sliced
1 kg sirloin or stewing beef cut into 3 cm pieces
4 cups coconut cream
1 tbsp fish sauce or oyster sauce

2 tsp brown sugar
2 fresh red chillis, seeded and chopped, or 1/2 tsp crushed bottled chilli
2 young tender lime leaves, sliced
1/3 cup basil leaves, chopped

RED CURRY PASTE

8 small fresh red chillis, seeded and chopped, or 3 tsp crushed bottled chilli
1 tsp cracked black pepper
2 tsp crushed fresh garlic
1 tbsp freshly grated ginger
juice and grated rind of 2 limes or 1 lemon

6 young lemon or lime leaves
1 tbsp oyster sauce, or 2 tsp shrimp paste or anchovy essence
1/3 cup fresh coriander, roughly chopped
1 1/2 tbsp paprika
1 tsp salt

Put all the curry paste ingredients into a food processor or blender, and process till smooth.

Heat the oil in a large saucepan or wok and fry the onions till soft. Add the curry paste and cook for 3-4 minutes. Add beef pieces and cook for 3 minutes. Add 3 cups coconut cream and simmer gently until the beef is tender. Add the fish sauce, brown sugar, chillis, sliced lime leaves and remaining 1 cup coconut cream. Adjust seasoning to taste. Remove from heat, transfer to a serving dish, and sprinkle with the chopped basil.

This recipe can be used on less expensive cuts of steak than tenderloin, as well as on pork fillet or lamb loin.

Serve steaks with kumara chips or taro chips, and a simple green salad.

Tournedoes with Sauce Tropicale

6 tournedoes (beef tenderloin steaks) weighing about 180g each
6 long strips rindless bacon to fit around tournedoes
salt and pepper
1-3 tbsp butter
1/4 cup brandy

Trim any fat and sinew from steaks, sprinkle with salt and pepper, and wrap with bacon, securing well with toothpicks. Either grill steaks, handling carefully, on a hot grill, or pan fry in the 3 tbsp butter in a large or 2 smaller frying pans, turning from time to time, until almost cooked as desired. If grilling steaks, put in a large frying pan or two smaller pans with the 1 tbsp butter after grilling. Add the brandy to the pan and ignite. Once the flame subsides, continue with the preparation of the sauce.

SAUCE TROPICALE

1/2 small, firm ripe pawpaw
2 tbsp butter
1/4 cup chopped spring onions or 1 small onion, very finely chopped
1 clove garlic, crushed
juice of 1 small lime or 1/2 lemon
1/2 tsp grated lime or lemon rind
1 tbsp fresh rosemary or tarragon, chopped, or 1 tsp dried
2 tbsp guava jelly or similar
1/4 cup dry white wine
1/2 tsp beef stock powder or crumbled bouillon cube
1 tsp freshly ground black pepper or crushed green canned peppercorns
1 1/2 cups coconut cream
6 small canned or fresh pineapple rings
2 tsp cornflour softened in 2 tbsp water
sprigs of rosemary for garnish

Peel and seed pawpaw and cut into 6 even slices. Heat butter in a small saucepan and sauté spring onion and garlic until soft. Add lemon juice and rind, rosemary or tarragon, guava jelly, white wine, beef stock powder, and black or green pepper. Cook, stirring, until jelly is dissolved.

Stir in 1 cup coconut cream. Pour this sauce over the ignited steaks in the frying pan. Cook for 2 minutes. Remove steaks to preheated serving plates, and remove toothpicks. If using 2 frying pans, pour sauce from one into the other. Add pineapple and pawpaw slices to the frying pan containing the sauce, and cook 2 minutes, handling gently. Remove fruit from pan and arrange fruit evenly on top of steaks. Add remaining 1/2 cup coconut cream to frying pan, together with cornflour mixture, and cook sauce until thickened. Spoon over steaks. Serve garnished with sprigs of rosemary.

This is a superb lamb dish, and does not take long to prepare. Other meat such as beef or pork could be prepared in the same way.

Serve with roasted kumara, Green Beans with Coconut (p. 51) and creamed pumpkin.

Leg of Lamb with Tropical Fruit Stuffing and Guava Sauce

1 leg of lamb (about 1.5 kg)
2 tbsp vegetable oil

2 tsp mild prepared mustard

TROPICAL FRUIT STUFFING

1 under-ripe mango, peeled and chopped, or 2 apples, peeled and chopped
1/4 ripe pawpaw, peeled and chopped

1/2 cup pineapple, chopped
2 tbsp butter
1 onion, finely chopped
grated rind of 1 orange
1/2 tsp ground cinnamon

GUAVA SAUCE

2 tbsp butter
4 tbsp guava jelly (or other jelly such as redcurrant)
1/2 cup orange juice

juices from roasting pan
2 tsp cornflour mixed with 4 tbsp water
1 tbsp port

Using a sharp knife, remove the bone from the lamb or have the butcher do so for you. Lay lamb out flat on a board.

Make the stuffing. Melt the 2 tbsp butter in a saucepan and sauté the onion and mango or apple till soft. Add the ripe pawpaw and pineapple, together with the grated orange rind. Cook for a few minutes. Add the cinnamon.

Spread the fruit mixture evenly at one of the short ends of the lamb. Roll up the lamb and tie securely with string. Put the lamb in a baking dish or tray. Brush with the 2 tbsp oil and rub on the mustard. Roast in a moderate oven (180°C), basting frequently for 40 minutes or until cooked as desired. Remove lamb and keep warm. Strain pan juices into a bowl.

Make the sauce. Melt the butter in the saucepan with the guava or other jelly and orange juice and stir until jelly has melted. Add the strained pan juices, cornflour mixture and port, and simmer for 1 minute, stirring.

Slice the lamb and serve with the sauce poured over.

I first tasted this delicious stir-fried lamb dish in Singapore. The touch of curry powder enhances the dish beautifully.

This recipe is good to serve to guests, as much of the preparation can be done in advance, leaving the cook free to socialise.

Serve with plain steamed rice or noodles and stir-fried vegetables (p. 40) or salad.

Oriental Stir-fried Lamb with Celery and Tomatoes♥

450g lean lamb leg
4 tbsp cooking oil, or less
2 tsp grated fresh ginger
2 cloves garlic, crushed
1-2 tsp crushed chillis, or less
1 cup water or beef stock
1 tbsp cornflour mixed in 1/4 cup water

1 medium onion, cut into wedges
2 stalks celery, sliced
1 capsicum, seeded and cut into small squares
3 medium tomatoes, each cut into 6 wedges
freshly ground black pepper to taste

MARINADE

4 tbsp soya sauce
1 tbsp dry sherry
3 tbsp tomato sauce

1 tbsp Worcestershire sauce
2 tsp curry powder

Combine the ingredients for the marinade. Cut the lamb into thin strips and marinate for 30 minutes.

Heat 2 tbsp oil in a wok and stir-fry the ginger, garlic and chillis for a few seconds. Drain the lamb, reserving the marinade, and add the lamb to the wok. Stir-fry the lamb till brown. Add the marinade, the 1 cup beef stock or water, and the cornflour mixture, and cook, stirring, until the lamb is tender. (The recipe can be prepared in advance up to this stage.)

In a separate wok or large frying pan, heat the remaining 2 tbsp oil, and stir-fry the onions, capsicum and celery for 1 minute. Add a little water if necessary. Add tomatoes and cook for 1 minute. Reheat lamb in wok and add vegetables to lamb, tossing together gently. Add black pepper to taste. Serve immediately.

This is a special-occasion lamb dish created at The Flame Tree. It is remarkably easy to prepare if using either phyllo or even ready-rolled puff or shortcrust pastry. The mango sauce is equally good with beef, pork or chicken. However, if mangos are not in season, use other tropical fruit of your choice.

Serve with Brown Rice Pilaf (p. 30) and a green salad.

Pecan Lamb Parcels with Mango and Coconut Sauce

6 lamb loins
18 sheets phyllo pastry
1/2 cup cream cheese
1/2 cup pecans (or walnuts), chopped

1 tbsp mint sauce
1 tsp prepared mustard
60g butter, melted
2 tbsp vegetable oil
salt and pepper

MANGO AND COCONUT SAUCE

2 mangos, peeled
1 tbsp vegetable oil
1 small onion, very finely chopped
1 1/2 cups thick coconut cream
1 tsp chicken stock powder

1/2 tsp cinnamon
1/4 tsp ground cloves
1 tsp dried rosemary or 2 tsp fresh
1/2 cup yoghurt
1 tbsp Rose's Lime Juice (or similar)

FOR THE LAMB

Mix together the cream cheese, pecans, mint sauce and mustard until well combined. Trim the skin and sinew from the lamb loins, and sprinkle with salt and pepper. Heat oil in a frying pan and seal the loins just until brown on all sides.

Keeping the rest of the sheets covered with a sheet of greaseproof paper topped with a damp cloth, take 3 sheets of phyllo and put on a lightly floured surface, then fold all 3 in half to make a rectangle 6 sheets thick. Brush lightly with melted butter.

Spread one-sixth of the pecan-cheese mixture over one lamb loin, then put loin pecan side down in the centre of the phyllo rectangle.

Brush edges of the rectangle well with melted butter. Fold the two longest edges in to the centre, to meet or slightly overlap in the middle. Brush the entire surface with melted butter. Fold one short edge in to the centre and brush with melted butter. Fold the other short edge in to the centre, overlapping the other edge, to make a neat parcel. Put seam side down onto a greased baking sheet, and brush the top well with melted butter.

Continue with remaining lamb, pecan mixture and phyllo pastry. Bake the phyllo parcels in a 190°C oven for 20-30 minutes, until golden and crisp.

MANGO SAUCE

Heat the oil in a small saucepan, and cook the onion until soft. Add the coconut cream and chicken stock powder, cinnamon and cloves. Chop 1 mango, and add to the sauce with the dried rosemary, and cook the sauce over a gentle heat for 10 minutes. Stir in the yoghurt and lime juice, and remove from heat.

Slice the remaining mango into thin slices. Serve the lamb parcels on individual plates with mango sauce underneath, and garnished with mango slices.

Pork dishes are a regular feature of Balinese cuisine, although much of Indonesia is predominantly Muslim. This is a quick, spicy and delicious pork dish, suitable for any occasion.

Serve with plain steamed rice or noodles, and a selection of sambals or a green salad.

Balinese Pork with Chillis and Tomatoes♥

1 kg pork leg or shoulder (fat removed)
3 tbsp vegetable oil
2 medium onions, finely chopped
6 cloves garlic, crushed
1 tbsp grated fresh ginger
2 cups peeled tomatoes, chopped, with juice
1 tbsp tomato paste
1/2 cup chicken stock or broth
1 tbsp paprika
3 tsp chopped fresh chillis, or more to taste
2 tbsp soya sauce
1 tbsp brown sugar
2 tbsp tamarind pulp or lemon juice
8-10 young lemon leaves, sliced
3 capsicums, thinly sliced
1 cup sliced fresh mushrooms
1 tbsp oyster sauce or fish sauce
3 tbsp chopped fresh basil
salt and pepper

Cut the pork into thin strips. Heat the oil in a large pan or wok, and cook the pork until it changes colour. Remove pork from pan. Add onions, garlic and ginger, and cook gently until onion is soft. Add tomatoes, tomato paste, chicken stock, paprika, chillis, soya sauce, brown sugar, tamarind or lemon juice, and lemon leaves, and cook for 5 minutes. Return the pork to the pan, together with the capsicum, and simmer gently for 20 minutes. Add the mushrooms and oyster sauce, and cook for another 10 minutes or until the pork is tender. Add salt and pepper, and extra chilli to taste. Stir in the chopped fresh basil.

In Far Eastern cuisine, plum sauce is often teamed with pork, much as apples are in European pork dishes. This plum sauce is very easy to make, as all the ingredients are stocked in most kitchens. The sauce is also delicious with other cuts of pork, and with chicken.

Serve the chops with plain steamed rice and Oriental Stir-fried Vegetables (p. 40).

Barbecued Oriental Pork Chops with Plum Sauce♥

6 lean pork chops

MARINADE
1 tbsp vegetable oil
1 tbsp sherry
2 tbsp soya sauce

1/4 cup chopped spring onions
1 tbsp grated fresh ginger
2 cloves garlic, crushed

PLUM SAUCE
1 tsp juice squeezed from freshly grated ginger
425g can plums, with juice
1 tbsp dry sherry

1 tbsp soya sauce
1 tbsp honey
1 tbsp cornflour mixed with 1/4 cup plum juice

Mix all the marinade ingredients together. Marinate the chops for several hours or overnight. Barbecue or grill the chops, brushing with the marinade, until done.

Remove stones from plums and blend all the ingredients for the sauce together until smooth. Heat in a small saucepan until thickened. Serve the chops with the sauce poured over.

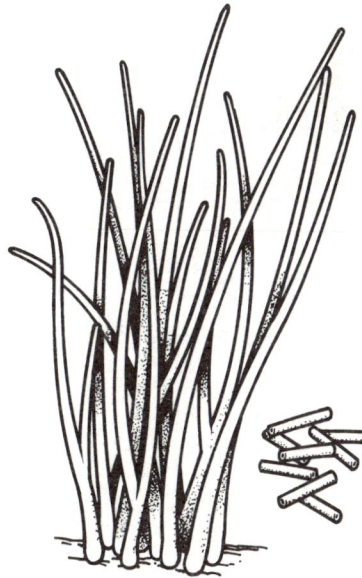

This delicious pork dish, which reflects the French influence in the local cuisine of Vanuatu, can be served as a simple family meal or at a dinner party.

Serve with plain steamed rice or noodles and a green salad, or with Creamed Breadfruit (p. 52) or mashed kumara.

Blanquette of Pork Vanuatu

1 kg stewing pork (leg or shoulder), cut into cubes
2 cups well-flavoured chicken stock
1 bay leaf
2 tbsp chopped parsley
2 stalks celery, washed and cut into thin slices, with leaves, chopped
1 1/2 tsp chopped fresh thyme, or 1/2 tsp dried
1 1/2 tsp chopped fresh oregano or 1/2 tsp dried
1/2 tsp chilli powder

1 tsp freshly ground black pepper
3 onions, peeled and quartered (or 12 tiny onions)
6 small carrots, sliced lengthways
3 tbsp butter
3 tbsp flour
1 cup coconut cream, and extra for garnish
juice of 1/2 lemon
salt to taste
extra chopped parsley for garnish

Put pork, chicken stock, bay leaf, parsley, celery, thyme, oregano, chilli and black pepper with 1 tsp salt (depending on the saltiness of stock) into a large saucepan. Bring to the boil, cover the pan, reduce heat and simmer gently for 30 minutes, or until the pork is half tender. Skim off any foam. Add onions and carrots and simmer gently, covered, until the vegetables and pork are tender. Drain stock from meat (use a large metal colander), reserving stock and straining stock again through a fine sieve into a bowl.

In a clean saucepan, melt the butter and stir in the flour to make a smooth roux. Gradually add the reserved stock, stirring until smooth. Add coconut cream, pork and lemon juice, and extra salt and pepper to taste. Heat through, and serve garnished with a few spoonfuls of coconut cream and sprinkled with extra parsley.

This is a wonderful stew that is delicious enough to serve at a party as part of a hot buffet. This stew appeals to children as well as adults.

Serve with brown rice and a green salad.

Pacific Pork Stew♥

1.5 kg lean stewing pork
3 tbsp vegetable oil, or less
2 onions, finely chopped
1 stalk celery with leaves, chopped
1 tsp crushed garlic
1 cup sliced salami or spicy sausage
1 tbsp fresh coriander, chopped
1 bay leaf
1 tsp crushed chilli, or more or less
1 tbsp vinegar

1/4 cup fresh orange juice
300g kumara, peeled and cut into small cubes
1 carrot, sliced
1 cup sliced pumpkin
1 cup taro root, cut into small cubes
1 cup corn kernels, fresh or canned
1 tbsp fresh lime or lemon juice
salt and pepper to taste

Cut pork into 4 cm cubes. Season pork cubes with salt and pepper. Heat the oil in a large saucepan and sauté the onions, celery and garlic until soft. Add the pork and cook for a few minutes. Add salami, coriander, bay leaf, chillis, vinegar and orange juice. Add just enough water to cover. Bring to the boil, reduce heat, cover and simmer for 20 minutes. Add the kumara, carrot, pumpkin and taro root. Cover the pot again and cook until the vegetables and pork are tender. Season to taste with salt and pepper. Add the lemon juice and the corn, and heat through until the corn is cooked.

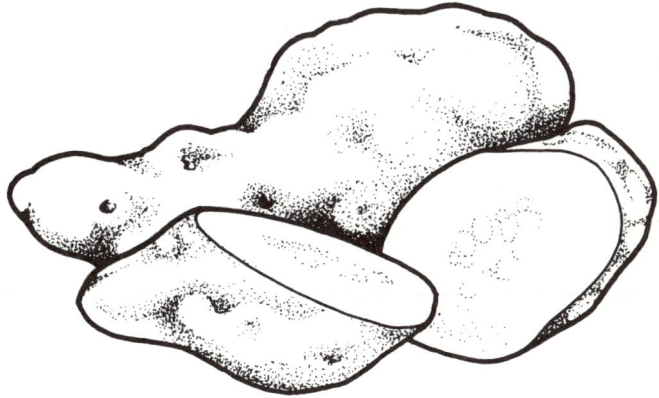

This dish is a Flame Tree creation that brings together pork and tropical fruit in a combination that is exotic and very appealing.

Serve with Scalloped Breadfruit (p. 52) and Green Beans with Coconut (p. 51).

Pork Loin with a Pawpaw and Cumin Coulis♥

6 small pork loins
2 tbsp vegetable oil, or less
salt and pepper

1/4 cup orange juice
1/4 cup dry white wine

PAWPAW AND CUMIN COULIS

1/2 small onion, chopped
2 tsp ground cumin
1/4 cup chicken stock
1/2 small pawpaw, peeled and
 seeded
1/2 tsp prepared mustard

juice of 1 small lime
1 tbsp honey
4 tbsp yoghurt
1 tbsp vegetable oil, extra
extra pawpaw slices and parsley
 sprigs for garnish

Trim the pork of any fat or sinew. Sprinkle with salt and pepper. Heat oil in a large pan and seal the pork loins on all sides. Reduce heat, add orange juice and white wine, and continue cooking until the pork is done.

FOR THE COULIS

Heat the extra 1 tbsp oil in a small saucepan and sauté the onion until softened. Add the cumin and cook for 1 minute without scorching. Add the chicken stock and cook for 30 seconds. Put into a food processor or blender with the pawpaw, mustard, lime juice, honey and yoghurt, and purée until smooth. Return to the saucepan and heat through gently.

Slice each pork loin into 8. Pour sauce onto 6 warmed plates. Arrange pork slices in a semi-circle on each plate, and garnish with pawpaw slices and parsley sprigs.

This is the hottest curry that we serve at The Flame Tree and the dish has a faithful following of customers who have cast-iron throats. We always warn people about this curry, having seen some of them dissolve into tears, clutch their throats and demand gallons of iced water to put out the fire. Meanwhile at the next table, another customer who is a lover of hot curries is claiming that the curry could be a bit spicier!

The chillis could be reduced if you wish.

Iced water is not the answer to a chilli overdose – a glass of milk or a piece of bread or chapati will cool down the throat much more effectively.

Beef Vindaloo, Lamb or Mutton Vindaloo
This recipe is equally delicious using stewing beef or lamb or mutton (or goat).

South Indian Pork Vindaloo

1.5 kg pork shoulder or lean
   stewing pork
1/4 cup oil or ghee
3 onions, thinly sliced

2 tsp garam masala
2 tsp brown sugar
1/2 cup cream
chopped coriander or basil

CURRY PASTE
1 cup white vinegar
1 tbsp grated fresh ginger
2 tbsp (6-8 large) chillis, seeded and
   chopped, or equivalent bottled
   crushed chilli
1 tbsp crushed garlic
1 tsp ground cinnamon
1 tsp ground cardamom

1 tsp freshly ground black pepper
1/4 tsp ground cloves
1/2 tsp ground nutmeg
2 tsp salt
1 tbsp paprika
2 tbsp curry powder
1 tbsp tomato paste

Put all the curry paste ingredients in a food processor or blender and process till smooth.

Cut the meat into cubes and put into a bowl with the curry paste. Marinate for 2 hours – do not marinate longer.

Heat the ghee in a large saucepan and cook the onion till soft. Drain the meat from the marinade in a colander, reserving the marinade. Add the meat to the onion mixture and cook till the meat changes colour, then add the marinade and cook the curry, covered, over a gentle heat until the meat is tender. Be careful not to overcook, as the vinegar can 'over-tenderise' the meat. Add a little water during the cooking time if necessary.

Add the brown sugar, garam masala and cream, stir to combine, and turn the curry out into a serving dish. Sprinkle with chopped coriander or basil.

This delicious spicy curry recipe was given to me by Wyomi Fernando from Sri Lanka, who lived here on Rarotonga for several years.

Serve with plain rice and your choice of sambals.

Sri Lankan Chicken Curry with Pineapple

This recipe is also wonderful with chicken. Use 1.5 kg chicken portions with skin and fat removed. Brown in hot oil and drain well on kitchen paper, then cook in the curry sauce till done.

Sri Lankan Pork Curry with Pineapple

SPICE BLEND

1 tbsp chilli powder
2 tsp turmeric
2 whole cloves or 1/4 tsp ground cloves
1 stick cinnamon or 1 tsp ground cinnamon
6 cardamom pods
1 tbsp curry powder
2 tsp salt

CURRY

1 kg shoulder or stewing pork
3 cloves garlic, crushed
1 tbsp grated fresh ginger
juice of 2 limes or 1 lemon
1/2 cup water
2 large onions, sliced
2 capsicums, thinly sliced
1 1/2 cups coconut cream
1 1/2 cups pineapple cubes, canned or fresh

Mix the spice blend together in a bowl.

Cut the pork into cubes. Mix the pork with the spice blend, garlic, ginger, lime juice and 1/2 cup water. Marinate with the marinade in a covered saucepan for 30 minutes.

Cook the pork over a gentle heat until almost tender – do not add any water unless the pork gets very dry. Add the onion and capsicum and cook for 8-10 minutes. Add the pineapple and coconut cream. Cook for 3 minutes.

This is a quick recipe for pork fillet that also tastes good with chicken.

Serve with buttered noodles such as fettuccine and a green salad or Coconut Creamed Taro Leaf (p. 69).

Tahitian Pork with an Orange Basil Sauce

4-6 pork fillets weighing 1 kg
salt and pepper to taste

flour
2-3 tbsp oil

ORANGE SAUCE
2 tbsp butter
2 tbsp flour
2 cups fresh orange juice

1 tbsp orange marmalade
1 tsp nutmeg
2 tbsp chopped fresh basil

Trim any fat off the pork and cut into slices about 3.5 cm thick. Flatten the pork slices gently with a meat hammer. Dust lightly with flour seasoned with salt and pepper. Heat oil and cook the pork slices a minute or two on each side. Remove from pan.

Add the butter to the pan, stirring with a wooden spoon. Add flour and keep stirring to make a smooth roux. Slowly add the orange juice, then the marmalade, nutmeg and fresh basil. Return the pork slices to the pan and cook gently till the pork is heated through. Transfer to a serving dish and garnish with twists of fresh orange slices.

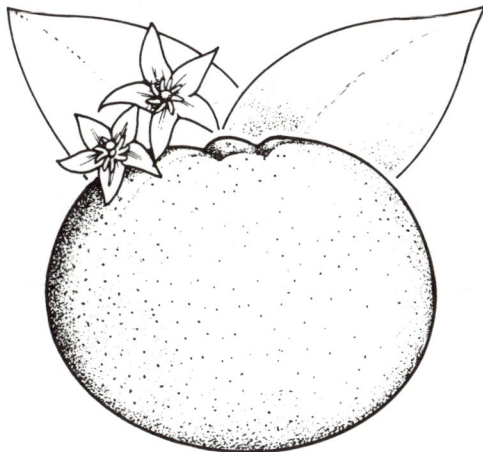

Tropical Fruit and Desserts

A Guide to Tropical Fruit

Avocado

Avocado is one of the few fruits that contains fat, which gives it a delicious flavour and texture. Choose firm fruit that is free of bruises. In most varieties, fruit is ripe if it feels fairly soft when pressed with the fingers; in some varieties, it is ripe when the stone rattles when the fruit is shaken. To hasten ripening, wrap the fruit in paper or put in a brown paper bag and keep in a dark place.

Uses
Avocado is mostly used as a salad vegetable. If using in a hot dish, never boil, as this causes it to taste bitter. Avocado is excellent incorporated into mayonnaise and hollandaise sauces, in soups and dips, and with fish and chicken dishes. Avocado also makes an excellent dessert in the form of a mousse, fool or ice cream.

Avocado flesh exposed to the air tends to go brown – sprinkle flesh with lemon juice to prevent discolouring.

To Freeze
Mash avocado flesh and mix with lemon juice, and put in plastic containers. Frozen avocado is good to use in sauces, soups, dips and desserts.

Bananas

Bananas are plentiful throughout the year. It is best to buy firm, slightly unripe to green bananas in a bunch, and ripen by placing in a brown paper bag.

Uses
Bananas can be used in ice cream, mousse, custard, cakes, bread, scones, jam, chutney, as well as sliced in fruit salad. Sprinkle freshly peeled and sliced fruit with lemon juice to prevent browning. Ripe bananas can be refrigerated to prevent further ripening. The skin will darken but the fruit will not discolour.

To Freeze
Bananas can be frozen in the skin, or the fruit can be mashed with lemon juice and packed in plastic containers. Frozen banana can be used in any recipe calling for mashed bananas.

Carambola or Starfruit

This fruit when cut cross-ways makes attractive star-shaped slices that are excellent as a garnish. Choose unbruised, firm fruit, and store on a wire rack at room temperature until ripe. Some varieties are sweeter than others.

Uses
Ripe sweet fruit is excellent in fruit or savoury salads. Carambola can be used in a sauce for meat, fish or chicken, or poached as a dessert in a sweet syrup. To use in sweet or savoury sauces, cook the cut-up fruit in a little water until soft, then purée. Garnish meat and fish with slices that have been simmered for a minute in stock or water, and garnish dessert with slices that have been poached in sugar syrup for 1 minute.

To Freeze
Carambola freezes best cut into star-shaped slices and poached in a light sugar syrup. Cool and pack in plastic containers in the poaching syrup.

Citrus: Orange, Lemon, Lime, Grapefruit, Pomelo, Ugli Fruit, Mandarin, Tangerine

All these fruits grow well in the Pacific Islands at various times of the year, and are excellent as fruit juice. Oranges, mandarins and the grapefruit family, which includes pomelo and ugli fruit, are good peeled and divided into sections and added to fruit salads. The juice and grated rind of the fruit is used in many curries, stews, casseroles, sauces, cakes and desserts. Lemon and lime juice and rind especially have a multitude of culinary uses, and in Asian countries the young leaves are also used in flavouring soups and curries. All citrus fruit, either alone or combined or with other fruits, makes excellent jam or marmalade.

To Freeze
Whole fruit can be frozen for later use in fruit juice and sauces, but it is best to freeze the squeezed juice in plastic containers or in conveniently sized ice-cube trays. The grated rind freezes well in tiny containers or bags. Orange, mandarin and grapefruit segments can be poached in a light sugar syrup before freezing.

If fresh coconuts are unavailable, coconut cream can be made from first soaking desiccated coconut in enough hot water to cover, and then squeezing as described for fresh coconut.

Store-bought desiccated or unsweetened flaked coconut can be used in any recipe in this book calling for grated coconut. Always taste before using to ensure the product is not rancid.

Coconuts

The coconut palm is the most useful plant in the tropics, and is put to a multitude of practical uses.

As a food source, the water of both the green and the mature coconut is a superb, thirst-quenching drink. The grated flesh of the mature coconut is used in baking, desserts and many other dishes, and is far superior to the packaged flaked or desiccated coconut widely available in supermarkets. The coconut cream which is extracted from the grated flesh is used extensively in the cuisine of every tropical country around the world.

Note: coconut water, or the liquid inside the coconut, is often called coconut milk. Coconut cream, from the grated flesh, is also referred to in some recipe books as coconut milk. In this book, coconut cream always refers to the liquid extracted from the grated flesh. Excellent canned coconut cream is available in New Zealand, and as a time-saver is recommended for use in curries and similar dishes. For desserts, sauces and in recipes such as marinated fish, the flavour of freshly squeezed coconut cream is far superior, and well worth the effort of making.

To grate coconut and extract cream

A simple rough-tipped grater attached to a plank of wood is the most commonly used grater. A standard kitchen cheese grater is not recommended – it may not be strong enough, and makes the task of grating extremely time consuming. The grating attachment of an electric food processor may also be used to grate coconut meat, but remember to remove all traces of the outer coconut shell from the flesh before processing.

Grated coconut can be blended again in a food processor or blender, for a finer product. This is also recommended before squeezing for coconut cream, as it allows the liquid to be extracted more quickly.

To extract liquid, put the grated coconut in a damp cloth bag, or put in several thicknesses of damp muslin squares and twist into a bundle. Then, holding the bag over a basin, squeeze out as much liquid as possible. For a thin coconut cream, useful as a liquid in the initial stages of cooking curries and so on, add 1/2 cup boiling water to the coconut left in the cloth, and squeeze again.

To Freeze

Coconut cream and freshly grated coconut flesh both freeze well. It is also best to store commercial desiccated and unsweetened flaked coconut in the freezer to prevent it going rancid.

Custard Apple, Sugar Apple, Cherimoya, Soursop

These fruits are all from the Annona tree family, originating in the American tropics.

Custard or sugar apples and cherimoya have green, knobbly outer skins and a sweet, white, creamy pulp. Soursop is similar but has rows of soft, dark spines along the outer skin. The flesh has a more acidic but delicious sweet-sour flavour.

Uses

The pulp of Annona fruits is good scooped out with a spoon and eaten as is or added to fruit salads. The seeds are inedible. The flesh can be sieved to remove the seeds, and the resulting purée used in custards, fools, ice cream, sorbets and mousses. The fruit can also be used in jams and jellies, either alone, with lemon added, or teamed up with other fruit.

To Freeze

The fruit purée freezes well. Add lemon to keep the colour white. The whole, washed fruit can also be frozen.

Guava

Tree-ripened fruit can often be infected with fruitfly, so it is best to pick or buy this aromatic fruit when it is half-ripe and to allow it to ripen. Canned guava is widely available, and is an acceptable substitute in many desserts.

Uses

The guava is excellent in ice cream, mousses, cakes, sponge puddings, jams, jellies, chutneys and in guava butter. The fruit can be used in fruit salads, preferably with the seedy pulp removed. Guavas can also be halved and simmered in a sugar syrup, then chilled, to make a delicious dessert. Alternatively, poach in a sugar syrup with lemon, then purée for use in sauces and drinks.

To Freeze

Whole washed fruit, poached fruit or purée can be frozen.

Jackfruit

Jackfruit is a huge fruit of the same family as breadfruit, and can weigh up to 28 kg. When ripe, the tender fruit around the seeds is good to eat, and the ripe fruit, prepared in sweet syrup, is commonly eaten as a sweet dish in many Asian countries.

In Fiji, the green jackfruit, when it is mature but unripe, is often used to make a delicious curry. However, the fruit in this stage of development produces a very sticky sap. To prepare the fruit, oil your hands well with vegetable oil, and also oil the chopping board and the knife. Use the oiled knife to remove the skin, then cut the fruit into manageable sections. Sprinkle with lemon juice to prevent the flesh from darkening. Cut the flesh into cubes or slices. Follow any good vegetable curry recipe, and cook the fruit in the curry sauce until tender.

To Freeze
The ripe fruit prepared in syrup freezes well. The green jackfruit, once cooked, also freezes well.

Jambo (Rose Apple, Malay Apple)

This is a rather bland fruit, the size of an apple, and with crisp flesh. Some varieties have a green outer skin, some a pink skin. Fruit bruises easily, so take care with handling.

Uses
Fruit can be poached in sugar syrup of 1 part sugar to 2 parts water, with a few cloves or a cinnamon stick added, and chilled to serve as a dessert fruit. Fresh sliced fruit, sprinkled with lemon to prevent darkening, can be used in fruit salads. Half-ripe or ripe fruit can be used in jellies, jams and chutneys.

To Freeze
Sliced fruit sprinkled with lemon, or fruit poached in sugar syrup, can be frozen.

Lychee, Rambutan

Although originating in China, lychees are now being grown in many tropical countries. The fruit has juicy, pearly-white flesh and a rough, leathery skin. The skin is easy to remove. Rambutans are of the same family as the lychee, but are native to Malaysia. The white flesh is similar to the lychee, but less aromatic. The outer skin is completely covered with soft, brownish-red spines. It is easiest to peel the fruit by cutting open through the skin first with a knife.

Canned lychees and rambutans are widely available in supermarkets and Asian food shops. They are softer in texture than the fresh fruit, but still excellent in fruit salads and other dishes.

Uses
Both fruits are delicious slightly chilled, then eaten as they are. They can be added to fruit salads after removing the seed, and also team up well in a salad with chicken and pork. Add to Chinese sweet and sour sauce to go with fish, chicken or meat.

To Freeze
Both fruits freeze well, unpeeled and left whole and put in plastic bags.

Mangos

The mango is one of the most delicious of all tropical fruits. There are many varieties grown, some of which have a stringy flesh and some of which have a 'turpentine' flavour. The best eating varieties have plenty of non-fibrous, juicy flesh and a comparatively small stone. Select mangos that are firm and free of bruising. To hasten ripening, wrap in paper and put in a dark place. Store ripe mangos in the refrigerator to prevent further ripening.

Uses
Ripe mangos are good eaten uncooked, as they are, or sliced into fruit salads. Both ripe and unripe mango are also used in a variety of sweet and savoury dishes. Never eat the skin of the mango, as this can cause mouth and gum ulcers. Also avoid the area immediately around the stalk, as this has the highest acid content. Always wash mangos well. To prepare a mango for eating, hold the mango upright, and with a sharp knife slice off the thick sides of the cheeks. Make a few cuts lengthwise then crosswise into the flesh, then pull the skin back from the mango. The flesh should pop out easily. When firm the whole fruit can also be peeled with a sharp knife or a potato peeler.

To Freeze

Cubes and slices of peeled fruit freeze very well in plastic bags for use in fruit salads and other dishes. Puréed fruit also freezes well. The whole washed and unpeeled fruit can also be frozen.

Passionfruit, Granadilla

The small, purple granadilla and a number of varieties of the larger, yellow passionfruit grow well in the tropics. The pulp of both passionfruit and granadilla is aromatic and delicious, with small, black edible seeds.

Uses

For fruit salads, cut fruit in half, remove pulp and seeds, and add this to the fruit salad. For drinks and some desserts, and for passionfruit butter, rub the pulp through a sieve. Pulp, with or without seeds, can be used in ice cream, gelatine desserts, and cream filling for cakes, meringues and pastries.

To Freeze

Passionfruit pulp, with or without seeds, freezes very well in plastic containers.

Pawpaw (Papaya)

There are several varieties of pawpaw, some of which are more flavoursome than others. Fruit is available almost all the year round, and on most Pacific islands is abundant. Choose firm, slightly unripe and unbruised fruit and allow to ripen. Immediately upon ripening, store fruit in the refrigerator.

Uses

Pawpaw has many uses, either green or ripe, in savoury and sweet dishes, as well as jams and chutneys. To serve as a fruit, halve the ripe pawpaw and remove seeds. Serve with lime wedges, and a spoon for scooping out the fruit. For dishes where peeled fruit is required, peel before or after halving and seeding.

To Freeze

Freeze, peeled, as cubes, slices, or made into balls with a melon-baller. Serve straight from the freezer, if desired. Pawpaw also freezes well as a purée for use in pies, ice cream, and so on.

Pineapple

Pineapples are available throughout most of the year in the Pacific. Select fruit that has been ripened on the plant, with a reddish-yellow colour. Picked unripe or very green fruit will never ripen, and will be sour and tasteless. Over-ripe fruit will taste fermented. Fruit will spoil if left for more than a few days unrefrigerated.

To Cut
Remove the top and base of the fruit and cut downwards with a sharp knife. Remove the 'eyes' by cutting diagonal wedges about 1/2 cm deep. Cut fruit in halves or quarters and remove the fibrous core.

Uses
Pineapple has many culinary uses in savoury dishes, baked goods, ice cream, jams and chutney, as well as being popular as a juice. Note: pineapple must be cooked before being included in any dish which contains gelatine, eggs or milk. Pineapple has an enzyme that breaks down protein and prevents gelatine from setting and curdles eggs and milk. The fruit, sliced or puréed, can be poached in a little sugar syrup, or cooked for 5 minutes in just a small amount of water, and then used in recipes where cooked or canned pineapple is required, such as mousse, custard, cakes, pie fillings, gelatine desserts, and so on.

To Freeze
Peeled, sliced, uncooked pineapple, sprinkled with a little sugar and put in plastic bags, freezes very well. Pineapple slices or chunks, cooked in sugar syrup or just a little water, also freeze well. Pineapple purée for later use in juice etc. also freezes well.

Tahitian Apple

This green-skinned fruit with yellow flesh has a crisp texture and rather acid flavour. Some of the flesh is stringy. As the fruit spoils easily, it should be washed well and stored in the refrigerator.

Uses
Peel the apple and cut flesh from seeds. Peel, slice or grate the fruit and use in fruit salads, chutney or jam. Non-fibrous fruit can be poached in a sugar syrup or water and used in desserts, or puréed and rubbed through a sieve for use in drinks, ice cream, or as an 'apple' sauce for pork.

To Freeze
Tahitian apple purée can be frozen.

Watermelon

Different sizes and varieties of watermelon are available during many months of the year. Fruit should have a firm, shiny skin, and have a hollow sound when tapped. The inside of a ripe melon should have a rich, dark red colour. Many vendors will cut the watermelon open to show you the inside.

Uses
Watermelon is delicious eaten as it is, chilled, or in fruit salads. The seeds are edible. The flesh can be scooped with a melon-baller, or cut into cubes. The flesh with seeds removed can be puréed for use in juices and sorbets. The white flesh between the red, sweet flesh and dark green skin, can be used in chutneys and pickles, and makes a good jam combined with ginger.

To Freeze
Watermelon purée for later use in juice and sorbets can be frozen.

This pie is very quick and easy to make. However, if you prefer, you can spoon the recipe for the filling into dessert glasses or a serving bowl, then chill, instead of spreading it into a biscuit crust.

To press the biscuit crumbs evenly into the pie dish, use a small, straight-sided glass, rather than your fingers. This is a quick way of making a smooth, firm, even crust.

Desserts

Avocado Cream Pie

CRUST

2 cups plain, coconut, or ginger
    biscuits, finely crushed

80g (1/3 cup) butter, melted
1/2 tsp cinnamon

Combine the finely crushed biscuits with the butter and cinnamon, and line a 23 cm pie dish.

FILLING

1/2 cup caster sugar
2 large avocados
juice of 1 lemon
1 tsp vanilla essence

2 tbsp plain gelatine
1/4 cup boiling water
1 cup cream, chilled

Peel avocados and remove stones. Mash the flesh (or purée in a blender or food processor). Beat together with the sugar and lemon juice for a few minutes. Add vanilla. Mix gelatine and boiling water together until dissolved, cool, then stir into avocado mixture. Beat cream in a clean bowl until it holds its shape, then fold into the avocado mixture. Spoon into the pie dish and chill for at least 4 hours, until set. Serve topped with extra whipped cream.

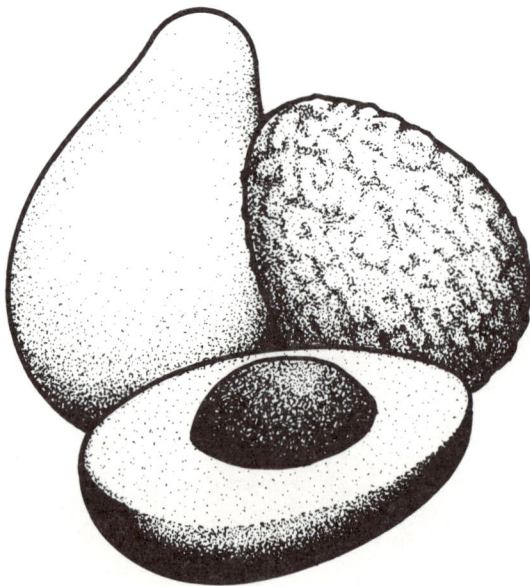

People (including myself) who have traditionally disliked bread pudding have been converted after tasting this version.

Other fruit, or combinations of fruit, can be used instead of bananas, and you can use either wholemeal or raisin bread in place of white.

If you prefer, the crusts can be removed from the bread.

Cinnamon and Banana Bread Pudding

8 slices white bread
5 large bananas
1 tbsp lemon juice
1/2 cup chopped dates, prunes or
    whole raisins
120g (1/2 cup) butter
4 eggs
3 cups milk

1 cup cream
1/2 tsp ground nutmeg
1 1/2 tsp ground cinnamon
1/2 cup brown sugar
1 tbsp golden syrup
1 tsp vanilla
1 tbsp rum (optional)

Peel and slice bananas and toss in the lemon juice. Keep crusts on bread, butter each slice and cut into cubes. Place a layer of bread cubes in a buttered ovenproof dish 30 cm x 20 cm, followed by a layer of bananas and dates. Repeat layers till all buttered bread, bananas and dates are used up.

Beat together the milk, cream, brown sugar, golden syrup, eggs, nutmeg, cinnamon, vanilla and rum till well combined. Pour over the bread. Bake in a moderate 180°C oven for 40-45 minutes, or until egg mixture is set.

Serve warm or cold accompanied by whipped cream.

These two tropical fruits make a delicious fruit crumble, and this is a very easy dessert to make when unexpected guests arrive. The crumble is best served warm with whipped cream and/ or ice cream.

Other combinations of fruit can be used. Adjust the amount of sugar according to the sharpness of the fruit. For a low fat version, reduce butter used in crumble topping.

Port Vila Banana and Mango Crumble

FILLING

5 large bananas
juice of 1 lemon
flesh of 3 large mangos, sliced

1/4 cup brown sugar
1/4 cup water or orange juice
1 tbsp cornflour

CRUMBLE TOPPING

1 1/2 cups plain white or wholemeal
    flour
3/4 cup rolled oats
1/2 cup grated coconut

80g (1/3 cup) cold butter, chopped
1/4 tsp cinnamon
3/4 cup brown sugar

Butter a baking dish approx. 20 x 30 cm. Preheat oven to 180°C.

Peel and slice the bananas, and sprinkle with the lemon juice. Lay the bananas and the mango slices in the baking dish. Mix together the cornflour, water or orange juice and brown sugar, and pour over the fruit.

Rub all the ingredients for the topping together, using your fingers, until well combined. Do not use a food processor, as the texture of the crumble should not be fine. Sprinkle the topping evenly over the fruit, and bake the crumble for 40-45 minutes, or until the topping is crisp and golden.

This is a rich and creamy tropical version of the French classic.

Coconut Cream Caramel

2 cups thick coconut cream
1/3 cup milk
2 eggs
2 egg yolks, extra

1/2 cup caster sugar
3 tbsp coconut liqueur (optional)
1 cup freshly grated coconut

CARAMEL
1/2 cup water

1/2 cup white sugar

Scald the coconut cream and milk in a small saucepan. Beat the eggs and egg yolks together in a bowl, but do not allow to get frothy. Add sugar and whisk lightly, then gradually whisk in the hot coconut cream mixture. Strain into a large jug, and stir in the grated coconut and coconut liqueur.

Put the sugar and water for the caramel into a small saucepan, dissolve the sugar, stirring, over a gentle heat, then boil rapidly without stirring until a rich golden colour. Stop the boiling by dipping the bottom of the saucepan quickly into a basin of cold water for 3 seconds only. Take care as caramel could splatter and burn you.

Add 2 tsp boiling water to the caramel mixture. Using a 15 cm soufflé dish or cake pan as a mould (or 6 x 1/2 cup individual moulds), pour three-quarters of the caramel into the dry *warm* mould. Pour the rest onto an oiled baking sheet. Turn the mould around carefully to coat the bottom and sides evenly with the caramel. Pour in the coconut mixture. Place in a baking dish, and pour in enough hot water to come half-way up the sides of the mould.

Bake at 180°C for about 40-50 minutes for the large mould and about 20 minutes for the individual moulds, or until set. Remove from the water and cool, then refrigerate overnight.

Crush the caramel on the oiled baking sheet by covering with greaseproof paper and hitting gently with a rolling pin. Turn out the coconut cream caramel(s), and serve with the crushed caramel around the edge.

The rich creaminess of the coconut mousse is complemented perfectly by the crisp flavour of the passionfruit sauce.

Coconut Mousse with Passionfruit Sauce

1 1/2 tbsp plain gelatine
1/4 cup cold water
1 1/2 cups thick coconut cream
1 cup dairy cream
4 eggs, separated

1/2 cup sugar
1 tsp vanilla essence or 2 tbsp
   coconut liqueur
1/2 cup grated fresh coconut

Soften the gelatine in the water. Heat the coconut cream and cream in a medium-sized saucepan over a gentle heat, then stir in the gelatine until completely dissolved. Beat the egg yolks and sugar together in a bowl until thick and creamy. Slowly stir this mixture into the hot coconut cream/gelatine mixture in the saucepan. Cook, stirring with a wooden spoon, over a *very gentle* heat for 2 minutes or until slightly thickened. Add vanilla or coconut liqueur. Remove from heat and allow mixture to cool completely, but do not allow to set.

Beat the egg whites until stiff, fold a little of the egg white mixture into the cool coconut custard, then fold in the remainder until well combined. Pour into a serving bowl or individual glasses, and chill until set. Allow at least 4 hours. Serve topped with or accompanied by the Passionfruit Sauce, and decorated with the grated coconut.

PASSIONFRUIT SAUCE

1 cup passionfruit pulp
1 tbsp cornflour

1/2 cup water
1/2 cup sugar

Mix cornflour with water until smooth. Put all ingredients into a small saucepan, and heat through, stirring, until sugar is dissolved and sauce is thickened. Cool, then chill.

This delicious rice pudding is a perfect dessert to serve after a hot and spicy main course.

Indonesian Coconut Rice Pudding

3 cups milk
4 cardamom pods or 1/4 tsp ground cardamom
1 cinnamon stick or 1/2 tsp ground cinnamon
1 cup sugar
60g (1/4 cup) butter
2 cups coconut cream

3/4 cup short-grain rice, uncooked
1/2 tsp rosewater (optional)
1/4 tsp nutmeg
1/3 cup raisins or chopped dates
1/4 cup cashewnuts or other nuts, toasted
1 cup canned, crushed pineapple, drained (optional)

Bring the milk with the cardamom pods and cinnamon stick slowly to the boil. Turn off the heat and leave for 5 minutes. Strain milk through a fine sieve. Stir the sugar and butter into the hot milk. Add the coconut cream and the rice, nutmeg and rosewater. Bring to the boil again, then reduce heat and simmer gently for 20 minutes, uncovered. Do not stir.

Pour into a buttered 30 cm x 20 cm baking dish, and bake tightly covered in the oven for 15 minutes. Remove from oven and stir in the raisins or chopped dates, pineapple and cashewnuts, and bake tightly covered for a further 15 minutes. Remove from oven. Stand for 5 minutes.

Stir well and serve warm or chilled in a large bowl or individual dishes.

This is a very easy recipe. Other nuts such as pecans, walnuts, almonds or macadamias can be used if cashews are unavailable.

To toast or roast nuts, place on a flat baking tray in a medium oven until golden, or put on a plate and microwave on High for 5 minutes, stirring from time to time. Whichever method you use make sure you watch carefully so as not to burn the nuts.

Cashew and Coconut Pie

BASE
1 recipe Sweet Short Crust Pastry, p. 183, or Rich Sweet Flan Pastry, p. 184

FILLING
1 cup brown sugar
1/2 cup white sugar
1 level tbsp flour
2 eggs
2 tbsp milk
1/4 tsp ground cinnamon

1 tsp vanilla essence
120g (1/2 cup) butter, melted
1 1/2 cups cashewnuts, toasted and roughly chopped
1 cup finely grated coconut

Roll out pastry to fit a 17 cm pie dish.

Mix the sugars and flour together. Add the eggs and beat well, then add the milk, cinnamon, vanilla and melted butter. Fold in the nuts and coconut. Pour the mixture into the unbaked pie shell, and cook in a moderate oven (180°C) for about 30-40 minutes, or until the filling is set.

I first tasted this cheesecake at a friend's house at Port Antonio, Jamaica, where the famous Blue Mountain coffee comes from. It makes a delicious dessert for coffee lovers anywhere.

Coffee Kahlua Cheesecake

BASE
2 cups gingernuts or coconut biscuits

80g (1/3 cup) butter

FILLING
1 1/4 tbsp plain gelatine soaked in 3 tbsp hot water
1 cup boiling water
1 tbsp instant coffee powder

2 tbsp Kahlua or other coffee liqueur
3/4 cup brown sugar
240g cream cheese
1 cup dairy cream

TOPPING
1/2 cup dairy cream, chilled
2 tbsp icing sugar
2 tsp instant coffee powder mixed with 1 tsp hot water, then cooled

1 tbsp Kahlua or other coffee liqueur

Combine the crushed biscuits and butter and press into the base of a deep 20 cm cake pan with removable base. (See notes on biscuit crusts, p. 184.) Chill while preparing filling.

Soak the gelatine in 3 tbsp hot water. Combine the 1 cup boiling water, sugar, coffee and coffee liqueur together in a saucepan, and stir in the softened gelatine. Keep stirring until the sugar is dissolved.

Beat the softened cream cheese (a food processor or blender is ideal for this), and then combine with the coffee mixture until smooth. Cool the mixture completely. Lightly whip the cream and fold into the cheese mixture. Turn into the biscuit case and chill for at least 4 hours until set.

TOPPING
Whip the cream and icing sugar together until the cream holds its shape. Fold in the coffee liquid and liqueur. Spread or pipe on top of the cheesecake.

This cobbler, with its guava base and cashewnuts added to the scone topping, is delicious. Other seasonal fruits of your choice can be used in the cobbler, and other nuts in the scone topping.

Guava and Cashewnut Cobbler

FILLING

1 kg guavas
1 cup sugar
finely grated rind of 1 lemon
juice of 1 lemon

1/2 tsp ground cinnamon
1 cup water
1 tbsp butter

Peel and remove core and seeds of guavas, and put guava shells with the sugar, lemon rind and juice, cinnamon and the water in a saucepan. Poach for 15-20 minutes or until the guavas are tender. Stir in the 1 tbsp butter. Cool. Put into a 23 cm pie dish.

TOPPING

1/2 cup cashewnuts, lightly toasted
2 tbsp sugar
1 1/2 cups plain or wholemeal self-raising flour

60g (1/4 cup) butter
1/2 cup milk, approx.

Preheat the oven to 200°C. Finely chop the nuts (use the food processor for this and all the following steps if you have one). Combine sugar, nuts and sifted flour together in a bowl (or food processor). Rub in the butter (or cut in with food processor blade) till mixture resembles fine breadcrumbs. Gradually add milk until a soft ball of dough is formed. Do not over-handle or over-process. Roll or press out the dough on a well-floured surface to a 1 cm thickness. Cut out into rounds using a 5 cm pastry cutter (or leave uncut).

Overlap the pastry rounds over the fruit, leaving a gap in the centre (or place uncut dough over the fruit and cut slits in several places). Brush the top of the pastry with milk and bake for 15-20 minutes until golden-brown.

If the Caramel Sauce appears complicated (it will not seem difficult after you have made it once, and it is certainly worth the initial effort) try the much easier Caramel Sauce on p. 177 or serve with the Sweet Mango Sauce (p. 180) or Sweet Coconut Sauce (p. 180).

Mango Bavarois with Coconut Sauce

Use 1 1/2 cups mango purée and reduce the amount of lime juice to 1 tbsp. Reduce the amount of cream to 1 1/2 cups.

Serve with the Sweet Coconut Sauce (p. 180) or the sauce of your choice.

Lime Bavarois with Caramel Sauce

1 1/2 tbsp plain gelatine softened in
   4 tbsp hot water
1 cup milk
4 egg yolks
1/2 cup caster sugar
2/3 cup lime juice (about 6 small limes)

1 tbsp grated lime rind
2 cups chilled cream (or very well chilled evaporated milk)
1/3 cup caster sugar, extra

Dissolve gelatine in a heatproof bowl (microwave on High for 30 seconds, or stand bowl in a pan of hot water and stir till dissolved).

Scald the 1 cup milk in a small saucepan. Beat the egg yolks and 1/2 cup sugar together, preferably with an electric beater, till thick and pale. Add the egg yolk mixture to the pan with the scalded milk and stir over a low heat until the mixture is thick enough to coat the back of a spoon. Add the dissolved gelatine, and the lime juice and rind. Turn into a bowl. Allow to cool, stirring to prevent a skin forming, or set the bowl in a larger pan of ice and water, and stir till thickened and cold. Do not allow to set.

Beat the cold cream with the extra 1/3 cup sugar in a separate bowl till soft peaks form (or the evaporated milk has doubled in size). Fold into cooled lime mixture. Pour into a 1.4 litre mould or 6-8 individual dessert dishes. Chill for at least 4 hours, until set.

CARAMEL SAUCE

1 cup sugar
1/3 cup water

1/2 cup cream or evaporated milk
2 tbsp lemon or lime juice

In a heavy saucepan, combine the sugar and water, and bring the syrup to a boil, stirring occasionally and pushing down the sugar that crystallises on the sides with a wooden spoon. (This step may seem to be a bit of a chore, but as the sugar and water starts to caramelise it becomes more fluid and easy to stir.) Once the caramel is golden-brown, immediately remove the saucepan from heat. Let the caramel cool or, if in a hurry, put quickly into a sink of cold water for 2 seconds, taking care not to let the caramel splatter and burn you. As the caramel cools, carefully add the cream or evaporated milk. Put the mixture in a bowl and add the lemon or lime juice. Add extra cream if the mixture is too thick. Allow to cool completely.

Serve the Lime Bavarois with the cool Caramel Sauce.

This is a lovely, melt-in-the-mouth cheesecake that is very easy to make.

Fresh Mango Cheesecake

CRUMB CRUST

1 1/2 cups finely crushed biscuits, such as gingernuts

80g (1/3 cup) melted butter

1 cup grated coconut, lightly toasted

1/2 tsp ground cinnamon

FILLING

3 medium mangos, chopped

240g cream cheese, softened

3/4 cup caster sugar

1 1/4 cups cream

1 1/2 tbsp gelatine

1/4 cup water

grated rind and juice of 1 large lemon or 2 small limes

Combine crushed biscuits, coconut, butter and cinnamon in a bowl, then press firmly into a 20 cm deep round cake pan with a removable base. Chill while preparing filling.

In a food processor or blender, process the cream cheese, sugar and half the chopped mango until very smooth. Add the cream and process for 30 seconds only.

Sprinkle the gelatine over the 1/4 cup water in a heatproof bowl, and either dissolve by standing the bowl in a pan of simmering water, or by microwaving on High for 30 seconds. Cool the gelatine mixture, then stir into the mango/cream cheese mixture, together with the remaining chopped mango and grated lemon rind and juice. Pour into the prepared crust and chill for at least 4 hours, until set.

This is a superb mousse with an exotic flavour. If mangos are not in season, 1 1/2 cups canned mango pulp can be used. Reduce sugar to 1 cup if using sweetened mango pulp.

Other tropical fruit can be used in this recipe.

Mango and Coconut Mousse

5 eggs, separated
1/4 cup rum
3 tbsp fresh lemon or lime juice
1 1/2 cups white sugar
1 tsp vanilla
pinch of salt
1/2 cup milk

1/4 cup thick coconut cream
2 tbsp plain gelatine
1/4 cup cold water
1 cup cream
flesh of 2 fresh mangos, puréed
2 cups freshly grated coconut,
    lightly toasted

In the top of a double boiler, beat the egg yolks with the rum and the lemon or lime juice until light and frothy. Using a hand-held balloon whisk, whisk in the sugar, vanilla and salt, and keep whisking until the mixture is slightly thickened. (For a superior flavour I prefer to use a heatproof non-aluminium bowl that sits over, not in, a pan of simmering water. Using a metal whisk in an aluminium container dislodges tiny flakes of metal, and this adversely affects the colour and taste of the contents.) Heat the milk and coconut cream together in a small saucepan, stirring (or microwave to heat). Soften the gelatine in the 1/4 cup cold water and whisk into the hot coconut cream mixture. Stir until gelatine is completely dissolved. Pour the coconut mixture into the egg yolk mixture. Stir till well combined and let cool for 30 minutes (or place the bowl in a larger bowl of iced water and cool, but do not allow mixture to set).

Meanwhile, using an electric beater if possible, beat the cream until it holds its shape, and in a separate clean bowl with clean beaters whip the egg whites until soft peaks form. Fold the mango purée into the completely cooled coconut mixture, then fold in cream, 1 cup grated coconut and the egg whites. Pour into a prepared mould or individual glasses or moulds, sprinkle remaining coconut on top, and chill for at least 4 hours, until firm.

This recipe also works well with firm ripe pawpaw and melons, and sliced carambola.

Poached Green Pawpaw in Ginger Syrup

Use 2 small green pawpaw, seeded, peeled and cut into even chunks. Add the pawpaw to the Ginger Syrup as soon as the sugar is dissolved. Poach for 20-30 minutes or until tender, then remove pawpaw and put in serving bowl. Strain the liquid as in the recipe, return to the heat and reduce by half. Pour syrup back over the pawpaw and chill.

Mangos in Lime and Ginger Syrup♥

2 mangos, peeled
2/3 cup dry white wine
1 1/4 cups water
1 stick cinnamon

1/2 cup white sugar
1 small lime
1 tsp crystallised ginger, plus 1 1/2 tbsp crystallised ginger

Cut the mango flesh into thin slices, and arrange in a serving bowl. Put the white wine, water, cinnamon stick and sugar in a small saucepan. Peel the lime, avoiding the white pith. Cut the lime peel into strips and add to saucepan. Squeeze the lime juice and add to the saucepan, together with the 1 tsp ginger. Stir over a low heat until sugar is dissolved. Bring to the boil, then reduce heat and simmer until the liquid is reduced by half. Strain the mixture back into the saucepan, bring to the boil, reduce heat and simmer until reduced again. Stir in the 1 1/2 tbsp ginger. Pour over the fruit in the serving bowl. Chill for several hours.

Mango and Lime Meringue Pie

CRUST
2 cups crushed biscuits such as gingernuts, coconut or plain sweet biscuits

1 tbsp plain flour
80g (1/3 cup) butter, melted
1/2 tsp ground cinnamon

FILLING
3 ripe mangos
3/4 cup fresh lime juice or lemon juice
1/4 cup plain flour

2 x 400g cans sweetened condensed milk
4 eggs, separated
grated rind of 1 lime or lemon
1 cup caster sugar

This is a delicious pie to make when fresh mangos are in season.

Pawpaw can also be used to replace the mango. Use 1 small ripe pawpaw, peeled and seeded.

Preheat oven to 180°C. Combine crushed biscuit crumbs, flour, cinnamon and butter together (this is easy with a food processor). Press into a deep 23 cm cake pan with removable base. (See notes on biscuit crusts, p. 184.) Chill while preparing filling.

Peel two mangos and purée with the lime juice in a food processor or blender. Stir in the flour, condensed milk, egg yolks and lime rind. Mix until well blended. Pour into crust and bake for 7-10 minutes only. Beat egg whites until they stand in stiff peaks (an electric beater makes this step much easier). With the beaters running, gradually add the 1 cup caster sugar in 3 lots, beating well between each. The meringue should be very thick and glossy, with a consistency like mobile marshmallow.

Reduce the oven temperature to 140°C. Spread the meringue over the pie filling and bake for a further 20-30 minutes, or until the meringue is golden-brown.

The mousse can, if necessary, be made without a food processor or electric beater, using a hand whisk.

For an even more impressive dessert, put the mousse into a very lightly oiled mould or individual moulds and turn out when set onto a serving dish with Caramel Sauce (p. 177) or Sweet Coconut Sauce (p. 180).

Fijian Pawpaw and Ginger Mousse

1 large (1 kg) pawpaw, weighed before peeling and seeding
1 cup caster sugar
2 tsp chopped crystallised ginger, or more to taste
1/4 cup fresh lemon juice

2 eggs, separated
1 1/2 tbsp gelatine
1/4 cup water
1 1/2 cups thick cream (or well-chilled evaporated milk)

Cut pawpaw in half, peel and remove seeds. Purée chopped flesh in a food processor or blender. Add sugar, egg yolks, ginger and lemon juice, and process till well combined. Turn into a bowl. Soften gelatine in water and microwave on High for 30 seconds (or dissolve by standing bowl in a pan of simmering water). Let the gelatine mixture cool slightly, add to the pawpaw mixture, and process.

Whip the cream until it holds its shape, and fold into pawpaw mixture. Fold in egg whites that have been beaten with an electric mixer till stiff but not dry. Pour into serving bowls or glasses and leave to chill for at least 4 hours, until set.

Orange and Yoghurt Mousse

juice of 3 oranges
1 1/2 tbsp gelatine
grated rind and juice of 1 lemon
grated rind of 1 orange
4 eggs, separated
1/2 cup caster sugar

1/2 cup plain yoghurt
3 tbsp orange liqueur
1 cup cream
candied or fresh orange slices to decorate
extra whipped cream to decorate

Pour fruit juices into a heatproof bowl, and sprinkle with the gelatine. Stand the bowl over a saucepan of hot water, and heat until the gelatine is dissolved (or microwave on High for 30 seconds, until gelatine is dissolved). Put fruit rinds, egg yolks and sugar in a large heatproof bowl and stand over a pan of gently simmering water. Whisk, using a hand-held beater, until mixture is thick. Remove bowl from heat and beat in gelatine-fruit juice mixture, yoghurt and orange liqueur. Leave mixture until cool and beginning to set.

Whip cream until it holds its shape. In a clean bowl, with clean whisk or beaters, whisk egg whites until stiff. Fold cream into orange mousse, and then fold in egg white, combining gently until evenly blended. Pour into a prepared serving dish or individual glasses, and chill until set – allow at least 4 hours. Decorate with a swirl of whipped cream and orange slices.

Passionfruit Mousse

The passionfruit filling can be spooned into dessert glasses or a large dessert bowl, instead of being put into the biscuit crust. Chill until set.

Passionfruit Chiffon Pie

CRUST

2 cups crushed biscuits, such as gingernuts, coconut or plain sweet biscuits

1 tbsp flour
80g (1/3 cup) butter, melted
1/2 tsp ground cinnamon

FILLING

4 eggs, separated
3/4 cup caster sugar
1 cup sour cream
1 1/2 tbsp gelatine

1 1/2 tbsp lemon juice
1/4 cup water
3/4 cup passionfruit pulp (8-10 passionfruit)

Combine crushed biscuit crumbs, flour, cinnamon and butter (this is easy with a food processor). Press into a deep 23 cm cake pan with removable base. (See notes on biscuit crusts, p. 184.) Chill while preparing filling.

With an electric mixer, beat egg yolks and caster sugar until thick and creamy. Stir in sour cream until mixture is smooth. Soften gelatine in water, add lemon juice, and dissolve by standing in a pan of hot water (or microwave on High for 30 seconds). Cool, then stir into egg/sour cream mixture. Refrigerate until beginning to set, then stir in passionfruit pulp.

Whip egg whites in a clean bowl until stiff but not dry, then fold 1/3 into the passionfruit mixture, followed by the remainder, until well combined. Pour into prepared biscuit crust and chill for at least 4 hours, until set. Serve topped with whipped cream.

This is a recipe that is very easy to prepare, and particularly pleasing to make on Rarotonga where pawpaw, like avocados, are so plentiful that they fall to the ground and get fed to the pigs.

Other fruit such as fresh mango or canned, drained pineapple can be used, mashed or puréed, instead of pawpaw.

Rarotongan Pawpaw Cream Pie

Serves 8-10

BASE

2 cups crushed plain biscuits
1 cup finely grated coconut
1/3 cup brown sugar

1 tsp cinnamon
80g (1/3 cup) melted butter or
    margarine

FILLING

3 eggs
400g can sweetened condensed
    milk

1/2 cup lemon juice
grated rind of 1 lemon
2 1/2 cups mashed ripe pawpaw

BASE

Combine the biscuit crumbs, coconut, sugar and cinnamon. Melt the butter and mix well into the crumb mixture. Press over base and sides of a deep 23 cm baking pan or ovenproof dish (see notes on biscuit crusts, p. 184), reserving about 4 tbsp crumbs for topping.

FILLING

Separate eggs. Combine the egg yolks with the condensed milk, pawpaw, lemon juice and rind. Beat egg whites until stiff but not dry, and fold into pawpaw mixture.

Pour the pawpaw mixture into the dish, top with remaining crumbs and bake in a moderately slow (160°C) oven for 1 hour. Serve warm or cold.

Pineapple and Coconut Meringue Pie

BASE

1 recipe Rich Sweet Flan Pastry, p. 184, or Sweet Shortcrust Pastry, p. 183

FILLING

1 1/2 cups canned or cooked
   crushed pineapple, very well
   drained
rind and juice of 1/2 lemon
1 cup thick coconut cream
1/2 cup white sugar

1/4 cup brown sugar
1 cup grated fresh coconut, lightly
   toasted
2 1/2 tbsp cornflour, mixed until
   smooth with 1/4 cup water
4 egg yolks, lightly beaten

Put all the ingredients in a saucepan, and cook, stirring, over a gentle heat until thickened.

Prepare topping after pastry is cooked and filling is prepared.

TOPPING

4 egg whites
1 cup caster sugar

1 cup grated coconut, lightly
   toasted

Beat egg whites until they stand up stiffly. Gradually add the sugar in three lots, beating continuously. The meringue should be very thick and like mobile marshmallow. Gently fold in the coconut — do not beat it in.

Preheat oven to 190°C. Roll out the pastry to fit a 23 cm pie dish. Cover with greaseproof paper filled with rice and beans, and bake for 20 minutes. Carefully remove paper and rice or beans, and bake for 5 more minutes. Fill with the pineapple mixture, and spread meringue over the top. Reduce oven heat to 140°C and bake the pie for 20-30 minutes, or until top is golden.

This pumpkin pie with coconut is a really delicious dessert, perfect to serve at any time of year. Serve slightly warm or cold, with whipped cream.

It is best to microwave or bake the pumpkin for this recipe. Do not use water to cook the pumpkin.

Pumpkin and Coconut Pie

BISCUIT BASE

1 recipe Rich Sweet Flan Pastry, p. 184, or Sweet Shortcrust Pastry, p. 183, or 1 recipe Biscuit Crust with coconut added, p. 184.

FILLING

3 eggs, lightly beaten
1 1/2 tbsp flour
3/4 cup brown sugar
1/4 cup white sugar
1 tsp vanilla essence
3/4 cup thick coconut cream
3/4 cup dairy cream
1 1/2 cups cooked mashed pumpkin
1/4 tsp salt
1/8 tsp ground cinammon
1/8 tsp ground nutmeg
1/8 tsp ground ginger
1 cup freshly grated coconut, lightly toasted

Roll out pastry to fit a 23 cm pie dish, or press biscuit mixture into dish. Preheat oven to 180°C. Beat together the eggs, flour, sugars and vanilla with the coconut cream and cream. Purée the pumpkin in a food processor or blender until smooth, and add to the mixture together with the salt, spices and grated coconut. Pour into the pastry or biscuit base and bake for 35-40 minutes or until set.

Many people who try this pie for the first time are amazed at how delicious it is. Serve cool with whipped cream.

Sweet Potato and Pecan Pie

This is an even more festive version of the pie. Omit the 1/2 cup brown sugar used in the recipe, but otherwise prepare the recipe exactly as described. Bake in the preheated oven for 20 minutes. Remove and top with Pecan Topping. Return to the oven and bake for a further 35-40 minutes, or until a knife inserted in the centre comes out clean.

PECAN TOPPING

3/4 cup soft brown sugar
1/4 cup golden syrup
2 eggs
1 1/2 tbsp melted butter
1 tsp vanilla essence
1/8 tsp ground cinnamon
3/4 cup pecan pieces or halves

Combine all the ingredients except the pecans, and mix together till well combined. Pour over the partially baked pie, top with pecans and return to the oven.

South Seas Kumara Pie

CRUST
1 recipe Sweet Shortcrust Pastry, p. 183, or Rich Sweet Flan Pastry, p. 184

FILLING
2 cups cooked kumara, drained
3 tbsp butter, melted
1/4 cup golden syrup
1/2 cup white sugar
1/4 tsp each ground cinnamon, nutmeg and cloves

3/4 cup milk or thin coconut cream
3 eggs, separated
1/2 cup brown sugar

Preheat the oven to 180°C. Roll out pastry to fit a deep 23 cm pie dish. In a large bowl mash the warm kumara with the butter, then stir in the golden syrup, white sugar and spices. Beat in the egg yolks and milk. In a separate bowl beat the egg whites until soft peaks form, and fold into the kumara mixture.

Sprinkle the brown sugar over the top and bake the pie for 55-60 minutes, or until a knife inserted in the centre comes out clean.

Choux puffs make an excellent dessert or tea-time treat filled with fresh tropical fruit and whipped cream, then topped with a caramel glaze.

Choux puffs or eclairs work beautifully every time, as long as the oven is preheated to the correct temperature. Never try to bake too many puffs at one time, and do not open the oven door while the choux puffs are baking. It is also important to follow the recipe exactly and to measure ingredients accurately. Do not try to double or triple the recipe. Only make one recipe of choux pastry at a time, even if you need to make a large quantity of choux puffs. Prepare the next batch while the first is baking in the oven.

Choux puffs freeze very well. To re-crisp, place thawed puffs on an oven tray, and bake at 180°C for 5 minutes. Cool before filling.

Choux Puffs with Tropical Fruit

Makes 12-14

CHOUX PUFFS

75g butter, chopped	1 cup flour, sifted
1 cup water	4 eggs

Preheat oven to 220°C. Combine the butter and water in a medium saucepan, and bring to the boil. Add flour all at once. Stir vigorously with a wooden spoon until the mixture leaves the side of the saucepan and forms a smooth ball.

Transfer the mixture to the bowl of an electric mixer (a hand beater can be used, but is not as easy to use). Add the eggs, one at a time, beating constantly, and beating well between each egg, until the mixture is smooth and glossy. The mixture should hold its shape when spooned or piped onto baking trays – it should not be at all runny. To be sure of success, lightly beat the fourth egg in a small bowl before adding, and add a little at a time until the right consistency of choux paste is achieved. Possibly not all of the egg will be required if the eggs are large.

Pipe, using a star nozzle, or drop heaped teaspoonfuls onto lightly and evenly greased trays, spacing 5 cm apart. Bake in the hot, preheated oven for 10 minutes, then reduce heat to 180°C for a further 10 minutes, or until puffs are golden and crisp.

Remove from oven, and quickly prick each puff with a wooden skewer to allow steam to escape. Return to the oven for 5-6 minutes to allow insides to become drier. Cool completely. Make a slit in each choux puff wide enough to spoon in filling, then fill and glaze as desired.

TROPICAL FILLING

1 cup cold cream, whipped with 4-5 tbsp sifted icing sugar until it holds its shape.	perhaps with some passionfruit pulp added
1 cup chopped fresh fruit, such as mango, banana, pawpaw, etc,	sugar to taste (optional) lemon or lime juice to taste (optional)

TOPPING

1 cup brown sugar	1/4 cup cream
2 tbsp butter	1/2 cup icing sugar, sifted

Heat together the brown sugar, butter and cream, stirring until sugar is dissolved. Cook for 2 minutes more. Remove from heat and beat in icing sugar. Cool slightly, then spoon over cooled choux puffs.

These crepes make a lovely dessert, and either one kind or any combination of fruit can be used. We often make them when we are short of time.

The rum or orange liqueur gives the crepes an exotic flavour, but can be replaced by orange juice if desired.

Although the first crepe may stick to the pan, once the pan is greased properly and hot enough, the remaining crepes should be easy to make.

Tropical Fruit Crepes

Makes approx. 12 crepes

CREPES

1 cup plain flour, sifted	2 tbsp melted butter
1 tbsp caster sugar	2 eggs
1 1/2 cups milk	1 tsp vanilla

Place all the ingredients in the bowl of a food processor with blade (or beat by hand), and process till well combined. Let the batter rest for 30 minutes.

Heat a lightly greased 15 cm crepe pan on a medium heat. Pour about 2 tbsp batter into the pan and tip the pan from side to side to make a thin coating of batter on the bottom of the pan. Loosen the edges with a spatula and turn over once bubbles start to appear and the batter is golden-brown. Cook the other side.

Repeat the process, greasing the pan with a little butter after each crepe.

FILLING

30g (1 1/2 tbsp) butter	1/4 cup coconut cream or cream
3 bananas, sliced	1/4 cup brown sugar
3/4 cup pawpaw (or mango), cubed	1 tsp vanilla essence
3/4 cup pineapple, cubed	2 tbsp rum or orange liqueur
pulp of 2 passionfruit	pinch of cinnamon and nutmeg
juice of 1 lemon	

Melt the butter in a large frying pan. Add the fruit and lemon juice, and cook for 5 minutes over a gentle heat. Add the coconut cream or cream, brown sugar, rum, vanilla, cinnamon and nutmeg, and remove from heat.

Fill each crepe with several tablespoons of fruit mixture and fold over into 4.

TOPPING

1/2 cup orange juice	1 tsp grated orange rind
2 tbsp icing sugar	

Mix the topping ingredients together.

Preheat oven to 200°C. Arrange the filled crepes neatly in an ovenproof dish. Spoon the topping mixture over the crepes, and bake in a hot oven for 5-10 minutes, or until heated through.

This luscious gateau is very quick and easy to make, and looks stunning. It makes a perfect dessert to serve at a special dinner party.

Tropical Fresh Fruit Gateau

BASE
1 x 23 cm slightly stale and firm sponge cake, either bought or home-made

FILLING
1 recipe thick Vanilla Custard,
  p. 178
1/4 cup sugar
1/4 cup water
2 cups thinly sliced fresh fruit such
  as pawpaw, pineapple, banana,
  guava, mango

juice of 1 lemon
1/4 cup rum and/or 2 tbsp orange
  liqueur
2 tbsp apricot or a tropical fruit
  jam, warmed

TOPPING
1 cup cream
2 tbsp icing sugar
1 tsp vanilla essence
1 cup toasted grated coconut or
  toasted chopped nuts

extra sliced fresh fruit and some
  glacé cherries (optional)

Dissolve the sugar for the filling in the water in a medium saucepan, and cook for 5 minutes. Add fruits such as pineapple and guavas (remove seedy pulp from guavas). Do not add soft fruit such as bananas, or pawpaw, but sprinkle these fruits with lemon juice. Poach the pineapple and guavas for 5 minutes, and then drain and cool, reserving the syrup. Add rum and liqueur to the syrup. Mix all the fruit into the Vanilla Custard.

Using a long serrated knife, cut the sponge cake into 3 even layers (use toothpicks to mark the layers for more accurate cutting). Using a flat metal sheet such as a Swiss roll pan to help, place the first layer of cake onto a serving plate. Using a teaspoon, sprinkle the cake layer with 1/3 of the syrup/liqueur mixture. Spread with a thin layer of jam, then half the fruit custard. Repeat with the next layer of cake, soaking with 1/3 of the syrup, then spreading with jam and remaining custard. Top with the last layer of cake, and sprinkle on remaining 1/3 syrup. Chill cake.

Whip cream and icing sugar together for topping until the cream holds its shape. Add vanilla. Spread the cake completely with the whipped cream, then sprinkle the entire cake with coconut or nuts. Chill cake for at least 4 hours. Garnish if desired with extra sliced fresh fruit and glacé cherries.

Tropical fresh fruit, coated in batter and deep fried, makes a very quick dessert that is always popular. Use any or all of the fresh fruit suggestions listed. Accompany with whipped cream and/or ice cream.

For a very light batter, separate the egg and beat the white stiffly. Fold the egg white into the batter after the other ingredients are combined.

Coconut Fruit Fritters

For a really delicious version of tropical fruit fritters, roll the fruit in finely grated fresh coconut after dipping in the batter, then deep fry.

Tropical Fruit Fritters

whole or sliced bananas
pineapple rings
sliced firm but ripe pawpaw
sliced firm but ripe mango

guava shells, with seeds and inner pulp removed
icing sugar for dusting

BATTER

1/3 cup flour
1/3 cup cornflour
1/2 tsp baking powder
2/3 cup milk

2 tsp caster sugar
1/2 tsp vanilla essence
1 egg

Beat the batter ingredients together by hand, or in a food processor, until well combined. Stand for 30 minutes. Dip the prepared fruit into the batter, so each piece is well coated. (For very juicy fruit, dip first into plain flour, and then into the batter.)

Deep fry in hot oil (a bread cube dropped in should turn golden-brown in less than a minute) until puffed up and golden. Drain on kitchen paper and serve immediately, dusted with icing sugar.

This 'upside-down' tart is the easiest fruit tart I have ever made, and it tastes wonderful. Any fruit in season can be used.

Tropical Fruit Tart

TOPPING

2 tbsp brown sugar
1 mango, sliced
1/4 small firm ripe pawpaw, sliced
1 banana, sliced

3 pineapple rings, halved
2 tbsp lemon juice
1/4 tsp cinnamon

PASTRY

1 1/4 cups self-raising flour
good pinch nutmeg
1/2 cup soft brown sugar

1/2 cup grated coconut
120g (1/2 cup) butter

Preheat oven to 150°C. Butter a 23 cm pie pan. Sprinkle in the brown sugar. Arrange the sliced fruit to cover the bottom of the pan, sprinkle with the lemon juice and cinnamon.

Sift the flour and nutmeg into a bowl. Add the brown sugar and coconut. Rub in the butter until the mixture resembles coarse breadcrumbs. Pack firmly over the fruit. Bake for 1 1/4 hours. Leave in the pan for 10 minutes, then turn out upside-down onto a serving plate. Serve with cream and/or ice cream.

Making ice cream with an ice-cream maker is very easy, but the following recipes are for making ice cream by hand. For a smooth-textured ice cream, it is important in most recipes to beat the ice cream once or twice during the freezing process to break down the ice crystals that have formed. This is easiest to do with an electric beater or food processor with blade. In all but the hottest climates, it is best to put the ice cream in the refrigerator 20 minutes before serving to soften slightly and make it easier to serve.

This basic recipe always works well and makes a delicious ice cream with a good texture.

Coffee

Add 1 tbsp instant coffee powder mixed until smooth with 1 tbsp hot water to the custard mixture at the same time as the gelatine.

Chocolate

Add 2 tbsp cocoa mixed until smooth with 1 tbsp hot water to the custard mixture at the same time as the gelatine.

Tropical Fruit

Fold in 2 cups fruit pulp such as avocado, mango, banana, soursop, etc, using one fruit or a combination of fruits, at the same time as the gelatine.

Nut

Add 1 cup toasted nuts such as macadamias or pecans to the Basic Ice Cream after beating, to break down ice crystals.

Tropical Ice Cream and Sorbets

Basic Ice Cream

1 tbsp custard powder	2 cups milk
1/3 cup caster sugar	1 tbsp gelatine
1 egg, separated	2 tbsp water
1 tsp vanilla essence	1/2 cup cream, chilled

Put custard powder, sugar, vanilla and egg yolk into a bowl, and stir in a little milk. Mix until smooth and creamy. Scald remaining milk and strain, then pour onto custard, stirring constantly. Put in saucepan and cook until thick enough to coat the back of a spoon. Soften gelatine in a bowl with the 2 tbsp water, then completely dissolve by standing the bowl in a pan of simmering water (or microwave on High for 30 seconds). Stir the dissolved gelatine into the custard mixture. Cool, then chill the custard for 1 hour.

Beat the egg white until stiff, and fold into the cold custard. Freeze for several hours or until mushy. Remove from freezer and beat to break down ice crystals. Beat the cream until it holds its shape, and fold into ice cream. Freeze in a covered container until firm and ready to serve.

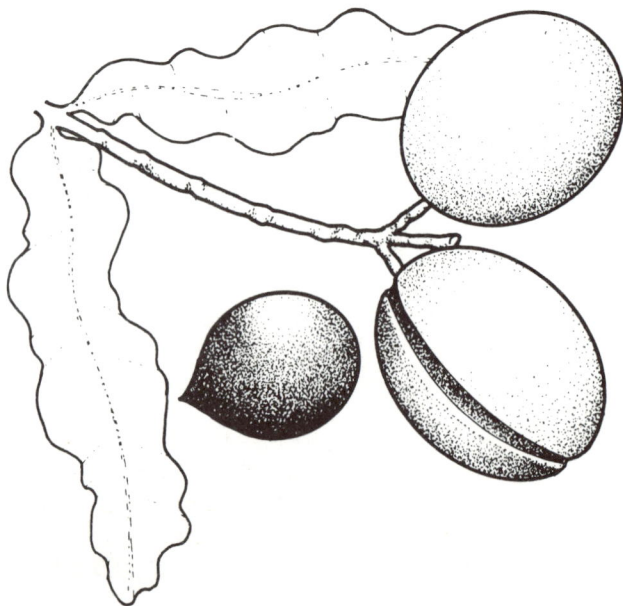

Many people request the recipe for this very creamy and delicious ice cream, which has a very appealing pale-green colour.

Avocado and Ginger Ice Cream

Reduce lime juice to 1 tbsp, and add 2 tbsp chopped, crystallised ginger to the recipe.

This is a really superb tropical ice cream.

Avocado Lime Ice Cream

2 large avocados
3 egg whites
2/3 cup caster sugar

1/4 cup fresh lime (or lemon) juice
3/4 cup cream

Peel avocado and remove stone. Mash the flesh. With an electric beater (or a food processor), beat egg whites until stiff. Gradually add sugar, beating well. Mix lime juice and mashed avocado together, beating until smooth. In a clean bowl beat cream until it holds its shape and fold into avocado mixture, then fold in egg whites. Spoon mixture into a shallow freezing tray, cover and freeze until mushy. Remove and beat until smooth. Refreeze until firm and ready to serve.

Coconut Ice Cream

2 cups thick coconut cream
2 eggs
2 egg yolks
1 tsp vanilla essence or 1 tbsp
    coconut liqueur

1 cup sugar
pinch salt
1 cup cream
1/2 cup grated coconut, lightly
    toasted

Put coconut cream in a medium-sized saucepan and heat gently until almost boiling, but do not allow to boil. In the top of a double-boiler, put eggs, egg yolks, vanilla, sugar and salt, and beat lightly with a hand whisk until mixture is light and creamy. Slowly add the hot coconut cream, then cook, stirring, until the mixture is thick enough to coat the back of a spoon. (A microwave can be used in the preparation up to this point – follow microwave instructions for making custard.)

Remove from heat and cool, stirring occasionally, then freeze in a covered container for several hours, until mushy. Remove ice cream from freezer. Beat with an electric beater or food processor with blade to break down ice crystals. Whip cream until it holds its shape, then fold into the coconut ice cream and freeze again until firm and ready to serve. Sprinkle with the lightly toasted grated coconut just before serving.

This recipe does not require cream.

Guava Ice Cream

480g guavas
1/2 cup white sugar
1/2 cup water

1 1/4 cups milk
4 egg yolks
90g caster sugar

Cook guavas with the white sugar and water until very soft, stirring gently from time to time. Pass mixture through a sieve. Cool the strained pulp. Heat the milk in a small saucepan, then strain through a sieve. Beat the egg yolks and caster sugar together until very pale, and gradually add the hot strained milk, beating constantly. Combine this mixture with the chilled guava pulp, and then freeze for several hours in a covered container until mushy. Beat well to break down ice crystals, freeze again for several hours, beat again, then freeze until firm and ready to serve.

This recipe does not require any eggs.

Pawpaw and Lime Ice Cream

Use 450g ripe pawpaw, weighed before peeling and seeding, and 1/4 cup fresh lime juice, and proceed as in the recipe.

Mango Ice Cream

2 large ripe, fleshy mangos
  weighing 450g after peeling and
  removing stones
3/4 cup sugar

1/2 cup water
1 1/2 tbsp plain gelatine
1/4 cup fresh lime or lemon juice
1 1/4 cups cream

Peel the mangos, cut off the flesh and purée in a food processor or blender, or chop very finely. Heat the sugar and water in a small saucepan and cook for 5 minutes, stirring. Soften gelatine in a small bowl with the lime juice, and stir into the hot sugar/water mixture. Cool. Add this sugar syrup to the mango purée, mixing thoroughly. Whip the cream until it holds its shape, and fold into the mango mixture. Freeze in a covered container for several hours until mushy. Remove and beat well to break down ice crystals. Freeze again for several hours, then remove and beat again. Freeze until required.

This wonderful ice-cream pie is very easy to make. It needs to be made 24 hours before serving.

To turn out the pie, dip the pie pan quickly into warm water. To cut the pie, dip the knife into a container of hot water.

Caramel Nut Ice Cream Pie

CRUST

2 cups crushed biscuits
120g (1/2 cup) melted butter
1 tsp cocoa

1/2 tsp cinnamon
1/2 tsp nutmeg

FILLING

1 litre vanilla ice cream
1 cup golden syrup
1 cup peanut butter

2 cups chopped almonds, or
    macadamias, or cashewnuts,
    lightly toasted

Make the crust by melting the butter, then stirring in the remaining ingredients. Press into a 20 cm deep pie dish with removable base.

Stir the golden syrup and peanut butter together until well mixed. Soften the ice cream but do not allow to melt. Put half the ice cream onto the pie crust, then half the peanut butter mixture and half the chopped almonds. Put in remaining ice cream and top with the rest of the peanut butter mixture and chopped almonds. Cover with plastic wrap. Return to the freezer for at least 24 hours.

This dessert looks very impressive, and is surprisingly easy to prepare.

Pawpaw Baked Alaska

Pawpaw can be prepared in the same way. Use a firm, ripe pawpaw, cut in half, and remove seeds and discard. Remove flesh, taking care not to damage shell, and cut into small cubes and soak in liqueur of your choice, then add melted jam. Proceed as described for Pineapple Baked Alaska.

Pineapple Baked Alaska

1 ripe pineapple
2 tbsp orange liqueur
3 tbsp warmed jam, such as the
    Tropical Fruit Jam, p. 205

1 litre vanilla ice cream
3 egg whites
1/4 cup caster sugar
1/2 tsp vanilla essence

Cut pineapple in half. Remove flesh from inside of pineapple, cut out hard centre core and discard. Chop pineapple flesh and put in a bowl with the liqueur for several hours. Stir in the melted jam. Soften ice cream slightly, and mix with the pineapple. Spoon mixture into pineapple shells, cover with plastic wrap, and freeze until very firm.

Twenty minutes before serving Baked Alaska, heat oven to very hot (240°C). Using an electric beater, beat the egg whites until stiff, then add the sugar in two separate lots, beating constantly. Add the vanilla and continue beating until the meringue is very thick and stiff. Remove pineapple shells from the freezer, and remove plastic wrap. Working quickly, spread (or pipe using a large star nozzle) the meringue to cover the top of the pineapple shells completely. Bake for 5 minutes in the hot oven until the meringue is a delicate brown, and serve immediately.

Tropical fruit makes a superb sorbet. Experiment with different fruit in season.

A food processor with blade is best for beating sorbets during the freezing process.

Lime, Orange, Mandarin or Grapefruit Sorbets

Prepare as for Lemon Sorbet. Use juice and rind of either 5 small limes, 2 oranges, 3 mandarins or 1 grapefruit.

Weight Watchers' Sorbet

Use artificial sweetener instead of sugar to make any of the following sorbet recipes.

Basic Sorbet♥

BASIC SYRUP
1 1/4 cups water   1/2 cup sugar

Put sugar and water into a heavy-based saucepan and heat gently until sugar is dissolved, stirring occasionally. Bring to the boil for 2 minutes without stirring. Remove from heat and cool.

Lemon Sorbet♥

1 recipe Basic Syrup (above)   1 egg white
grated rind and juice of 3 lemons

Prepare syrup to the point of dissolving sugar. Add lemon rind and simmer gently for 10 minutes. Stir in lemon juice then strain into a freezer container. Freeze for about 3 hours, until frozen but still mushy. Whisk egg white until stiff. Put sorbet in a bowl and beat to break down ice crystals. Fold in egg white. Return to freezer and freeze until firm. Soften in refrigerator for 20 minutes before serving.

Mango/Pawpaw/Soursop Sorbet♥

Use the flesh from 2 large peeled mangos, or 1 small, ripe pawpaw or 1 large soursop, with the juice of 1 large lemon or lime and 1 recipe cooled Basic Sorbet, above. Freeze as for Lemon Sorbet, beat to break down ice crystals, then fold in 1 stiffly beaten egg white, and re-freeze.

Passionfruit Sorbet♥

10 medium passionfruit   1 recipe Basic Syrup, cooled
4 tbsp orange juice   2 egg whites

Scoop out passionfruit pulp. Purée with orange juice in a blender or food processor briefly. Pass through a nylon sieve. Add strained juice to sugar syrup, and freeze until mushy. Beat to break down ice crystals. Fold in stiffly beaten egg whites, and freeze again. After 1 hour, beat again, as the egg whites tend to separate. Freeze.

This sauce, which is delicious hot on ice cream, or cold as a cake filling and topping, is very quick to make. The amount of brown sugar and golden syrup can be reduced slightly if preferred. Extra cream can be added if a thinner sauce is required.

Dessert Sauces

Caramel Sauce

1 cup cream
1 cup brown sugar
2 tbsp golden syrup

2 tbsp butter
1 tsp vanilla essence

Put all the ingredients except for the vanilla into a saucepan. Bring to the boil, then boil, stirring, for 6-7 minutes. Add vanilla. Remove from heat and stir well.

Many people request the recipe for this chocolate sauce, which is best served hot on vanilla ice cream. The addition of the dark chocolate in the recipe makes for a richer sauce, but it can be omitted and the sauce will still taste delicious.

Chocolate Fudge Sauce

4 tbsp cocoa
1 cup sugar
4 tbsp boiling water
1 1/2 cups evaporated milk, or 1 cup
    milk mixed with 1/2 cup cream

1 1/2 tbsp butter
1 tsp vanilla essence, or 1 tbsp
    coffee liqueur
60g dark chocolate, chopped
    (optional)

Put the cocoa and the sugar in a heavy saucepan, and stir (off the heat) to remove lumps. Add the boiling water, and stir until the mixture is smooth. Put the saucepan onto a medium heat and gradually add the evaporated milk or the milk and cream, stirring constantly. When the mixture comes to the boil, add the butter and cook, stirring constantly, for 6-8 minutes. Do not allow to boil over. Remove from heat, stir in vanilla (and chocolate if using).

This quick and easy custard requires no eggs. If no cream is available, use 2 cups milk instead of 1 1/2 cups milk.

For a low-fat version, use skim milk instead of milk and cream, and omit butter.

Tropical Fruit Custard

Add 1 cup puréed fruit such as mango, soursop, banana, and so on, to the Vanilla Custard recipe, at the end of cooking time. Replace vanilla essence with 1 tbsp orange liqueur or rum, or the juice of 1/2 small lemon, if desired.

Vanilla Custard Sauce

1 tbsp custard powder	1/2 cup cream
1 tbsp cornflour	1 tsp vanilla essence
1/4 cup sugar	2 tsp butter
1 1/2 cups milk	

In a saucepan, mix the custard powder, cornflour and sugar with enough milk to make a smooth paste, then slowly stir in the remaining milk and the cream, stirring well with a wooden spoon to keep the mixture smooth. Cook the custard over a medium heat, stirring constantly, until the mixture begins to boil. Reduce heat and cook, stirring, until the custard is thickened and smooth. Stir in vanilla and butter. Turn into a bowl or jug. (If not using immediately, cover with plastic wrap, with the wrap resting on the custard to prevent a skin forming.)

Warm Crème Anglaise, or custard, is good to serve with fresh fruit, warm sponge puddings, crumbles, cobblers and crepes. It is also good, chilled, to serve as a dessert sauce with a Bavarian Cream or jellied fruit mould, or with fresh fruit.

Mango Crème Anglaise

Add 1 medium mango, puréed and sieved, to the Crème Anglaise recipe, and replace vanilla with 1 tbsp orange liqueur or rum.

Crème Anglaise

2 eggs	1 vanilla pod, split, or 1 tsp vanilla
2 tbsp caster sugar	essence
1 1/4 cups milk	

Beat eggs, sugar and 3 tbsp milk together in a bowl. Heat the rest of the milk with the vanilla pod, if using, in a saucepan until lukewarm (or microwave on Low for 2 minutes). Strain though a fine sieve. Beat the warm milk into the eggs. Pour mixture into the top of a double-boiler or bowl standing over a pan of simmering water, and cook, stirring continuously with a wooden spoon, until custard is thickened enough to coat the back of a spoon. (Or microwave mixture on High for 1 minute, then Low for 4 1/2 minutes, stopping to whisk frequently.) Remove vanilla pod, rinse and dry for use at another time. Stir in vanilla essence if using instead of a vanilla pod. Pour custard into a jug if serving warm. Put into a bowl if serving cold, cover with plastic wrap resting on top to prevent a skin forming, and chill until required.

This is delicious served chilled with fresh fruit salad, or hot with the ice cream of your choice, or with warm fruit crepes.

Guava Coulis♥

500g guavas, peeled and chopped   juice of 1 lemon
1 cup sugar syrup, p. 176

Purée the fruit in a food processor or blender. Add the sugar syrup and lemon, and strain through a fine sieve. Discard the seeds.

Serve with vanilla or soursop ice cream, or with sliced bananas or fresh fruit salad.

Pawpaw and Ginger Purée♥

1/2 ripe pawpaw   1 tbsp sugar
2 tbsp crystallised ginger   juice of 1 lime

Purée all ingredients together. Heat or chill as desired.

This is particularly good with a passionfruit dessert such as a Bavarian Cream, or passionfruit ice cream, or over a fresh fruit salad.

Sweet Avocado Purée♥

1 ripe avocado   1 tbsp honey
2 tbsp sugar   juice of 2 limes

Peel avocado and remove stone. Blend the flesh with remaining ingredients in a food processor or blender until smooth. Chill until ready to serve.

This is delicious hot with fruit crepes or with ice cream, or cold with fruit salad, a fruit mousse or Bavarian Cream.

Sweet Coconut Sauce

1/4 cup milk
1 1/2 tbsp cornflour
1 1/4 cups coconut cream

2 1/2 tbsp white or brown sugar
1 tbsp coconut liqueur (optional)
1 tsp vanilla essence

Mix cornflour with milk in a bowl until smooth. Heat coconut cream and sugar in a saucepan, then add to cornflour mixture, stirring. Return mixture to saucepan and cook over a gentle heat, stirring, for 2 minutes or until mixture is thickened. Stir in coconut liqueur and vanilla essence.

Serve hot with ice cream or crepes, or chill and serve with a dessert such as the Coconut Mousse (p. 154) or Lime Bavarois (p. 158).

Sweet Mango Sauce♥

2 mangos, peeled and chopped
1/3 cup caster sugar

1/4 cup water
1 tbsp lemon juice

Combine half of the mangos with the sugar, water and lemon juice, and bring to the boil in a small saucepan. Reduce heat and simmer, uncovered, for 3 minutes. Blend or purée the mixture until smooth, and return to the saucepan. Add remaining chopped mango and heat through.

Tropical Baking

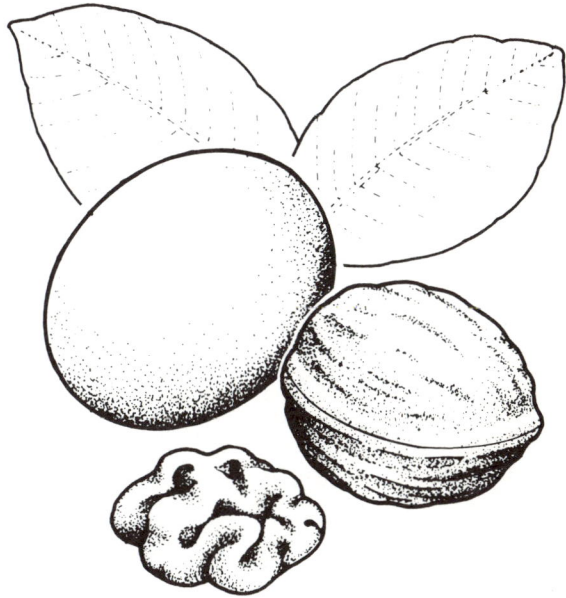

For successful results when making pastry, always handle dough as quickly and gently as possible. Always measure ingredients exactly, have butter or margarine very well chilled, and after making the pastry, rest the dough in the refrigerator, wrapped in cling film, for 30 minutes before rolling.

When rolling pastry, especially a very short, crumbly pastry such as the Rich Sweet Flan Pastry, roll between 2 lightly floured sheets of greaseproof paper to desired size. Carefully peel off top sheet of paper and turn pastry over into dish or pan, then peel off bottom layer of paper.

The recipes here make more than enough pastry to line a 23 cm pie dish or pan. Any extra can be wrapped and frozen for later use. Double the quantities given for a two-crust pie.

Basic Shortcrust Pastry is suitable for most pies.

Pastry Making

Basic Shortcrust Pastry

1 1/2 cups white flour or 1 cup
   white and 1/2 cup wholemeal
80g (1/3 cup) cold butter or
   margarine, chopped

pinch of salt (if butter is unsalted)
2-3 tbsp chilled water

Sift flour and salt together into a bowl, and rub in butter until mixture resembles coarse breadcrumbs. Add just enough water to form a ball with the pastry, handling the pastry as little as possible. Wrap and chill for 30 minutes.

FOOD PROCESSOR METHOD
Put flour, salt and chopped butter into bowl of food processor. Using the Pulse button, mix in the butter using a few short pulses at a time. Add the chilled water through the feed tube, and pulse just until the mixture starts to form a ball. Take care not to over-process. Remove pastry, wrap and chill.

TO MAKE SWEET SHORTCRUST PASTRY
For fruit pies, etc: Add 2 tbsp icing sugar or white sugar to the flour in the recipe above. Add 1 tsp vanilla essence or lemon juice with the chilled water.

TO MAKE CHEESE PASTRY
Delicious with quiches and savoury pies: Reduce the butter in the recipe to 60g (1/4 cup) and add 1/2 cup grated cheddar cheese at the same time as the butter.

This is an excellent light pastry for fruit and dessert pies. We use this recipe for nearly all our dessert pies at The Flame Tree.

Rich Sweet Flan Pastry

1 cup plain white flour (or mixture of wholemeal and white)
1 cup white self-raising flour
150g (5/8 cup) margarine or butter

1 small egg
3 tbsp sugar
1 tsp vanilla essence

Sift flours into a bowl and rub in butter by hand (or use food processor) until mixture resembles coarse breadcrumbs. Beat egg, sugar and vanilla together and add to the flour mixture. Stir with a wooden spoon until ingredients are just combined and mixture forms a ball. (If using a food processor, pulse until just combined.) Add 1 tbsp chilled water if pastry is too dry, or 1-2 tbsp flour if pastry is sticky. Do not over-handle. Wrap and chill.

To press the biscuit crumbs evenly and easily into the dish or cake pan, use a small, straight, smooth-sided glass or custard cup and not your fingers. This saves a lot of time and makes a smooth, firm and even crust.

Biscuit Crusts for Sweet Pies

2 cups plain sweet biscuit crumbs   80g (1/3 cup) butter (approx.)

Melt the butter and add to the biscuit crumbs in a bowl. (The biscuit crumbs must be very finely crushed, and a food processor with blade is best for this.)

Biscuits such as coconut biscuits and gingernut biscuits can be used to make a biscuit crust. 1/2 tsp nutmeg or cinnamon can be added to the crushed biscuits, or 1/2 cup biscuit crumbs can be replaced by 1/2 cup finely chopped nuts or finely grated coconut. (If using chocolate biscuit crumbs, reduce the amount of butter used by about 1 tbsp.)

Spring rolls are very popular with adults and children. It is easiest to make spring rolls with purchased wrappers but if you are unable to buy them, this recipe is a very acceptable substitute. The wrappers will not be quite as crisp as the kind you can purchase, but they are very good all the same.

The Egg Roll Wrappers are slightly thicker than the Spring Roll Wrappers.

The wrappers can be prepared in advance and kept stacked and wrapped with plastic wrap in the fridge for several weeks or in the freezer for months.

Spring Roll Wrappers

2 cups flour
4 cups water or more

pinch salt

Mix flour and water together, and add a pinch of salt – the batter should be pourable. Leave to stand for 1 hour. Wipe a small cast-iron frying pan lightly with oil. Pour in 2 tbsp batter and tip the pan to spread the batter evenly. Cook for slightly less time than you would a crepe.

Carefully remove from the pan and continue with remaining batter, lightly oiling the pan frequently, until all the batter is used.

Note: It is important to make the wrappers as thin as possible.

Chinese Egg Roll Wrappers

1 egg
1 tsp sugar
2 cups flour

2 tbsp cornflour
1 tsp salt
3 cups water

Put all the ingredients in a food processor or blender for 30 seconds, or beat by hand till well mixed. Proceed as in the recipe for making Spring Roll Wrappers, making the wrappers as you would crepes, loosening the edges and turning the mixture over when bubbles appear on the surface.

When frying filled egg rolls, fry until the outside is very crisp.

Note: Try to make Egg Roll Wrappers as thin as possible.

This is a banana cake that is economical to make and never seems to fail. It always rises beautifully and tastes good.

Serve plain, or iced with double the quantity of Cream Cheese Icing (p. 196), or split the cake in two, and fill and top with Caramel Cake Filling (p. 195).

Cakes and Muffins

Banana Cake

2 1/2 cups plain flour	1 cup vegetable oil
2 tsp baking powder	1 cup white sugar
1 tsp baking soda	1 cup brown sugar
1/4 tsp salt	1 tsp vanilla essence
1 tsp ground cinnamon	4 large ripe bananas, mashed
4 eggs	

Preheat the oven to 180°C. Butter a 23 cm cake pan. Sift the flour, baking powder, baking soda, salt and cinnamon together twice into a large bowl. In a separate bowl, beat the eggs, oil and sugars together until light and creamy, and stir in the mashed bananas and the vanilla.

Make a well in the centre of the flour mixture and pour the egg and banana mixture into the well. Stir and fold until the two mixtures are just combined. Do not beat or over-stir. Turn into the prepared cake pan. Bake the cake for 40-50 minutes, until springy to touch and a cake tester comes out clean.

This unusual chocolate cake is moist and delicious, and is one of my favourite chocolate cakes.

The cake can be split when cool, and filled and topped with the icing of your choice, see p. 196.

Chocolate Kumara Cake

80g (1/3 cup) butter, softened	2 tbsp water
1/2 cup brown sugar	3 eggs, separated
1/2 cup white sugar	1 cup plain flour
1/2 cup hot mashed kumara	1 tsp baking powder
2 tbsp milk	1/4 cup milk
90g dark chocolate, chopped	1 tsp vanilla essence
1/2 tsp baking soda	

Butter and line a 20 cm cake pan with buttered greaseproof paper. Preheat oven to 190°C. Beat the butter until pale and soft, add the sugars and beat until well mixed. Mix the hot mashed kumara with the 2 tbsp milk and add to the butter mixture with the melted chocolate.

Mix the baking soda with the 2 tbsp water and add to the butter mixture. Beat in the egg yolks one at a time. Sift the flour and baking powder together two times and fold into the batter alternately with the 1/4 cup milk, then add the vanilla. Beat the egg whites in a clean bowl until stiff but not dry. Gently fold in 1/3 of the egg whites and then the remainder into the cake batter. Pour into prepared cake pan and bake for 45 minutes to 1 hour, or until a cake tester comes out clean.

This recipe is perfect for when you need to make a cake in a hurry. It needs no electric beater or machinery, and is inexpensive and easy to make. We often use this recipe at the restaurant when we get a request for a birthday cake at short notice.

The cake is best eaten on the day it is made, but can be frozen while still almost warm, with the filling frozen separately.

For a quick filling or icing, use the Easy Butter Cream (p. 196).

The Flame Tree Special Cake

1 cup white sugar
80g (1/3 cup) butter, melted and cooled
2 eggs
1/3 cup milk
2 cups self-raising flour
6 tbsp boiling water
1 tsp vanilla essence

Preheat oven to 190°C and prepare cake pan(s). Any of the following can be used: a 1 kg loaf tin; a 20 cm round or square cake pan; a Bundt pan or ring pan; or small cake, patty or muffin pans. Cake pans with removable bases need to be greased and lined with buttered paper. Other pans can be sprinkled evenly with flour after greasing.

Put the ingredients in a mixing bowl *strictly in the following order*.

Sift in the sugar. Using a wooden spoon, stir in the melted butter and eggs together. Stir in the milk. Sift in the flour. Stir in the boiling water and vanilla.

Stir mixture with the wooden spoon until smooth. Pour into prepared pans and bake for 30-40 minutes for a large cake, and 15-20 minutes for small cakes, or until a wooden skewer inserted into the centre comes out clean.

Cool on a cake rack. Split in two if desired (for large round or square cake), and fill and ice with frosting of your choice.

Easy Chocolate Cake
Replace 4 tbsp self-raising flour with 4 tbsp cocoa. Sift the cocoa in with the sugar.

Add 1/2 tsp baking powder sifted in with the self-raising flour.

Easy Coconut Cake
Replace 3/4 cup self-raising flour with 1 1/4 cups finely grated coconut, which has been dried slightly in a hot oven or microwave. Add coconut at the same time as the butter and eggs.

Add 1/2 tsp baking powder sifted in with the self-raising flour.

Easy Orange or Lemon Cake
Add grated peel of 2 oranges or 2 lemons at the same time as the butter and eggs. Replace milk with 1/3 cup orange or lemon juice.

Easy Coffee Cake
Add 1 tbsp instant coffee powder to the boiling water.

Easy Fruit Cake
Sift the flour into a separate bowl. Stir 1 1/4 cups dried fruit such as sliced cherries, chopped dates, prunes, raisins or sultanas (or a combination of dried fruit) into the flour, and stir until fruit is well

187

coated with the flour. Add some grated or candied citrus peel if desired. Stir fruit and flour into the cake mixture.

The fruit cake may need to bake for 1-1 1/4 hours until done. Bake at 180°C instead of 190°C. Cover cake with foil if it becomes too brown while baking.

Hawaiian Carrot Cake

This is a delicious cake that, covered, keeps well in the refrigerator for up to a week.

The recipe makes a large cake to feed a crowd. The recipe can be halved to make a 20 cm round cake (or make two cakes and freeze one).

1 cup of the plain flour can be replaced by wholemeal flour. Other nuts such as pecans, macadamias or lightly toasted cashews can be used instead.

3 cups plain flour
2 cups white sugar
1 tsp salt
1 tsp baking soda
1 tsp baking powder
1/2 tsp ground cinnamon
1 1/4 cups vegetable oil
1 1/2 tsp vanilla essence

4 eggs
2/3 cup canned crushed pineapple, well drained
3 cups finely grated carrots
1 cup freshly grated coconut, lightly toasted
1 cup chopped walnuts

Lightly butter a large loaf tin, or a 20 x 30 cm baking pan, or two 20 cm round cake pans. Preheat oven to 180°C. Combine the flour, sugar, salt, baking soda, baking powder and cinnamon. Sift together into a large bowl. Stir together the oil, vanilla and eggs until well combined. Stir into the flour mixture with the carrots, pineapple, coconut and walnuts. Bake for 1 hour, or until a cake tester comes out clean.

Ice with the Cream Cheese Icing (p. 196) or Coconut Cinnamon Icing (p. 196).

This cake is also delicious with other tropical fruit. It is wonderful served at an afternoon tea or morning coffee, and also makes a super dessert, served slightly warm with cream and/or ice cream. The cake is best eaten on the day of baking, unless serving warm as a dessert, when it can be reheated briefly in the oven or microwave.

Mango Custard Cake

CUSTARD

1 1/2 tbsp custard powder	30g (2 tbsp) butter
2 tbsp caster sugar	2 tsp vanilla essence
1 cup milk	

CAKE

2 large or 3 small slightly unripe mangos	90g (6 tbsp) butter
juice of 1 lemon	3/4 cup brown sugar
1 1/2 cups self-raising flour	2 eggs
1 tsp cinnamon	1/2 cup milk
1/4 tsp nutmeg	1 tsp cinnamon
	2 tsp caster sugar

CUSTARD

Combine custard powder and sugar in a pan, then gradually stir in milk until mixture is smooth. Bring to the boil, stirring, then reduce heat and simmer, stirring, until thickened and smooth. Stir in butter and vanilla, pour into a bowl, cover with plastic wrap and cool to room temperature.

CAKE

Lightly grease a deep 23 cm round cake pan, and line with buttered greaseproof paper. Preheat oven to 180°C. Peel mangos, remove stones and slice into thin slices. Sprinkle with lemon juice. Sift flour and spices together three times. Beat butter and brown sugar together until light and creamy. Beat in eggs one at a time. Add flour alternately with the milk. Stir just until combined.

Spread half the cake mixture into the pan, then spread with all the cooled custard. Top with half the mango slices. Spread in the remaining cake mixture, then arrange remaining mango slices on top. Sprinkle with the cinnamon and caster sugar. Bake for 50-55 minutes, or until firm. Cool in pan.

This cake is really delicious, and is good to serve at a special morning coffee or afternoon tea. The marmalade and pawpaw flavours go together very well. The cake is best eaten on the day it is made, but will keep for up to two days in the refrigerator.

Pawpaw and Orange Streusel Cake

240g firm, ripe pawpaw, chopped
1 tbsp lemon juice
3 cups self-raising flour
120g (1/2 cup) butter
3/4 cup caster sugar
4 eggs

1 tbsp orange marmalade
grated rind of 1 orange
1/4 tsp ground cinnamon
1/4 tsp ground nutmeg
pinch ground cloves
1/2 cup natural yoghurt

STREUSEL TOPPING

1/2 cup brown sugar
1/2 cup sifted flour
1/4 tsp cinnamon
3 tbsp softened butter

3 tbsp chopped nuts
few drops vanilla essence
1/2 cup freshly grated coconut

Make topping: mix sugar, flour and cinnamon together thoroughly. Rub in the butter till mixture resembles coarse breadcrumbs, then add vanilla, nuts and coconut. Set aside.

Sprinkle the pawpaw with the lemon juice and 1/2 cup self-raising flour. Preheat oven to 180°C. Butter a deep 23 cm cake pan and line with buttered greaseproof paper. Beat together the butter and caster sugar until creamy. Beat in the eggs, one at a time. Stir in the marmalade and orange rind. Sift the remaining 2 1/2 cups self-raising flour with the cinnamon, nutmeg and cloves. Fold the flour alternately with the yoghurt into the egg and butter mixture until the mixture is smooth.

Spread 1/3 of the batter into the base of the prepared cake pan, then arrange 1/2 the pawpaw on top. Repeat layers, ending with the last 1/3 of the cake batter. Sprinkle topping evenly over the cake. Bake for 1 hour 20 minutes to 1 1/2 hours, or until a cake tester comes out clean. *Cover the cake with foil half way through baking to prevent the top getting too brown.*

Fresh pineapple, cut into rings with cores removed, can be used in this recipe.

Guava Upside-Down Cake

This cake is also delicious with guavas instead of pineapple. Use 4 large or 5 small guavas, cut into quarters with seeds removed. Place rounded side down into the cake pan on top of the brown sugar mixture. Use 3 extra tbsp milk in the cake in place of the pineapple juice. Omit cherries. Use whole blanched almonds instead of pecans.

Pineapple Upside-Down Cake

TOPPING

225g can sliced pineapple in rings
80g (1/3 cup) butter
3/4 cup brown sugar

8-10 glacé cherries (optional)
8-10 pecan halves (optional)

CAKE

120g (1/2 cup) butter
1/2 cup caster sugar
1 tsp vanilla essence
2 eggs
1 1/4 cups self-raising flour

2 tbsp milk
3 tbsp reserved pineapple juice
1 tbsp lemon juice
1 tsp grated lemon rind

Preheat oven to 180°C. Melt the butter for the topping and stir in the brown sugar. Spread evenly over the base of a 23 cm cake pan. (If using one with removable base, butter pan and line with buttered greaseproof paper.) Arrange well-drained pineapple rings, pecans and cherries over the brown sugar mixture.

Cream the butter, caster sugar and vanilla essence together with an electric beater until smooth. Add eggs one at a time, beating well after each addition. Stir in the sifted self-raising flour, the milk and reserved pineapple juice, the lemon juice and rind. Do not over-stir. Pour into cake pan. Bake for 30–40 minutes or until a cake tester comes out clean. Leave in pan for 15 minutes before turning out onto a serving plate. The cake is best served warm.

This is a simple cake which does not include any flour.

Always mash taro while it is still hot. (A food processor with blade can be used. Chop the taro into cubes first.)

Taro and Coconut Cake

500g hot peeled and cooked mashed
  taro
60g (1/4 cup) melted butter
1 cup freshly grated coconut
1/2 cup white sugar

2 eggs, beaten
1/4 tsp each ground nutmeg and
  cinnamon
1 cup milk
1/2 tsp vanilla essence

Butter a shallow 20 cm cake pan. Preheat the oven to 180°C. Combine the hot taro with the melted butter, mashing again as you work in the butter. Add the coconut, sugar and beaten eggs, and mix in well. Add the cinnamon, nutmeg, milk and vanilla, and beat all together by hand or with an electric beater for 1 minute. Pour into cake pan and bake for 45 minutes to 1 hour, or until firm. Remove from oven and cool completely.

Sprinkle top with sifted icing sugar if desired.

These are delicious to serve with after-dinner coffee, or as a sweet treat at any time.

Chocolate Cashew Fudge Bars

BASE

1/2 cup cashewnuts (or almonds)
1 cup plain flour
1/2 cup sugar

120g (1/2 cup) butter
1 egg, lightly beaten

TOPPING

400g can sweetened condensed milk
2 tbsp sugar
2 tbsp butter

1 tbsp vanilla essence
360g milk chocolate, chopped
30g cashewnuts (or almonds), chopped and lightly toasted

Preheat the oven to 180°C. Grease a 33 x 23 x 5 cm pan. Put the nuts in a food processor or blender and process till finely ground. In a bowl stir together the nuts, flour and sugar. Chop the butter, then rub into the mixture until it resembles coarse breadcrumbs. Add the egg and blend in well. Spread evenly into pan. Bake for 18-20 minutes, or until golden.

Make the fudge topping while the crust is baking. In a large saucepan combine the condensed milk, sugar, butter and vanilla, and heat over a low heat, stirring, until the sugar is dissolved. Remove from heat and stir in the chocolate, and beat until the mixture is smooth. Spread the fudge evenly over the warm crust, and sprinkle with the chopped nuts. Let the fudge cool completely, then chill. Cut into slices, about 5 cm x 3 cm.

This very moist coconut slice is very easy to make. Serve cold or warm.

If using freshly grated coconut, allow it to dry out by baking in a moderate oven for 10 minutes, or microwave on a shallow plate on High for 3 minutes, stirring occasionally.

Malaysian Coconut Slice

4 eggs
1 1/2 cups white sugar
2/3 cup flour
1/2 tsp baking power
120g (1/2 cup) melted butter, cooled

1 1/2 cups grated fresh coconut or desiccated coconut
1 tsp vanilla essence
1/4 cup brown sugar, for topping
1/2 cup grated coconut, for topping

Beat the eggs lightly. Add the white sugar 1/2 cup at a time, and beat till well combined. Sift the flour and baking powder together and fold into the egg mixture with the butter, the 1 1/2 cups coconut, and vanilla. Spread into a greased 20 cm square cake pan preferably with a removable base lined with greased paper.

Mix the remaining 1/2 cup coconut and the brown sugar together and sprinkle on top of the cake. Bake in a moderate oven (180°C) for 40-50 minutes until firm to touch and leaving the sides of the cake pan. *Cover with foil after 20 minutes to prevent cake getting too brown.*

Cashewnut and Banana Muffins

120g (1/2 cup) butter
1 1/4 cups sugar
2 eggs
2 cups plain flour
1/2 tsp salt
2 tsp baking powder

1/2 tsp vanilla essence
1/2 cup plus 2 tbsp milk
3 ripe bananas, chopped
1 cup chopped cashewnuts, lightly
    toasted

Cream the butter and sugar together until light and fluffy, then add the eggs, one at a time, beating after each one. Sift the dry ingredients together twice and fold into the creamed mixture just until combined – it is important not to overmix. Add the vanilla and milk and stir very lightly. Fold in the bananas and cashews. Spoon the batter into the muffin pans and bake for 20 minutes, or until the tops are springy to touch and the muffins are golden-brown.

Other nuts besides cashews can be used. Half wholemeal flour can be used instead of all white.

Fijian Pumpkin Scones♥

Makes 10-12 scones

3 cups plain flour, or plain and
    wholemeal flour
1/4 tsp ground cinnamon
1 level tsp baking soda
pinch of salt
2 1/2 level tsp baking powder

1 tbsp butter
1 cup cold cooked pumpkin,
    mashed
1 egg
3 tbsp sugar
1/2 cup milk

Preheat oven to 230°C. Sift flour, cinnamon, baking soda, salt and baking powder together twice. Rub the butter into the flour mixture with your fingers until well mixed in.

Stir the pumpkin, egg and sugar together in a bowl until well combined. Stir into the flour mixture. Add *just enough* milk to make a soft dough, using a tablespoon to measure. Press out lightly on a floured surface and, handling the dough as little as possible, cut into scones. Place on a baking tray, brush the tops with milk or egg and water mixed, and bake for 10-15 minutes or until golden-brown.

If the pumpkin used is very moist, it may be necessary to add little or no milk to the scone dough.

For a low-fat version, reduce the butter and use skim milk.

To stop kumara from discolouring, grate into a bowl of cold water. Squeeze out water before putting kumara into cake mixture.

Kumara Loaf

The mixture can also be baked in a loaf tin (20 cm). Bake for about 1 hour. Serve sliced and buttered if wished.

Kumara Muffins

Makes 12 muffins

1/2 cup orange juice
1 cup chopped dates
2 cups plain white flour, or 1 cup plain and 1 cup wholemeal flour, mixed
2 tsp baking powder
1/2 tsp baking soda

3/4 tsp salt
3/4 cup sugar
1/4 tsp ground nutmeg
1 tsp grated orange rind
2 cups grated kumara
1/2 cup vegetable oil
2 large eggs

Mix the dates with the 1/2 cup orange juice. Microwave on High for 1 minute, or boil in a small pan on the stove till orange juice is absorbed into the dates.

Sift flour, baking powder, baking soda and salt into a mixing bowl. Stir in the sugar, nutmeg, orange rind and kumara. Add date and orange mixture. Beat oil and eggs together and stir into kumara mixture till just combined.

Divide mixture into a 12-hole muffin tray and bake at 180°C for 20 minutes or until springy to touch. Leave for 10 minutes before turning out.

It is essential that the nuts are fresh and not rancid for this easy recipe.

Orange Syrup

1/4 cup orange juice
1/4 cup sugar

Simmer together in a small saucepan for 5 minutes, stirring from time to time.

Orange Pecan Muffins

120g (1/2 cup) butter
2/3 cup brown sugar
1 tsp baking soda
1/2 cup sour cream
2 eggs, beaten lightly

1 1/2 cups plain white flour
1 cup chopped pecans
1 tsp vanilla essence
1 heaped tbsp grated orange rind
    (about 1 1/2 large oranges)

Preheat oven to 180°C. Grease a 12-hole muffin pan. Cream butter and sugar together (a hand whisk is adequate for this). In a separate bowl, mix the baking soda with the sour cream. Add the eggs and sour cream mixture to the butter/sugar mixture. Lightly fold in the flour, nuts, vanilla and orange rind – do not over-mix. Fill muffin holes three-quarters full, and bake for 25 minutes, until tops of the muffins are lightly browned.

If desired, brush while still warm with Orange Syrup.

To prevent a skin from forming on custard after making, cover with plastic wrap, with the wrap resting directly on custard.

Chocolate

Add 2-3 tbsp sifted cocoa with the custard powder. Increase sugar by 1 tbsp. Or stir 60g chocolate, chopped, into the hot custard, and stir until melted.

Coffee

Add 2 tsp instant coffee mixed with a little hot water at the end of cooking time.

Caramel

Substitute soft brown sugar for white sugar in the recipe.

Fruit

Fold 3/4 cup sieved and puréed or chopped fruit into the cold custard.

Coconut

Substitute coconut cream for milk and cream in the recipe.

Cake Fillings and Icings

Vanilla Custard Cake Filling

1 tbsp cornflour
1 1/2 tbsp custard powder
3 tbsp caster sugar
1 1/4 cups milk

1 cup cream
1 tbsp butter
1 vanilla pod or 1 tsp vanilla essence

If using vanilla pod, heat the milk with the vanilla pod in a small saucepan. Remove from heat just before the milk boils. Allow the vanilla pod to infuse in the milk for 30 minutes, then strain. (If using vanilla essence, omit this step.)

Put cornflour, custard powder and sugar in a saucepan, and slowly add the milk, stirring until smooth, then add the cream. Bring the mixture to the boil, stirring constantly. Reduce heat and cook, stirring, for 5 minutes or until thickened and smooth. Remove pan from heat and stir in the butter, and the vanilla essence if using.

Chocolate

Add 2-3 level tbsp cocoa, mixed with a little boiling water, to the mixture. Or add 60g melted and cooled dark chocolate to the icing at the same time as the vanilla essence.

Coffee

Add 2-3 level tsp instant coffee powder mixed with the hot water in the recipe.

Coconut

Add 1-2 cups lightly toasted, finely grated coconut to the recipe. Use coconut essence or liqueur instead of vanilla essence.

Orange or Lemon

Omit vanilla and hot water. Add grated rind to taste, and a little juice to make a smooth icing.

Easy Buttercream

80g (1/3 cup) butter	1 tsp vanilla essence
1 1/2 cups icing sugar, sifted	1-2 tbsp hot water

Cream butter in a bowl by hand or with an electric mixer, or use a food processor. Add icing sugar gradually, and beat until light and fluffy. Stir in the vanilla essence and hot water.
This is an easy recipe for a cake filling or icing. The quantity given should be doubled to fill and ice a 23 cm cake.

Cream Cheese Icing

4 tbsp cream cheese	1 tsp vanilla essence
30g (2 tbsp) butter	1 tsp grated lemon rind
1 1/2 cups icing sugar	

Put all the ingredients in a food processor or bowl, and process or beat until smooth.

Coconut Cinnamon Icing

30g (2 tbsp) butter	1 tsp grated orange rind
1 1/2 cups icing sugar, sifted	1/2 cup finely grated coconut,
1/4 tsp cinnamon	lightly toasted
1 tbsp sour cream or yoghurt	

Beat butter with electric mixer (or use food processor) until light and fluffy. Gradually add icing sugar, beating until well combined. Stir in cinnamon, sour cream and orange rind. Spread on cooled cake, then sprinkle with the coconut.

This is a delicious bread to serve with curries. It comes from North India and is a very close relative of pita bread. It is best served as soon as it is made, but can be frozen while very fresh, wrapped well with freezer wrap or in freezer bags and then thawed and reheated quickly in a hot oven.

Flat Breads

Naan (Punjabi Leavened Bread)

Makes about 8 naan

3 cups flour
1 tsp salt
1/2 cup plain yoghurt
1 1/2 tsp dried yeast
2 tsp sugar
1/2 cup warm water

extra warm water
extra flour
1 tbsp poppy seeds or sesame seeds
   (optional)
1 tbsp ghee or clarified butter

Sift the flour with the salt into a bowl and mix in the yoghurt. Stir the sugar and yeast into the warm water, and add to the yoghurt/flour mixture. Add a little extra flour or water to make a soft, pliable dough. Knead well for about 15 minutes by hand, or split into 3 balls, flour each ball well and put one ball into food processor with blade. Process for several minutes or until smooth. Remove and repeat with remaining balls, then quickly knead the three balls together by hand.

Put dough into a bowl, cover with a damp tea towel, and put in a warm place to prove for 4-5 hours. Preheat oven to 230°C. Divide dough into 8 balls, and let balls rest for 5 minutes. Roll out into circles about 15 cm in diameter and lay out on baking trays. Brush with a little ghee and sprinkle with poppy seeds or sesame seeds. Bake for about 10 minutes or until puffed and golden. Keep warm, wrapped in a cloth, and serve.

Chapatis are the easiest flat bread of all to make, and must be made just before serving. The dough can be made up some hours in advance, brushed with a little ghee and kept in a warm place covered with a cloth.

Atta flour is a wholemeal flour used in making chapatis.

Puris

Follow the recipe for chapatis, but cut the rolled dough out into smaller circles about 12 cm in diameter. Deep fry in hot oil until puffed up – about 30-45 seconds. Lift out of the deep fryer, shaking off excess oil, and drain on paper towels. Serve immediately with curries, or as a snack with dips or chutneys.

This is a delicious flat bread to serve with curries.

Chapatis♥

Makes about 12 chapatis

3 cups Atta flour (or 2 cups plain white flour and 1 cup wholewheat flour)

3/4-1 cup warm water
2 tbsp ghee or vegetable oil
1 tsp salt

Mix together the 3/4 cup warm water and ghee, and mix quickly into the flour, which has been sifted into a bowl with the salt. (Put into the bowl any bran left in the sieve.) Add extra warm water to make a smooth ball. Turn onto a lightly floured surface and knead by hand for about 10 minutes, or until smooth and elastic. (Or split into 2 balls and coat each with flour, then put one into a food processor with blade and process until smooth and elastic, adding extra flour if necessary. Repeat with the other ball, and then quickly knead the two balls together by hand.) Leave dough to rest, covered, in a warm place until ready to cook.

Divide dough into 12 balls, and roll out each one to about 18 cm in diameter. Lightly grease a frying pan with ghee, butter or oil and then wipe dry. Cook each chapati for 1-2 minutes on each side – each side should be dry and slightly 'bubbled'. Keep wrapped in a clean cloth in a warm place while the rest are being cooked.

Sri Lankan Coconut Roti

Makes 10-12 roti

2 cups plain flour
1 tsp salt

2 cups freshly grated coconut
boiling water

Stir the flour and salt into a large bowl. Stir in the grated coconut. Stir in 2 tbsp hot water, then gradually add more hot water, a tablespoon at a time, to form a ball. Knead lightly. Turn out onto a floured surface, and knead, adding more flour if the dough is sticky, until you have a smooth and pliable dough. This can take 5-10 minutes.

Form dough into small balls. Using a rolling pin, roll out the balls on a well-floured surface to about 15 cm in diameter. (I use a small side-plate and cut the roti to the exact size.) Cook the roti 2 at a time in a large well-oiled frying pan or on a hot plate over a low heat, turning when the underside is slightly brown.

Jellies, Jams, Chutneys and Relishes

Tropical fruit makes delicious jams, jellies, chutneys and relishes. Experiment with any tropical fruit or vegetable, except starch vegetables such as taro, kumara and breadfruit.

Hints for Best Results

1. Select fruit that is not over-ripe, and vegetables in good condition. Fruit should preferably be picked on a fine day.

2. Use a saucepan for cooking that is preferably non-aluminium and has a heavy bottom. A good-quality pressure cooker is ideal, and fruit and vegetables can be cooked to soften, using pressure in most cases, before the stage of adding sugar.

3. It is important to watch the mixture very carefully towards the end of cooking time as it can easily catch and burn. Reduce heat to very low at this stage.

4. To test if jams and jellies are ready, put a little on a cold saucer and put in the freezer for 1 minute. Check if a skin has formed. The mixture should wrinkle when pressed with a finger. Remove saucepan of jam or jelly from heat while testing.

5. Sterilise jars and lids – an easy method is as follows: Wash in hot soapy water, rinse, and then boil in a large saucepan of clean water for 5 minutes. Dry on a large tray in a 120°C oven for 15 minutes, or dry in the microwave on High for 5 minutes. Lids should be boiled for 5 minutes and allowed to dry in the oven for 5 minutes. Do not put plastic lids in the oven, or metal lids in the microwave.

6. Put boiling jams, jellies, chutneys and relishes into jars, and cover with a clean cloth until cool. If storing for an extended time, seal jams and jellies with boiling wax; once wax has set, fix on lid tightly. Store jars in a cool, dark, airy place or the refrigerator. Always store in the refrigerator after opening.

7. In hot climates, unopened jars of jams and jellies, chutneys and relishes stored outside the refrigerator can sometimes spoil, in spite of correct sealing, as described above. An extra precaution for extended shelf-storage is to add 1/2 tsp Benzoate of Soda to every 1 kg fruit used in a recipe, stirred in at the end of cooking time. Benzoate of Soda is a tasteless, harmless preservative available from the pharmacy.

Jellies

General Recipe for Jelly Making

Remove any blemished part of fruit, remove stones from fruit such as mango, but leave pips in fruit such as guava. Peel fruit such as mango, but leave fruit such as guava unpeeled. Simmer washed sliced or chopped fruit with barely enough water to cover until very soft and falling apart. Strain through a jelly bag – linen or a double thickness of muslin are ideal. Tie securely, hang over a basin and allow juice to drip into basin. Never squeeze the bag or jelly will be cloudy. Allow to drip for 4-6 hours or overnight.

For fruit low in pectin, such as guava and pineapple, add the juice of 1 lemon to every cup of strained juice. Add 3/4 or 1 cup sugar to every cup of juice, depending on sweetness of fruit used. Jellies can be made using a combination of fruit, such as carambola with surinam cherry, and pawpaw with passionfruit.

Never try to make jelly with more than 6 cups juice (and 4 1/2-6 cups sugar) at a time. After straining juice through the jelly bag and measuring, add lemon juice where necessary, measure again and put in a saucepan with the sugar. Stir over a medium heat until sugar is dissolved. Boil rapidly, without stirring, until jelly is ready.

Guava Jelly

2 kg slightly under-ripe guavas   lemon juice
sugar

Wash guavas, cut in half, put in a saucepan and just barely cover with water. Cook, uncovered, for about 1 hour until the fruit is soft and loses its colour. Strain as described in the general recipe. Measure the juice and add the juice of 1 lemon to every 2 cups guava juice. Measure again and add 3/4 cup sugar to every cup of fruit juice. Put juice and sugar in a saucepan suitable for jam-making, stir over a medium heat until sugar is dissolved, then boil rapidly, uncovered, without stirring, until jelly is ready to set. Bottle in sterilised jars and seal when cold.

Pawpaw and Passionfruit Jelly

Use 1 1/2 kg pawpaw, weighed after peeling and seeding, and 10 passionfruit. Follow the recipe for Passionfruit Jelly, cooking passionfruit skin and water together. Put the strained passionfruit-skin water and chopped pawpaw together in the saucepan, and cook until pawpaw is soft. Then add passionfruit pulp and cook for 10 minutes and strain through a jelly bag. Proceed as for Passionfruit Jelly.

Other Annona fruits such as custard apple can be used for this recipe. Add lemon juice where necessary.

Passionfruit Jelly

about 20 passionfruit   lemon juice
sugar

Remove pulp from fruit and set aside. Wash skins, and cut them up with scissors. Put skins in a saucepan, just cover with water and boil for 30 minutes. Strain, and add strained water to passionfruit pulp. Boil passionfruit pulp and strained water together for 10 minutes only, then strain through a jelly bag. Add 1 tbsp lemon juice to every cup of passionfruit juice, and 3/4 cup sugar. Proceed as for Guava Jelly.

Soursop Jelly

3 large soursop, peeled, seeded and   water
    chopped   sugar

Put the soursop flesh in a saucepan, just covered with water. Cover the pan and cook the soursop until water is well flavoured and fruit is tasteless. Strain through a jelly bag. Add 3/4 cup sugar to every cup of strained juice, and proceed as for Guava Jelly.

Jams

Lemon or Lime Butter

3 eggs, beaten
1 cup sugar
3 tsp grated lemon or lime peel

1/2 cup lemon or lime juice
60g (4 tbsp) butter

Combine all the ingredients in the top of a double saucepan, and cook, stirring, over simmering water until the mixture is thick enough to coat the back of a spoon. Cool, then store in a sterilised, covered jar in the refrigerator.

Pawpaw and Ginger Jam

1 1/2 kg pawpaw, weighed after
    peeling and removing seeds
1 cup water

1/2 cup fresh lime or lemon juice
2 tbsp grated fresh ginger
1 1/2 kg sugar

Cut the pawpaw into small cubes. Place in a heavy-bottomed saucepan with the water, lime juice and ginger. Cover and cook until the pawpaw is tender – about 15-20 minutes. Stir in sugar until dissolved, then boil rapidly until the jam is ready to set when tested. Bottle in sterilised jars and seal when cold.

Pineapple Jam

6 cups (about 1 1/2 kg) chopped
    fresh pineapple, core removed
grated rind and juice of 4 lemons

1 1/2 kg sugar
3 cups water

Combine all the ingredients in a bowl in the refrigerator for 24 hours. Put in a large, heavy-based saucepan and simmer, uncovered, for about 1 hour. Stir only toward the end of cooking time, when jam should be thick and ready to set when tested. Bottle in sterilised jars and seal when cold.

This is delicious as a Swiss Roll or Sponge Sandwich filling.

Ripe Mango Jam

1 kg ripe mangos, weighed after
    peeling and removing pips
1/2 cup water

1/4 cup fresh lemon or lime juice
1 kg white sugar (or slightly less if
    mangos are very sweet)

Chop mango and combine with water and lemon juice in a large, heavy saucepan. Bring to the boil and simmer, covered, for 15 minutes or until mango is tender. Add sugar, stirring until sugar is dissolved, then boil, uncovered and without stirring, until jam will set when tested (about 20-30 minutes). Bottle in sterilised jars and seal when cold.

A combination of tropical fruit makes a really delicious and exotic-tasting jam. Experiment with whatever fruits are in season. Never use over-ripe fruit. If fruit is very tart, increase the sugar by 450g.

Tropical Fruit Jam

Makes approximately 12 cups

750g pineapple, peeled with core
    removed
750g pawpaw, peeled and seeded
750g mango, peeled and seeded
750g bananas, peeled

1 cup passionfruit pulp, strained
juice of 2 large lemons
1/2 cup orange juice or water
3 kg sugar

Finely chop all the fruit and put into a large heavy saucepan with the passionfruit pulp, lemon juice and orange juice or water. Cover the saucepan and cook the fruit for 15-20 minutes over a gentle heat until soft. Add the sugar, and stir until dissolved. Bring the jam to the boil, then boil, uncovered and without stirring, for 20-30 minutes or until jam sets when tested on a cold saucer. Take care not to burn towards the end of cooking time. Bottle in sterilised jars and seal when cold.

For an extra special marmalade, 250g chopped crystallised ginger can be added to any of the marmalade recipes at the same time as the sugar, and/or 1/3 cup whisky, brandy or rum can be stirred in at the end of the cooking time.

The oil in the skins of tropical citrus fruit can make a marmalade that tastes very bitter. These first three marmalade recipes use a method that eliminates this bitterness to a great extent. If, however, you prefer this bitter tang in your marmalade, eliminate Step 3 completely.

A food processor with a sharp blade can be used to cut the peel for marmalade, but be careful that the peel does not become mushy. If the peel has been pre-boiled, as in Step 3, it is really preferable to cut it thinly by hand.

Tropical Orange Marmalade

1 1/2 kg oranges   juice of 2 lemons
8 cups water   extra water for cooking peel
2 1/2 kg sugar   (Step 3)

Step 1: Cut oranges in half across the widest part of their circumference. Squeeze out the juice through a sieve into a bowl. Discard the pips. (Many recipes suggest keeping the pips in a muslin bag and cooking with the marmalade to increase the pectin content, helping the jam to set. With the addition of lemon juice, this step is unnecessary.)

Step 2: Using a teaspoon, scrape out all the pulp from the orange halves and add to the bowl of juice.

Step 3: Put the orange halves in a saucepan and cover with water. Bring to the boil, then simmer for 10 minutes. Drain the orange halves under cold running water, and discard the water in which they were boiled. The orange halves will now be softened slightly, and be easy to cut by hand with a sharp knife into very thin slices.

Step 4: Using a clean board and a sharp knife, cut orange halves into very thin slices. Put sliced orange peel into a heavy-bottomed saucepan with the 8 cups of water, and cook, uncovered, for 20-30 minutes or until the peel is very tender.

Step 5: Add the reserved orange juice, pulp, 2 1/2 kg sugar and the lemon juice to the saucepan. Cook over a gentle heat, stirring, until sugar is dissolved, then bring to the boil and boil rapidly, uncovered and without stirring, until the marmalade will set (about 20-30 minutes).

The small tropical lime is excellent for this marmalade. Smooth-skinned lemons can also be used.

Tropical Lime or Lemon Marmalade

1 kg limes or lemons   extra water for cooking peel
6 cups water   (Step 3)
2 1/2 kg sugar

Follow the method exactly as for Tropical Orange Marmalade, but cook the lime or lemon peel for 20 minutes in Step 3. The sliced peel will also take a longer cooking time in the 6 cups of water before becoming tender.

Sweet Three Fruit Marmalade

1 1/2 kg mixed citrus fruit such as
    grapefruit, oranges, mandarins,
    lemons and limes

8 cups water
3 kg sugar
juice of 1 lemon

Follow the method exactly as in Tropical Lime Marmalade.

Pawpaw, Lime and Ginger Marmalade

5 small limes (or 2 big lemons)
4 cups water
1 1/2 kg pawpaw, weighed after
    peeling and seeding

2 tbsp grated fresh ginger
1/2 cup chopped crystallised ginger
2 kg sugar

Halve the limes, squeeze out the juice into a large, heavy-based saucepan, discarding the pips. Mince the lime shells in a food processor or hand mincer, and add to the pan with the 4 cups water. Add the pawpaw which has been finely chopped, and the fresh ginger. Cover and cook for 30 minutes. Add crystallised ginger and sugar. Stir over a gentle heat until sugar is dissolved, then boil rapidly, uncovered, until jam sets when tested (about 30 minutes).

Hawaiian Guava Marmalade

2 lemons
2 kg guavas
6 cups sugar

water
2 tsp grated fresh ginger

Wash lemons and cut in half, remove seeds and centre white pith. Cut into very thin slices. Wash guavas, cut in half and remove seeds and pulp. Cut shells into thin slices. Put guava and lemon slices into a heavy saucepan with just enough water to cover, and cook, uncovered, until soft. Put guava pulp and seeds into another pot with just enough water to cover, cover pot and cook until mixture is mushy. Strain this guava pulp through a sieve to give a smooth purée. Add to the saucepan containing the sliced guavas and lemon slices, and add the sugar and ginger. Bring to the boil, stirring until sugar is dissolved, then cook, without stirring, until jam will set when tested.

Combinations of tropical citrus fruit make delicious marmalade. Experiment with combinations of your own.

Chutneys and Relishes

Banana and Ginger Chutney

This recipe originates in the West Indies, and is a good way to use up an excess of bananas.

1 kg ripe bananas, weighed after
   removing peel
500g raisins
2 1/2 cups vinegar, preferably malt
2 cloves garlic, crushed
2 tbsp freshly grated ginger

1 tsp chilli sauce
1 1/2 cups brown sugar
1 tsp garam masala
1/4 tsp ground cloves
1/2 tsp cinnamon

Chop the bananas. In a food processor or blender, purée the raisins with 1 cup vinegar, the ginger, garlic and chilli sauce. Put all the ingredients into a large, non-aluminium saucepan and cook, stirring from time to time, over a gentle heat for about an hour, or until the chutney is thick and leaving the sides of the pan. Spoon into sterilised jars and seal.

Green Mango Relish

This is a really delicious relish, excellent with roast or cold meat, or on sandwiches.

Green Tomato Relish
Substitute 1 1/2 kg green unpeeled tomatoes for the mango in the recipe.

Green Pawpaw Relish
Substitute 1 1/2 kg green pawpaw (weighed after peeling and seeding), for the mango in the recipe.

1 1/2 kg green (unripe) mangos,
   weighed after peeling and
   seeding
4 large onions
6 medium green capsicums, seeds
   removed
2 cups vinegar, preferably wine or
   cider
2 cups brown sugar

1 cup white sugar
2 1/2 level tsp salt
1 tsp chopped, seeded, fresh green
   chilli
1/4 cup chopped fresh mint, basil or
   dill
1 1/2 tbsp mustard seeds
1 1/2 tbsp celery or dill seeds

Finely chop the mangos, onions and capsicum by hand or in a food processor. Combine in a large, heavy saucepan with all the remaining ingredients. Bring to the boil, stirring, and boil for 10 minutes only. Cover and let stand overnight in a cool place. The next day, bring back to the boil, reduce heat and simmer, uncovered (without stirring except towards the end of cooking time), until thick (about 35-45 minutes). Take care not to burn towards the end of cooking time. Pour into hot, dry, sterilised jars and seal when cold.

There is often an abundance of eggplant on Rarotonga. We created this recipe at The Flame Tree after being unable to find an eggplant chutney recipe anywhere. I am really pleased with this chutney, and can highly recommend it.

Flame Tree Eggplant Chutney

3 kg eggplant, washed
2 tsp crushed garlic
1 tbsp grated fresh ginger
2 tsp fresh chillis, seeded and chopped (or use bottled crushed chilli)

2 tsp salt
2 tsp ground cumin
1 tsp ground cinnamon
1/2 tsp ground cloves
1 kg white sugar
750 ml bottle white or wine vinegar

Cut the unpeeled eggplant into small cubes. Put all the ingredients into a large saucepan and bring to the boil, stirring. Reduce heat and simmer, uncovered, for about 1 1/4-1 1/2 hours, stirring regularly. The chutney should be thick and jam-like. Spoon into sterilised jars and seal when cold.

This recipe also works well with chokos.

Green Pawpaw Chutney

1 kg green pawpaw (unripe), weighed after peeling and seeding
3 onions, finely chopped
480g tomatoes, peeled and chopped (canned or fresh)
1 cup raisins
3 cloves garlic, crushed
1 tsp chilli sauce

3 capsicums, chopped
2 tsp ground ginger
2 tsp ground cinnamon
1/2 tsp ground cloves
2 tsp salt
grated rind and juice of 2 lemons
750 ml bottle vinegar, preferably malt
480g sugar

Finely chop the pawpaw. Put all the ingredients *except* for the sugar in a large, heavy saucepan. Bring to the boil. Reduce heat, cover the saucepan and cook for 20 minutes. Add sugar, stirring to dissolve. Bring back to the boil and cook, uncovered, until the mixture is thick and jam-like. Keep stirring from time to time while the chutney is cooking. Pour into sterilised jars and seal when cold.

This pawpaw chutney is easy to make and delicious. I have lots of pawpaws growing in the garden so I am always trying to find different ways to use them.

Ripe Pawpaw Chutney

Makes about 8 cups

4 or 5 large pawpaws (4 kg weight before peeling and seeding)
5 medium onions, chopped
2 cups sugar, preferably brown
750 ml bottle vinegar, preferably malt
1 1/2 tsp salt
1 tsp freshly ground pepper
1/2 tsp dry mustard powder, or 1 tsp prepared mustard

1 tsp cumin or fennel seeds
1/2 tsp ground nutmeg
1/4 tsp ground cloves
1 1/2 tsp ground cinnamon
2 tsp crushed chilli or 1 tsp chilli powder
2 tsp crushed fresh ginger or 1 tsp ground ginger
juice and grated rind of 1 lemon

Halve, seed and peel pawpaw, and chop flesh. In a large heavy-bottomed saucepan, combine all ingredients except pawpaw, bring to the boil, stirring, and boil for 10 minutes. Add chopped pawpaw and simmer over a reduced heat, stirring occasionally, for about 1 1/2 hours or until thickened. Ladle into sterilised jars and seal when cold.

Tomato Chutney
This recipe also works well with ripe tomatoes. Use 4 kg ripe tomatoes, peeled if desired, in place of the mangos.

Sweet Mango Chutney

4 kg ripe but firm mangos, weighed after peeling and seeding
3 onions, chopped (optional)
2 cups sultanas or seedless raisins, or chopped dates
3 tsp salt
2 tsp chilli sauce
2 tsp crushed garlic

1/4 cup chopped fresh ginger
4 tsp curry powder
1 tsp ground nutmeg
2 tsp ground cinnamon
1/2 tsp ground cloves
2 x 750 ml bottles vinegar, preferably malt
2 kg sugar

Chop mangos and put aside into a large bowl. Into a large, heavy saucepan, put sugar and 1 1/2 bottles vinegar. Put the remaining 1/2 bottle vinegar into a food processor or blender with sultanas, salt, chillis, garlic, ginger, curry powder, nutmeg, cinnamon and cloves, and blend until smooth. Add to the saucepan and bring the mixture to the boil, then simmer, uncovered, for 15 minutes. Add mangos, and onions if using, and simmer, stirring only occasionally, until thick and jam-like. (Stir gently more often towards the end of cooking time – about 1-1 1/2 hours – and take care not to burn chutney.) Pour into sterilised jars and seal when cool.

In all Asian countries, curries are accompanied by a variety of fresh chutneys or relishes, known as sambals in Indonesia and raitas in India. The plentiful Pacific Island ingredients like coconut and mango are superb in these fresh relishes.

These fresh coconut sambals keep in the refrigerator for up to 2 days.

Sambals, Raitas and Fresh Chutneys

Fresh Coconut Sambal

1 tbsp vegetable oil
1 tsp mustard seeds
1 medium red or green capsicum
1 tbsp finely chopped onion

1 tsp salt
1 tsp lime or lemon juice
1/2 ripe coconut, grated

Heat the vegetable oil in a small saucepan. Add the mustard seeds and cook until they start to pop. Remove pan from heat. Remove seeds and white pith from capsicum and cut into chunks. Blend in a food processor or blender with the onion, salt and lime or lemon juice (adding a little water to circulate the ingredients smoothly), for 1 minute. Add the grated coconut and blend for 30 seconds. Put into a bowl and stir in the mustard seeds.

Coconut Mint Sambal

1 cup freshly grated coconut
1/2 cup coconut cream
1/4 tsp salt
1 tsp freshly ground black pepper

a few drops chilli sauce
1 tbsp chopped fresh mint or mint
  sauce
1 tsp brown sugar

Combine all ingredients together in a bowl.

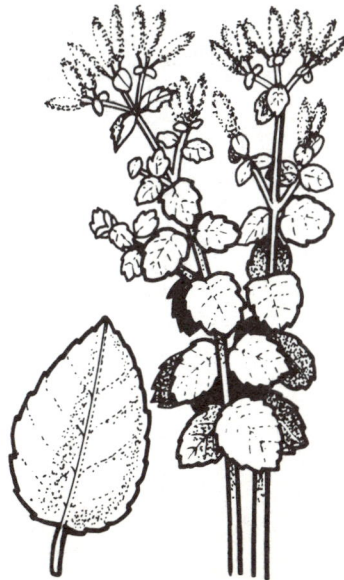

This fresh chutney keeps in the refrigerator for 2 days.

Green Coriander Chutney

1/2 cup chopped fresh coriander
1 small green chilli, chopped
2 tbsp lemon juice
1 tsp grated fresh ginger

1/2 tsp freshly ground black pepper
1 tsp sugar
salt to taste

Wash the coriander and put in a food processor or blender with all the other ingredients except for the salt. Purée until smooth. Add salt to taste.

This will keep for up to 4 days in the refrigerator. Green, unripe pawpaw can also be used in this recipe.

Green Mango Chatni

1 unripe, green mango
2/3 cup finely grated coconut
1 small chopped red chilli or 1 tsp
    chilli powder
1 tsp mustard seeds

1 tbsp natural yoghurt
1 tbsp oil
1 tbsp chopped fresh coriander or
    basil
salt to taste

Peel and chop the mango very finely (or grate). Put the coconut, chilli and half the mustard seeds in a food processor or blender, and blend together for 1 minute. Add to the chopped mango and stir in the yoghurt. Heat the oil in a small pan and fry the remaining mustard seeds until they have popped, then stir into the chatni with the coriander. Season with salt to taste.

This keeps for 2 days in the refrigerator.

Peanut Dressing

Add an extra cup of coconut cream to the sambal for a delicious salad dressing.

Peanut Sambal

2 onions, chopped
1 tbsp oil
1 cup natural peanuts, toasted
1 cup coconut cream
1/2 tsp garlic powder

1 tsp crushed chilli
1 tbsp brown sugar
1/2 tsp freshly ground black pepper
1 tbsp lemon juice
2 tbsp chopped basil leaves

Cook onions in oil until golden-brown and crisp. Add remaining ingredients and cook for 5 minutes. Cook and blend or process until fairly smooth.

This keeps for several weeks in the refrigerator.

Tamarind Sambal

1/4 cup tamarind pulp (strained)
1 tsp ground cumin
1/2 tsp chilli powder

1 tbsp lemon juice
2 tbsp brown sugar
1 tsp grated fresh ginger

Stir all the ingredients together. Chill until ready to serve.

Dressings, Sauces and Spices

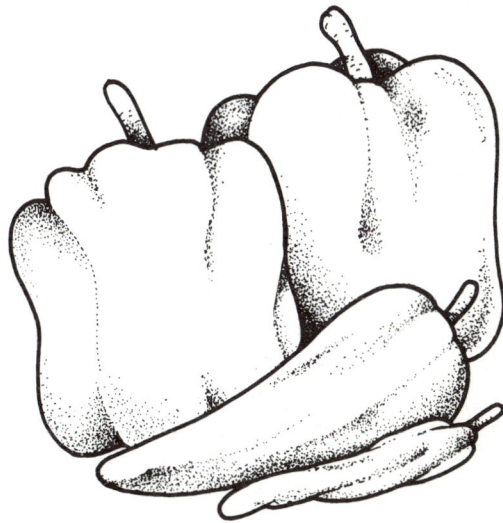

Salad Dressings

Avocado Yoghurt Dressing

Makes 6 cups

4 ripe avocados
1/2 cup vegetable oil
1 tbsp fresh lemon juice
2 cups plain yoghurt
2 cloves garlic, crushed

1 tsp salt
1/2 tsp freshly ground pepper
1 tsp paprika
1/4 tsp fresh chopped dill

In a food processor blend avocados, oil and lemon juice until smooth (or beat by hand with a whisk). Add the yoghurt, garlic, salt and pepper, paprika and dill. Blend the mixture for 1 minute until thick and smooth (or beat by hand).

Delicious on a crisp vegetable salad, or a prawn or chicken salad. This can be kept refrigerated for up to 24 hours, well covered.

Basic Mayonnaise

2 egg yolks
2 tsp French mustard
1-1 1/4 cups vegetable or olive oil

juice of 1 lemon
salt
freshly ground black pepper

Place the egg yolks and mustard into a bowl and beat with a wire whisk until well blended. Beating constantly, add the oil, drop by drop at first and then in a thin, steady steam as the mayonnaise thickens. Add the lemon juice, and salt and pepper to taste.

FOOD PROCESSOR METHOD
Put the egg yolks, lemon juice and mustard in the bowl of a food processor with blade, and blend until well combined. With the motor running, add the oil in a thin stream through the feed-tube. (Have the oil in a jug for easy pouring, and do not hurry – the oil should be dribbled in steadily.) Once the mixture thickens, stop the motor. Add salt and pepper to taste.

Making your own mayonnaise is very easy, and its flavour is quite superior to most commercial brands.

Mayonnaise will keep refrigerated for up to a week.

Herb Mayonnaise
2 tbsp or more of fresh herbs such as dill, parsley or basil, finely chopped, can be stirred into the thickened mayonnaise

Garlic Mayonnaise
2-4 cloves of crushed garlic can be added to the Basic or Herb Mayonnaise.

This curry mayonnaise is really delicious, and goes well with shellfish such as mussels, prawns or crayfish. It is also good in a potato salad, or with grilled fish – in fact it can add an exotic flavour to anything you care to add it to or serve it with. This recipe only makes 1 cup of mayonnaise, so double or treble the recipe for a larger amount.

Curry Mayonnaise

1 cup mayonnaise
1/4 tsp honey
3 tbsp chopped spring onions with
   green parts

3 tbsp chopped fresh tomato
2 tsp best-quality curry powder

Combine all the ingredients together. Keep chilled until required.

This mayonnaise is excellent in a coleslaw or pasta or rice salad, or with a chicken or seafood salad.

Tropical Fruit and Ginger Mayonnaise
2 tsp grated fresh ginger can be added to this recipe.

Tropical Fruit Mayonnaise

Makes 1 1/2 cups

1 cup mayonnaise
1/2 cup chopped tropical fruit, such
   as pineapple
1 tsp fruit chutney

1 tsp curry powder (optional)
1 tbsp chopped fresh herbs, such as
   mint

Combine all the ingredients together. Chill until required.

Garlic Yoghurt Dressing

1 cup natural yoghurt
1/2 cup mayonnaise
1 tsp brown sugar
1/4 cup chopped fresh herbs, such

as parsley, coriander or basil
4-6 cloves garlic, crushed
1 tbsp lemon juice
salt and pepper to taste

Blend all ingredients together in a food processor or blender until smooth.

Both this Honey Lime Dressing and the Honey Mustard Dressing are delicious on vegetable, chicken or seafood salads, as well as with cold pork, beef and lamb.

Honey Lime Dressing

1 cup fresh lime juice
1/2 cup honey
1 small onion, chopped

1 clove garlic, chopped
2 tbsp vegetable oil
4 sprigs fresh parsley

In a food processor or blender, blend all the ingredients except the parsley till well combined. Add the parsley and blend a few seconds only. Chill the dressing till ready to serve.

Honey Mustard Dressing

3 tbsp vegetable oil
1/4 cup chopped parsley
2 tbsp vinegar

3 tsp Dijon-style mustard
1 tsp honey
freshly ground black pepper

Put all in the ingredients in a screwtop jar and shake well until thoroughly mixed.

This salad dressing is delicious on vegetable, seafood, chicken, beef, pork and lamb salads.

Thai Coconut Dressing

1/3 cup coconut cream
2 tbsp lemon or lime juice

2 tsp fish sauce or oyster sauce
1 tsp sugar

Combine all the ingredients together in a screwtop jar and shake well.

This keeps for more than a week in the refrigerator.

Vinaigrette Dressing

1 cup vegetable or olive oil
1/3 cup cider, wine or herb vinegar
1 level tsp prepared mustard
2 cloves garlic, crushed (optional)
2 mashed egg yolks (optional)

1 tbsp sugar, or less
1 tbsp fresh or 1 tsp dried herbs
salt and freshly ground pepper to
  taste

Shake all ingredients well in a screwtop jar, or mix thoroughly in a food processor or blender.

Delicious on a crisp green salad, or on a seafood, avocado, chicken or pork salad, as well as with a savoury mousse such as the Cucumber and Cream Cheese Mousse (p. 18). It is also good on grilled fish, prawns or seafood kebabs. This vinaigrette keeps for 2 days in the refrigerator.

Tropical Fruit Vinaigrettes
Experiment using other tropical fruit in place of the mango in this recipe.

Mango Vinaigrette

250g mango flesh, peeled
1 cup vegetable oil
1/3 cup cider, wine or herb vinegar
1 tbsp green peppercorns, drained
  (optional)
1 tbsp chopped fresh basil or
  coriander

1 clove garlic, crushed
salt and freshly ground black
  pepper, to taste
1 tbsp sugar

Blend all the ingredients together in a blender or food processor until smooth.

Sauces

Avocado Sauce

This sauce is good with chicken, fish or egg dishes.

2 small avocados, peeled and stoned
2 tbsp lemon juice
1 cup cream
1 tbsp lemon juice

1 tbsp chopped spring onions
salt and pepper to taste
a few drops Tabasco

Put all the ingredients together in a blender or food processor and purée until smooth. Serve at room temperature.

Bechamel (White) Sauce

Makes 2 cups

2 cups milk
1 small bay leaf
1 small onion, peeled and quartered
1 sprig parsley
pinch dried thyme

1/4 tsp nutmeg
2 tbsp butter
1/2 cup plain flour
salt and pepper

Bring the milk to the boil with the bay leaf, onion, parsley, thyme and nutmeg. Remove from heat and stand for about 15 minutes. In a clean saucepan melt the butter, add the flour and stir to make a smooth roux. Strain the milk through a fine sieve into the roux and stir constantly with a wooden spoon till the sauce is thick and creamy. Cook the sauce for at least 10 minutes after adding the milk. Add salt and pepper to taste, and extra nutmeg if desired.

When making sauces, always use a wooden spoon. If your sauce is lumpy and needs a whisk, never let a metal whisk scrape against the sides or bottom of the saucepan, as this could ruin the colour and flavour of your sauce by loosening tiny flecks of metal into the sauce. Over the years I have seen many cooks make this mistake.

Cheese Sauce

Add 1 cup grated cheese to the sauce after it has thickened. Cook just until the cheese has melted.

This sauce is good with savoury crepes, and is also delicious combined with cooked chicken, vegetables or seafood and served on pasta or rice. It goes well with a savoury phyllo parcel such as the Smoked Fish Strudels (p. 88) or the Kumara and Zucchini Parcels (p. 38).

Coconut and Ginger Sauce

Add 1 tbsp grated ginger to the sauce at the same time as the onion.

Coconut and Coriander Sauce

Add 2 tbsp chopped fresh coriander to the sauce and omit the parsley.

This sauce is good with roast meat, chicken, barbecued or pan-fried pork or lamb loin, or chicken breasts.

Other tropical fruit jelly, jam or marmalade can be used in this recipe. Strain the sauce where necessary.

Coconut Sauce

Makes about 2 cups

2 tbsp butter
1 onion, very finely chopped
1 tbsp flour
1/2 cup chicken stock or vegetable
   stock

1 1/2 cups thick coconut cream
1/2 tsp brown sugar
salt and pepper to taste
1 tbsp chopped fresh parsley

Heat the butter and cook the onion over a gentle heat until softened but not brown. Add flour and stir for 30 seconds until smooth. Slowly add the chicken stock and 1 cup coconut cream, stirring constantly. When the mixture is smooth, stir in the brown sugar, salt and pepper, and chopped parsley. Cook, stirring for 3 minutes. Stir in remaining 1/2 cup coconut cream, and serve.

Guava and Orange Sauce♥

1 cup guava jelly
3 tsp grated orange rind
3 tsp grated lemon rind
1 cup orange juice
1 tsp grated fresh ginger

2 tbsp port
2 tsp French mustard
2 tsp cornflour
2 tbsp water

Combine all ingredients except for cornflour and water in a medium-sized saucepan, and bring to the boil, stirring. Mix cornflour with water, and add to the pan. Simmer the sauce for 5 minutes, stirring.

Hollandaise sauce is excellent on fish dishes, with steamed mussels, grilled oysters, with crayfish or lobster, and with steamed vegetables such as cauliflower or broccoli. Fresh herbs and many tropical fruits make a really delicious Hollandaise Sauce.

Pawpaw and Lime Hollandaise

Add 1 cup chopped pawpaw, drained in a sieve, and 2 tbsp lime juice to the Hollandaise after incorporating the butter. Process for just 20 seconds to combine the pawpaw with the Hollandaise.

Avocado and Lemon Hollandaise

Add 1 cup chopped avocado and 2 tbsp lemon juice to the Hollandaise, processing for just 20 seconds as described above.

Mango and Ginger Hollandaise

Add 1 cup chopped ripe mango, drained, and 2 tsp freshly grated ginger to the Hollandaise, as described for Pawpaw and Lime Hollandaise.

Curry Hollandaise

Replace peppercorns, bay leaf and thyme in Basic Hollandaise with 2 tsp curry powder and a pinch of sugar, cooking with wine vinegar until reduced to 1 tbsp liquid. Proceed as in Basic Hollandaise.

Basic Hollandaise Sauce

1 cup white wine
1 tbsp white vinegar
a few black peppercorns
1 bay leaf
a pinch of thyme, mixed herbs or
   tarragon

3 egg yolks
250g butter
1 tsp Dijon mustard (optional)
salt to taste

Put the ingredients except for the egg yolks, butter and mustard in a small non-aluminium saucepan, and boil until reduced to about 1 tbsp of liquid. Strain this liquid through a fine sieve into the bowl of a food processor. Add the egg yolks and mustard, and blend briefly. Heat the butter in a small saucepan until hot and bubbly. Transfer to a jug. With the motor running, pour the hot butter in a slow but steady steam through the feed-tube into the food processor. Do not add the white residue at the bottom of the jug. Stop the machine immediately the sauce thickens. Add salt to taste, if necessary.

TO MAKE BY HAND

Put the strained wine liquid in a stainless-steel bowl over a pan of simmering water. Add egg yolks and mustard, and beat for a few minutes with a hand balloon whisk until the yolks start to thicken. Whisk in the butter, pouring it into the bowl in a thin, steady stream. Continue until the butter is used up and the sauce is thickened.

This sauce is very versatile, and is delicious on steamed mussels, with grilled fish, with vegetables such as cauliflower, or with pork, lamb or steak – use vegetable or herb stock if the sauce is accompanying a vegetable dish. For steak or other meat, use beef stock instead of chicken, red wine instead of white wine, and omit the lemon juice.

Mustard Cream Sauce

1 tbsp butter
2 tbsp chopped spring onions or 1/2 small onion, very finely chopped
1/3 cup dry white wine
1 cup cream
2 tbsp whole-grain mustard

1/4 cup chicken stock
2 tbsp chopped parsley
1 tbsp lemon juice
salt and pepper
a pinch of brown sugar

Melt the butter in a small saucepan and cook the onions until very soft. Add the wine and cook until most of the liquid has been evaporated. Add the cream and, stirring with a wooden spoon, add the mustard, stock and chopped parsley. Stir in the lemon juice, brown sugar, and salt and pepper to taste. Heat through but do not boil. Serve immediately.

This delicious pesto is good on pasta, grilled fish or chicken, and is very easy to make with a food processor or blender.

To Roast Capsicum

Char the capsicum over an open flame, using a long fork to hold. Turn capsicum from time to time until the skin is completely blackened and blistered. (Or cook directly under a grill or broiler, turning, until blackened and blistered.) Put the hot capsicum into a paper bag and close the bag for 10 minutes, until the capsicum is cool. Scrape off the skin, halve the capsicum, remove the seeds and membrane, and cut the capsicum as required.

Red Pepper Pesto

Makes 2 cups

4 red capsicums, roasted and peeled
2/3 cup white nuts such as almonds, pinenuts, macadamias or cashews, or a mixture
1 cup peeled tomatoes, with seeds removed (canned or fresh)
3 cloves garlic, crushed
1 tsp salt

1 cup olive oil or vegetable oil
a pinch of chilli powder
juice of 2 lemons, or more to taste
freshly ground black pepper to taste
1/2 cup thick coconut cream or dairy cream (optional)
1/2 cup parmesan cheese (if serving with pasta)

Seed the roasted, peeled capsicum. Lightly toast the nuts in the oven (or microwave on High, stirring from time to time, for 5-8 minutes). Combine the capsicum, nuts, tomatoes, garlic, salt, oil, chilli powder and lemon juice in a food processor or blender, and blend until very smooth. Add freshly ground black pepper to taste and more salt if necessary. Stir in coconut cream or dairy cream if using. Serve at room temperature. Serve parmesan on the side if serving the pesto with pasta.

This is an excellent Oriental sauce that is good to use as a dipping sauce or to accompany lightly battered or stir-fried vegetables, chicken, fish or pork.

Sweet and Sour Sauce

1 cup water
1 tbsp soya sauce
1/4 cup vinegar
1/4 cup sugar
1/2 tsp grated fresh ginger
1 clove garlic, crushed (optional)
4 tbsp tomato sauce

1/2 cup chopped pineapple, with juice
1 cup finely sliced vegetables, such as onions, capsicums, carrots and mushrooms
1 tbsp cornflour mixed with 1/4 cup water

Combine all ingredients and bring to the boil, stirring until sugar is dissolved and sauce is thickened.

This is a very easy tomato sauce, with chilli added – it is excellent with crepes, pasta, rice and seafood.

Creole Tomato Sauce♥

1 tbsp vegetable or olive oil
1 onion, thinly sliced
1 capsicum, thinly sliced
2 cloves garlic, crushed
400g whole peeled tomatoes
1/2 tsp brown sugar

1/3 tsp salt
1/2 tsp freshly ground black pepper
1/2 tsp chilli sauce or powder, or more to taste
1 tbsp chopped fresh basil

Heat oil and cook onions, capsicum and garlic till onion is soft. Add tomatoes, sugar, salt and pepper, and cook, uncovered, over a gentle heat for about 30 minutes or until thick. Stir in basil and chilli to taste, and extra salt and pepper if necessary.

This is another easy tomato sauce that we use in many recipes, especially with pasta and fish dishes.

Fresh basil is preferable but 1 tsp dried basil can be used if necessary. This sauce freezes well for 1 month.

Tomato and Basil Sauce♥

4 cups chopped peeled tomatoes, canned or fresh
3 tbsp chopped fresh basil
2 tbsp butter or olive oil

1 tsp sugar
1 tsp crushed garlic
salt and pepper to taste

Put all the ingredients in a saucepan and cook until the sauce is reduced by half. Season to taste with salt and pepper, if necessary.

225

We use a lot of chillis in a variety of dishes, and have found that we save a great deal of time and energy if we make up a batch of chilli sauce every 2 weeks or so. This means that we do not have to stop and chop fresh chillis every time a recipe calls for them.

Commercial brands of bottled crushed chilli (Sambal Oelek) and various chilli sauces are very expensive on our island, so by making our own we also save a lot financially.

Remember when handling chillis to wear gloves if possible and never to touch your face or eyes.

Chilli Sauces

Indonesian Chilli Sauce♥

12 red chillis, seeds removed   1 tsp salt
3 tbsp vegetable oil

Cut the chillis into pieces. Heat the oil in a frying pan and fry the chillis until they are soft and beginning to brown. Add salt. Cool, then blend in a food processor or blender.

Keep refrigerated for 1 week. Serve as an accompaniment to curries and other dishes, or when a recipe calls for crushed or chopped chillis.

Easy Sambal Oelek♥

40 fresh red chillis   3 tsp salt
vinegar   1/4 cup brown sugar

Put the chillis with seeds into an electric blender. Add enough vinegar to keep the chillis moving, and blend to a paste. Add salt and brown sugar, and blend some more.

Put into sterilised jars and store for up to a month in the refrigerator. Use where a recipe calls for crushed or chopped chillis.

We use this sauce to make Singapore Chilli Prawns (p. 94) and as a base in curries and many other sauces. It can also be served on its own as an accompaniment.

The Flame Tree Chilli Sauce♥

250g chilli peppers, seeds removed, or 1/2 cup chilli powder
2 onions, chopped
2 capsicums, chopped
juice and grated rind of 1 lemon or 2 limes
240g peeled tomatoes with juice

1 tsp chopped fresh garlic
1 cup vinegar
1/2 cup brown sugar
2 tsp salt
1 tbsp soya sauce
1/8 tsp ground cloves
1/4 tsp ground cinnamon

Put the chillis or chilli powder, onion, capsicum, lemon rind and juice, tomatoes and garlic in a food processor or blender and grind the mixture till fairly smooth but not mushy. Put in a saucepan with the vinegar, brown sugar, salt, soya sauce, cloves and cinnamon, and bring to the boil, stirring constantly. Reduce heat and simmer over a gentle heat for 45 minutes. Cool and seal well in sterilised jars. Store in the refrigerator for up to 6 months. Refrigerate after opening.

Use this liquid as desired to spice up any recipe, as you would use Tabasco sauce.

Very Easy Hot Sauce♥

250g chillis

750 ml bottle sherry, vodka or gin

Prick a hole in the chillis with a toothpick and put into 2-3 sterilised bottles. Pour in the sherry. Seal and leave for several weeks.

Spices

Home-made Curry Powder

This is a quick and easy alternative to ready-made, store-bought curry powder.

4 tbsp ground coriander
2 1/2 tbsp ground turmeric
1 1/2 tbsp ground cumin
1 1/2 tbsp mustard seeds
1 tbsp ground cinnamon
2 tsp ground fenugreek

2 tsp ground cardamom
2 tsp (or more or less) chilli powder
2 tsp ground black pepper
2 tsp ground ginger
2 tsp garlic salt (optional)
1 tbsp poppy or fennel seeds

It is best to grind your own spices from the whole spice seeds. Use an electric grinder or small electric mill or coffee grinder. (After grinding spices in a coffee grinder, grind some hard crusts of bread to remove aroma of spices.) If buying ready-made spices, always check that they are fresh and aromatic.

Put all the ingredients in a food processor with blade, or a blender, and blend for 5 minutes. Store in an airtight container for 3 months, or in a plastic container in the freezer for up to 1 year.

Easy Garam Masala (*Flame Tree Spice Blend*)

This garam masala is used in the South Indian Chicken Curry (p. 112) and could be used with any curry in place of commercial curry powder or garam masala.

1 cup ground coriander
1/2 cup ground cumin
1 tsp ground black pepper
1 tsp cardamom seeds

1 tsp ground cinnamon
1/4 tsp ground cloves
1/2 tsp nutmeg
1/2 tsp cracked black pepper

Mix all the ingredients together. Keep in an airtight container, or in a plastic container in the freezer.

Curry Paste

We keep quite a few batches of this paste in the freezer so that we can make a curry without always having to reach for the different spice jars.

1 medium onion, chopped
1/4 cup coconut cream
juice of 2 lemons or 4 limes
1 tbsp chopped fresh ginger
1 tsp crushed fresh garlic
1 tbsp crushed fresh chillis, or hot chilli sauce or chilli powder
1 tsp mustard seeds

2 tbsp Easy Garam Masala (above)
2 tbsp good-quality commercial curry powder, or Home-made Curry Powder (above)
2 tsp turmeric
1 tbsp soya sauce
1 cup whole peeled tomatoes

Put all ingredients in a food processor or blender and process till chunky. Do not purée. Keep refrigerated in an airtight container for a week, or freeze.

Ghee (Clarified Butter)

Ghee is excellent for frying and for sautés, for use in curries, and cooking fish and seafood. It is less likely to burn than regular butter. Excellent New Zealand ghee is sold in cans, but it is easy to prepare your own.

Heat any amount of butter in a saucepan, and heat slowly until it begins to foam. The white milk solids will sink to the bottom of the pan. Remove pan from heat, skim off the foam and carefully pour out the clear yellow liquid, leaving the white residue behind in the pan. Discard the white residue.

Cool ghee, and keep in refrigerator for use when required.

Home-made Wholegrain Mustard

This recipe for mustard is both delicious and handy, as mustard seeds are often much easier to obtain on tropical islands than jars of ready-made mustard. It is also much cheaper to prepare your own, and always makes a nice gift.

120g yellow mustard seeds	1 tsp salt
160 ml wine vinegar	1/4 tsp cinnamon
3 tbsp honey or brown sugar	

Soak mustard seeds in vinegar for 36 hours. Put the seeds and soaking vinegar, honey, salt and cinnamon in a food processor or blender, and blend until smooth. Add a little extra vinegar or boiled water if mustard is too thick. Keep sealed in sterilised jars in the refrigerator for up to one year.

Index

231

233